MASCULINITIES, VIOLENCE, AND CULTURE

Suzanne E. Hatty

Sage Series on Violence Against Women

Sage Publications, Inc.
International Educational and Professional Publisher
Thousand Oaks ■ London ■ New Delhi

For information:

Sage Publications, Inc.
2455 Teller Road
Thousand Oaks, California 91320
E-mail: order@sagepub.com

Sage Publications Ltd.
6 Bonhill Street
London EC2A 4PU
United Kingdom

Sage Publications India Pvt. Ltd.
M-32 Market
Greater Kailash I
New Delhi 110 048 India

Printed in the United States of America

Library of Congress Cataloging-in-Publication Data

Hatty, Suzanne.
    Masculinities, violence and culture / by Suzanne E. Hatty.
        p.   cm. — (Sage series on violence against women)
    Includes bibliographical references and index.
        ISBN 0-7619-0500-6 (cloth: alk. paper)
        ISBN 0-7619-0501-4 (pbk.: alk. paper)
    1. Men.   2. Masculinity.   3. Violence.   4. Women—
Crime against.   I. Title.   II. Series.
HQ1090 .H377   1999
305.31—dc21   99-050747

00   01   02   03   04   05   06   7   6   5   4   3   2   1

Acquiring Editor:	C. Terry Hendrix
Editorial Assistant:	Kristine Lundquist
Production Editor:	Diana E. Axelsen
Editorial Assistant:	Cindy Bear
Typesetter:	Lynn Miyata
Indexer:	Mary Mortensen

MASCULINITIES, VIOLENCE, AND CULTURE

Sage Series on Violence Against Women

Series Editors

Claire M. Renzetti
St. Joseph's University

Jeffrey L. Edleson
University of Minnesota

Contents

1

Engendering Violence
Starting Points

The pressures to speak and act violently are everywhere. . . . Violence is not a deviant act; it is a conforming one.
—*Michele Toomey*

Murder is not weak and slow-witted. Murder is gutsy and daring.
—*Luke Woodham, convicted schoolboy killer*

Witness this: A 16-year-old male student, unable to tolerate rejection by a girlfriend or bullying by his peers, arms himself and goes to school. There, in the bright light of an October morning, he enters the crowded commons area, pulls a rifle from beneath his coat, and kills his former girlfriend. He also kills the girl standing next to her. Continuing on his lethal mission, he shoots and wounds several other students. He apologizes to one of his wounded victims, saying that he is not shooting anyone in particular.

Before beginning his killing spree, the boy pens a written statement. This is his manifesto, accounting for his actions, explaining that he has been wronged. In it, he writes, "I am not insane. I am angry. . . . I killed because people like me are mistreated every day. I did this to show society 'push us and we will push back.'" "A disgruntled girlfriend-boyfriend thing," says the local chief of police, yet the boy's mother also lies dead, killed earlier that morning with a knife.

The boy, Luke, looks soft and childlike, his dark hair curling over his forehead and brushing his collar. His school photograph, widely

1

broadcast after the killings, shows a young man who glances sideways at the viewer from behind wire-rimmed glasses. This image is the antithesis of the confident, assertive, and athletic masculine ideal. The media describe the boy as a failed male adolescent: overweight, artistic, introverted. In addition to these deficiencies, he is described as poor, attired in shabby clothes, and fatherless.

The killings occurred in Pearl, Mississippi, a small town firmly enclosed by the Bible Belt. It is a town of about 20,000 residents, complete with about 40 churches. Here, feelings of protest at personal injustice can readily assume the form of religious subversion, a turning away from Christian ideals. And so it was with Luke Woodham. After being rejected by his girlfriend, the one individual whom he believed had loved him, Woodham developed a powerful and perverse friendship with Grant Boyette, a young man who dabbled in Satanic spells and rituals. Boyette offered Woodham relief from the "16 years of crap" he claimed to have endured. For the first time, according to Woodham, he was affirmed—accepted, valued, and appreciated—by an older person. Boyette was the leader of a group of teenage boys called the Kroth. Boyette adopted the term *father* within the group. He appointed Luke Woodham the assassin.

In June, 1998, Luke Woodham was convicted of the murder of his mother and two female school students. He is currently serving three life terms for these offenses. Woodham also received 20 years for each of seven aggravated assault charges relating to the wounding of others at the school. He is serving all these sentences concurrently.

At his trials, Luke Woodham was variously described by the prosecution as "mean," "hateful," and "bloodthirsty." Woodham testified that he had been instructed by Grant Boyette to kill his mother and his former girlfriend, and to unleash a "reign of terror" over the school. A defense of insanity was rejected in both trials. As he left the courthouse after being convicted of his mother's murder, Luke Woodham declared to the waiting journalists, "I'm going to heaven now. This is God's will." As he was getting into the police car, he added "God bless you all."

This incident was the first of several fatal school shootings around the country, all committed by boys. Acknowledging this, the grandmother of Woodham's former girlfriend claimed that he had "initiated a chain of events across these United States that's wreaked havoc on our children." She also described Woodham as "genetic waste."

Although we might find such statements simplistic or offensive, we are still compelled to ask the question: Why are some young men so angry? Why does this anger translate into lethal violence? Who constitutes this "community of the afflicted," named by Luke Woodham, that threatens to "push back"?

During the same month that Luke Woodham vented his deadly anger, an army of Promise Keepers marched on Washington in a display of masculine solidarity. The founder of this movement spoke of the "severe shortage of integrity" within U.S. society, sparked largely by the "growing irresponsibility of men" and the tendency of men to betray or abandon relationships, commit violent crimes, and consume drugs to excess (McCartney, 1997, p. 1). Although these two incidents appear to be in strong opposition—one a gesture of annihilation and one a gesture of consolidation—these incidents bespeak the similarities in culturally valorized styles of masculinity. After all, "To be a man is to be in charge. To be gentle is to be a wimp, a weak excuse for a man, an object of derision, and ridicule" (Toomey, 1992, p. 44).

This book is an attempt to address some of the issues raised above and to explore some of the ramifications of the relationship between masculinity and violence. I contextualize this discussion within the larger debates about social dislocation, cultural change, and, of course, the "problem of men"—the perceived contribution of men to newfound levels of civil disorder, and the apparent retreat of men from civic responsibilities.

This chapter presents a brief portrait of visible violence in U.S. society. This involves a short excursion into the complex field of official crime statistics. The United States has been chosen as a case study because of the high levels of violence saturating this nation: the deep penetration of violence into public and private places and the extremes to which violence is taken (see McGuckin, 1998; Smith & Zahn, 1999). I explore the intricacies of defining, constructing, and theorizing violence in Chapter 2.

I concentrate, in this chapter, on the conceptual underpinnings of our current knowledge about social systems and their actors. This focus reveals the common philosophical legacy that binds together much contemporary theorizing about human beings and their social world. It also provides us with a departure point for our foray into postmodern readings of social institutions and practices. Arguably, our modern and postmodern understandings of violence and gender are derived from these larger bodies of theory; hence it is important for us to acquaint ourselves with their premises and arguments. The chapter concludes with a set of formulations about violence and masculinity that lay the groundwork for the material in the ensuing chapters. Now, let us turn directly to the topic of violence.

Forcefields

What are the patterns of crime, especially violent crime, in today's society? How are homicide, assault, and rape woven into the social fabric? Measuring the amount of crime in any community is, of necessity, a political activity. This is nowhere more evident than in the sphere of sexual and gender-based violence. Recent data collection on domestic and sexual violence, conducted under the auspices of the U.S. Violence Against Women Act (1994), reveals that the majority of states are collecting annual statistics on these offenses. However, the researchers discovered that there is wide variation among states in the definition of domestic violence and sexual assault (Travis, Chaiken, & Auchter, 1996). Clearly, this variability affects the measurement processes and seriously restricts the reliability and validity of data aggregated at the national level.

Official reports on the distribution and severity of crime in the United States are generally based on the Uniform Crime Reports (UCR), published by the Federal Bureau of Investigation, which contain details of the crimes reported, on an annual basis, to the police. Another official data source is the National Crime Victimization Survey (NCVS), which surveys a large sample of the populace to determine annual rates of victimization. Recent findings from the NCVS have pointed to a decline in the rate of reported violent crime, a trend that began in 1994; for example, in 1995, the rates of homicide (as measured by the UCR) and the rates of rape, robbery, and aggravated assault (as measured by the NCVS) were at their lowest ebb for 23 years (Rand, Lynch, & Cantor, 1997). This reduction in reported crime rates in large cities can be explained by three factors: the adoption of an aggressive and often controversial style of results-oriented policing; the stabilization of illegal drug markets; and the coordination of effort on the part of police, other government agencies, and local communities (Brady, 1996). However, we know that violent crime is concentrated in specific areas of large cities and that some individuals suffer repeat victimization. The social groups most vulnerable to victimization are the young, African Americans, and males (Rand, 1997). Murder victims are most likely to be relatively young and male; in the most recent national survey, 65% were under 35 years, and 78% were male (Rand, 1997). Forty-seven percent of these murder victims were related to or knew their attackers. In the case of aggravated assaults, the majority were committed by strangers. About half the reported incidents of simple assault were committed by strangers. In the case of rape or sexual assault, two-thirds of the victims were related to or acquainted with their assailant.[1] Low-income, urban residents between 16 and 19 years of age were most likely to be sexually victimized. The majority of these sexual attacks were not reported to the police.

Gender differences are apparent in the longitudinal patterns of criminal violence in the United States. The statistical trends show that the rates of victimization reportedly experienced by men and women are now converging. Violent victimization of males is decreasing, while violent victimization of women remains relatively unchanged. In 1994, women were about two-thirds as likely as men to be the victims of violent crimes, including rape, robbery, assault, and homicide. Twenty years ago, women were less than half as likely as men to be victimized.

Today, women are more than twice as likely to be murdered by an intimate partner than by a stranger. Similarly, women are more likely to report being assaulted by a relative or an intimate partner. Furthermore, such violent encounters are more likely to result in injury to the woman than assaults perpetrated by a stranger (Craven, 1996).

Violent crime committed by youths now appears to be in decline after a steady and alarming increase. In the United States, juvenile crime has been the subject of intense political, social, and media attention. It has been widely acknowledged that the rate of reported violent juvenile crime increased substantially during the last few years. A report issued by the Office of Juvenile Justice and Delinquency Prevention of the U.S. Department of Justice (1994) noted that "juveniles account for an increasing share of all violent crimes in the United States" (p. 1). In introducing an updated statistical report on juvenile offenders and victims, Bilchik (1995) noted that

> between 1988 and 1992 juvenile arrests for violent crime increased nearly 50%. . . . While juveniles may not be responsible for most violent crime, the growing level of violence by juveniles does not bode well for the future. If violent juvenile crime increases in the future as it has for the past 10 years, [we] estimate that by the year 2010 the number of juvenile arrests for a violent crime will more than double and the number of juvenile arrests for murder will increase nearly 150%. (p. 1)

The statistical evidence indicates that juveniles in the United States have been committing more violent crime than in the past. The number of Violent Crime Index arrests of youths under 18 years of age increased by 50% between 1987 and 1991. This compared with an increase of 25% for adults. The number of youth arrests for murder increased by 85% during the same period (compared with 21% for adults); the number of youth arrests for sexual assault increased by 16% (compared with 7% for adults); and the number of youth arrests for robbery increased 52% (compared with 29% for adults). By 1991, the youth arrest rate for Violent Crime Index offences had reached a level higher that at any other time in history (see Kelley, Huizinga, Thornberry, & Loeber, 1997).

The number of juvenile murders tripled between 1984 and 1994, and the number of juvenile murderers using guns quadrupled during this same time (Snyder, Sickmund, & Poe-Yamagata, 1996). Furthermore, the arrests of youths under 15 years of age for violent crime increased by 94% between 1980 and 1995 (Butts & Snyder, 1997). Indeed, this wave of youth violence was viewed with such gravity that researchers suggested that "it might be helpful to conceptualize violence as an infectious disease spreading among the Nation's youth" (Kelley et al., 1997, p. 2).

Recent statistical data suggest that this climb has been halted. It has been reported that the arrest rate of youths for violent crime fell by 2.9% in 1995 and 9.2% in 1996. Commenting on this reversal, Attorney General Janet Reno claimed that the Clinton "crime plan" had provided more financial support and harsher penalties for juvenile offenders. Reno also attributed the decreased arrest rate to greater cooperation between law enforcement agencies, communities, and young people themselves. However, she noted, with reference to the Luke Woodham case, among others, "We continue to hear of too many serious violent crimes committed by young people. We cannot be satisfied by this reduction in youth violence. . . . One crime committed by a 16-year-old, one crime of violence, is one crime too many" (press conference, October 2, 1997). Clearly, violence is still the prerogative of the youthful male, especially when confronted by the contradictions and paradoxes of thwarted desire and personal and social disempowerment. Reaching deep into the historical and cultural storehouse of masculinity, a young man may still retrieve the ultimate tool of manly self-assertiveness: omnipotence through violence. However, the broader picture of risk and harm is closely tied to sociostructural disadvantage.

Detected or reported violence—that which comes to the attention of the state—is generally enacted by and inflicted upon the more marginal groups in society. Being young, being poor, and being African American or Hispanic exposes the individual to violence—either as victim or offender. These positionings, or social identities, are associated with heightened risks of harm, directed toward the self or others.

Class, ethnicity, and youth combine to place the individual within potential networks of violent relations. Gender intersects with these flashpoints of vulnerability to exacerbate the likelihood of men's involvement in violent behavior and to decrease the likelihood of women's involvement. How is gender implicated in the commission of violence? By what processes is violence included in or excluded from the constructions of gender? What are the origins and explanations of violence in all its forms? How are gendered identities produced and reproduced in society? How are cultural industries and institutions, such as film and the mass media, involved in the formation of ideas, attitudes, and beliefs about gender and violence? How can the new politics of masculinity inform our discussion of the nexus between gender and violence? These are some of the specific questions explored in the next several chapters. This exploration draws on the knowledge bases of several disciplines or interdisciplinary clusters: psychology, sociology, history, anthropology, criminology, cultural studies, media studies, women's studies, and men's studies.

Before embarking on our journey into the distinct and overlapping terrains of gender and violence, I wish to work through the implications and ramifications of our current perspectives on knowledge. I do this in recognition of the centrality of knowledge systems for both experience and social action, and of the profound changes to the constitution of knowledge that are now apparent at the beginning of the 21st century. As Elizabeth Grosz (1995) asserts, "Knowledges are not purely conceptual nor merely intellectual. . . . Knowledge is an activity; it is a practice. . . . It does things" (p. 37). Let us reflect on our traditions of knowledge: our ways of organizing experience, of making sense of the world, and of doing things. Doing so provides us with vital signposts for the intellectual work ahead.

Knowing Violence/Gendering Knowledge

Many of our understandings about self, the social world, and the natural environment are grounded in the epistemological frameworks laid down during the Enlightenment. The conceptions of knowledge, integral to Enlightenment philosophy, were premised on assumptions about the objective nature of "reality," the accessibility of reality to human understanding, the accumulation of knowledge through the faculty of reason, and the universality of knowledge-generating processes.

These 18th-century Enlightenment beliefs continue to inform mainstream epistemological approaches to the investigation of social and political institutions. Culturally pervasive beliefs define the parameters of human experience; for example, such beliefs specify the existence of a stable, coherent self, built on the foundations of conscious awareness and, of course, the faculty of reason. However, within this belief system, reason has a life independent of the self; it transcends the particular and embraces the universal. Reason produces timeless knowledge, free of the constraints of location, and adrift from culture—in short, it produces "truth." Claims to the authority or legitimacy of knowledge are decided in the court of reason. Truth is harnessed to power, guaranteeing that both freedom and progress are possible and attainable. Scientific knowledge, as the apotheosis of the appropriate use of reason, is the paradigm of all valid knowledge. Language, as the transparent representation of reality, is the rationalist vehicle for scientific inquiry. Interrogation of the nature of self and of the social and natural world proceeds through the mechanism of science, which is established as the preeminent and privileged source of knowledge in Western society.

The Enlightenment credo, articulated by Kant as *sapere aude*— "Have courage to use your reason" (p. 85)—rests on a deeply gendered view of human existence. In its call to mobilize specific properties of mind, it betrays the biased character of an Enlightenment philosophy in which the embodied and ethical perspectives on human subjectivity were abandoned. In their place rose "an episteme of representation [that] presupposed a spectator conception of the knowing self, a designative theory of meaning, and a detonative theory of language" (Benhabib, 1990, p. 110). Aspects of this Enlightenment legacy bear close examination, especially those premises that strongly influence contemporary understandings of human action and human experience. In particular, it is important to consider the role played by the Enlightenment construction of self as a stable, coherent entity mindful of its capacity to utilize reason (see Mascuch, 1996). This examination serves as a bridge to an analysis of the "crisis of reason" that threatens to undermine the validity and utility of modern, disciplinary knowledges (see Grosz, 1995). Let us begin by thinking through what is meant by *the self*.

The Self

Our dominant definition of the self is founded on an understanding of human beings as "self-contained unitary individuals who carry their uniqueness deep inside themselves" (Burkitt, 1991, p. 1). The anthropologist Clifford Geertz (1975) provides us with a succinct portrait of the self. He claims that we see the self as

> a bounded, unique, more or less integrated motivational and cognitive universe, a dynamic center of awareness, emotion, judgement, and action organized into a distinctive whole and set contrastively both against other such wholes and against a social and natural background. (p. 48)

This self-contained being is separate and divided from other selves, and is seen as a self-protecting, self-controlling entity. Moreover, Giddens (1991) notes that the modern self is a "reflexive project for which the individual is responsible" (p. 75). The self is also understood as embodied—that is, bounded—by the physical body although not reducible to it: The boundary of the self is seen to match the boundary of the body (Sampson, 1993). This individualized perspective on selfhood may be described as the "independent construal of self" (Matsumoto, 1994, p. 20), or as the Cartesian view of the subject (Gergen, 1995).[2] It may also be labeled the "monologic view" (Sampson, 1993).

This construction of self is grounded in psychological essentialism: the belief that individuals possess identifiable mental structures or processes that constitute a psychic interiority (Gergen, 1996). The cultural conviction that individuals are enlivened by a psychic core is sustained by three principal conditions that emerged particularly from the Enlightenment. The first condition supporting psychological essentialism relates to the ontological configuration of reality (Gergen, 1996). In any culture, there is consensus about the categories that organize and lend meaning to existence. For us, at the beginning of the 21st century, these relate to specific descriptions or categorizations of emotional or cognitive life. For example, we talk of emotions such as fear, greed, and envy as motivating factors in our behavior (Gergen, 1996). The second condition supporting psychological essentialism relates to modes of expression. In order to communicate effectively, we acquire and utilize particular ways of interacting in society. We assume, for example, that rationality underscores intelligent forms of speech. We also read certain behaviors as indicative of particular mental states; we see tears, for example, as evidence of sadness or grief (Gergen, 1996). Finally, the third condition supportive of psychological essentialism relates to valued goals. We share a broad commitment to the worth of cultural outcomes, and this fashions our vocabulary of human experience and action.

The Ideal Self

It is in the image of the ideal self that we find perhaps the clearest representation of the dominant construction of Western selfhood. The ideal self is a portrait of how we would like to be and what we are striving to become. Callahan (1993) notes that the ideal self of Western society "has drawn heavily from the larger treasure chest of modern faith and sensibility" (p. 121). Among the most prized items in that chest are self-control and self-direction. Not surprisingly, a core ideal of the modern self is to be "independent and self-sufficient, not dependent upon the help of others" (Callahan, 1993, p. 140). Autonomy—equated with independence, stability, and rational functioning—is cultivated and highly valued. This emphasis on self-governance translates into a specific construction of the self. In this construction, individual responsibility is of central significance (see Pitch, 1995). As Callahan persuasively states,

> We have come, in modern life, to shape an ideal of the self and its character that is empty of all content save that of choice. Choice—and the control over life and death that is its necessary condition—has come to be understood as the final meaning of human existence: the capacity to make of ourselves what we want to be. (p. 154)

Furthermore, Callahan argues that

> we have come to think that we as individuals are our own invention, not creatures of the state, or convention, or the past. In the idea of self-determination—fashioned on a foundation of vaulting human rights, and the elimination of slavery to fixed notions of human good—we have written the final charter of freedom. (p. 121)

Rational, emotionally contained, competent, and in control of both internal and external forces, the modern self is the epitome of what Bauman (1992a) describes as modernity's relentless subjugation of the natural world, the banishing of contingency and the ruthless imposition of order and predictability. The modern self is concerned with the preservation of autonomy not only as a personal goal, but also as a manifestation of the self's allegiance to the order-imposing, self-determining spirit of modernity. Violence, in the service of the modern self, preserves individuality and forestalls the possibility of fusion with the dangerous not-self. Violence, as a modern strategy, guarantees both individual and social control, while maintaining and perpetuating hierarchy and inequality. Benjamin (1998) notes, "Violence is the outer perimeter . . . of the tendency of the subject to force the other to either be or want what it wants, to assimilate the other to itself or make it a threat" (p. 68). Violence, then, is the expression of extreme undifferentiation. I explore this in more detail in Chapter 6.

The spirit of modernity is typified by Lasch's (1984) notion of the "imperial self." As an autonomous, self-constituting subject with a predictable and relatively fixed identity, the imperial self is not content with domination as the mere instrument of order. The imperial self is also narcissistic, materialistic, and expansionist; hence exploitation, manipulation, and colonization of the natural and social world become allied drives. The narcissistic dimensions of the imperial self are manifest in the preoccupation with the cultivation of an image that accords with socially constructed symbols of perfection, status, and success. The body, relationships, and knowledge itself become objects to be exploited. Indeed, the imperial self of the modern era has a voracious appetite for expanding its domain of ownership and its territory of control in a bid to suppress all other competitors and to achieve omnipotence.

It is in this context that the duality between self and Other is articulated. This dichotomy informs and shapes social, cultural, political, and economic practices in modern Western society. It also legitimizes the altruistic claims of democracy and justice. However, the self/Other split may be read as a metaphor for both empowerment and oppression; the duality between self and Other reflects a hierarchical structure in which self is valued over the Other (see Plumwood, 1993), and in which the latter may be viewed as the repository of all that is negative, threatening, or devalued in modern Western society. As Jessica Benjamin (1998) observes, "what we cannot bear to own, we can only repudiate" (p. 95). The Other may also be viewed as all that is alien, strange, or different; the boundaries between self and Other are often vigilantly policed so that the specter of mergence can be held at bay. I expand on the significance of boundaries to the modern imagination a little later.

As we have seen, the themes of independence, self-reliance, self-regulation, and self-control are implicit in the individualism that underpins the definition and construction of the modern self. Dependence, from a Western perspective, is an indicator of developmental immaturity or emotional deficiency. It is also closely associated with femininity and the normalized status of womanhood. Indeed, Carole Pateman (1989) observes that "the meaning of 'dependence' is associated with all that is womanly" (p. 185). The valorized construct of independence is associated with the exercise of masculinities in the public sphere; for example, the rights and entitlements of the citizen in the modern democratic state are emblematic of independence. A central element of the citizen's independence is his capacity for self-government. This involves the provision to subordinates of protection and the buying and selling of labor power (Pateman, 1989; see Hatty, 1992). Indeed, the contemporary ideals of citizenship, embracing human rights and freedom of expression—inalienable expressions of self-government—are so inextricably intertwined with the dominant characteristics of Western society that they are considered innate or natural. However, as we shall see in later chapters, many social theorists fiercely contest this view.

Given the privileging of self-reliance and self-control within the dominant discourses of self in modern Western society, the modern self's experience of loss—especially loss of self-control or loss of control over the Other—is likely to have social, personal, and ontological ramifications. Loss, signified by common experiences such as physical or mental illness, divorce, retrenchment, and bereavement, is construed by both society and the individual as a form of defeat and as a failure to uphold our faith in modernity's power to shape our own destiny. Sander Gilman (1988) notes, with reference to illness,

> It is the fear of collapse, the sense of dissolution, which contaminates the Western image of all diseases, including elusive ones such as schizophrenia. But the fear we have of our own collapse does not remain internalized. Rather, we project this fear onto the world in order to localize it and, indeed, to domesticate it. For once we locate it, the fear of our own dissolution is removed. Then it is not we who totter on the brink of collapse, but rather the Other. And it is an-Other who has already shown his or her vulnerability by having collapsed. (p. 1)

The fear of loss is so profound and the ethos of control is so entrenched in modern Western society that there is a tendency to avoid associating too closely with an individual experiencing the trauma of loss: loss of self-control, loss of health, loss of a loved one, loss of material prosperity. Loss in all its manifestations represents an encroachment upon selfhood and is therefore a challenge to the continued integrity of the modern self (see Phelan, 1997). The effect of loss is to remind the self of its finitude and its mortality.

Loss clearly challenges the modernist notions of the self as a bounded, masterful, integrated, and autonomous universe, and it seriously threatens the illusory security of the modern self. For the modern self, the realization of the fragile and capricious nature of life is likely to be deeply disturbing, engendering feelings of fearfulness, insecurity, and pervasive anxiety, which may linger indefinitely. I examine the implications of this in our later discussion of post-modernism.

The Modern Self: Two Models

Within the context of this individualized view of the self, there are two models of personhood or subjectivity that operate concurrently in modern Western society (Gergen, 1991). These models circulate throughout popular culture and inform academic and professional discourses of self. Both of these models conform to the dictates of the "independent construal of self" (Matsumoto, 1994). I briefly explore the dimensions of these models here, because they bear directly on my analysis, in later chapters, of gender and violence.

The first model is derived from the Romantic (or, more properly, *romanticist*) conceptions of self that emerged during the 19th century. In this model, the hidden depths of the person are emphasized, and the individual is seen as driven or animated by invisible, but deeply significant, forces (see Gergen, 1991, 1997). The key to this model is the concept of interiority. Carolyn Steedman, in her book *Strange Dislocations* (1995), documents how, from the 18th century onward, the concept of the self began more and more to embrace interiority. Interiority implied the existence of the self located *within* the individual, a "richly detailed self" (Steedman, 1995, p. 4) whose identity "was constituted in memory" (Taylor, 1989, p. 288).

Paralleling the relocation of the self from the outside to the inside was a strong cultural interest in the figure of the child. The child came to represent both the interiorized self and the past history that each individual life contained. Steedman notes that "what was turned inside in the course of individual development was that which was also latent: the child *was* the story waiting to be told" (p. 11). Freud's work most clearly crystallized these ideas about interiority and childhood. His account of infantile sexuality, for example, rearticulated many 19th-century ideas and, most importantly, *theorized* childhood, giving it another name—the unconscious. We still live with the legacy of this spacialized view of the self. Many of our prevailing notions of love and romance are a testament to the persistence of this 19th-century perspective (Gergen, 1991).

There are other sites where *conflicting* views of the self are apparent. The recent controversy over the validity of the construct of repressed (or recovered) memories is indicative of the struggle over differing models of the self, particularly when these touch on gender issues. Based on the twin precepts of repression and the infantile capacity for memory (Yapko, 1994), the idea of recovered memories relies on the romanticist conception of self. Those who object to the Freudian or post-Freudian view of the self challenge this notion of repression (see Loftus, 1993, 1994). Some point to the need to distinguish between the processes of repression and dissociation. Kristiansen (1994) claims that repression implies the ejection from consciousness of traumatic material, whereas dissociation implies the displacement of conscious awareness during or after the traumatic event. According to Kristiansen, this has profound consequences for the encoding and retrieval of material from memory. Memory, as a result of traumatic dissociation, is likely to be iconic: that is, organized on a somato-sensory level. This may be expressed as flashbacks or somatic sensations.

Critics of recovered memories label the phenomenon False Memory Syndrome (FMS). This occurs when the alleged victim experiences distorted or confabulated memories. Proponents of FMS believe that the techniques of therapists and the ill-advised approaches of self-help groups are primarily responsible for generating false memories.

The second model of selfhood—the *modernist* view of self—is founded on the scientific imperative of observing, measuring, and recording the visible aspects of human behavior (see Gergen, 1991, 1997). In the modernist model, the self is seen as transparent and open to scientific scrutiny. It is also viewed as predictable and accessible. The self is understood to be a product, in the main, of environmental influences. The modernist self, therefore, is knowable, and it constitutes a complex source of knowledge (or data) for the contemporary scientist.

The discipline of psychology has been critical to the formulation and application of the modernist view of self. In his influential book, *Governing the Soul: The Shaping of the Private Self* (1991), Nikolas Rose claims that

> our selves are defined and constructed and governed in psychological terms, constantly subject to psychologically inspired techniques of self-inspection and self-examination. And the problems of defining and living a good life have been transposed from an ethical to a psychological register. (p. xiii)

Furthermore, as Gergen (1997) argues, "Psychological expertise now holds out the promise not of curing pathology but of reshaping subjectivity," leading us to conclude that psychological categories and terms are now core constituents of contemporary cultural practices.

We were witness, in the second half of the 20th century, to the rise of the "desiring, relating, actualizing self" (Rose, 1991, p. xiii). This led to the advent of what might be called the therapeutic culture of the self, in which the vocabulary of the psychotherapeutic penetrates every aspect of life. Rose (1991) nominates four aspects of this psychotherapeutic culture: first, the subjectification of work (the installation of a concern with identity, fulfillment, and personal success at the heart of work); second, the psychologization of the mundane (the translation of everyday occurrences into "life events"); third, the therapeutics of finitude (the renaming of endings, closings, and limits as therapeutic opportunities); and, fourth, the neurotization of social intercourse (the recasting of our relationships into a series of categories, such as normal/abnormal or functional/dysfunctional).[3]

This suggests that the modernist self is amenable to being reshaped; it further suggests that invitations to self-change flicker across our everyday lives, enticing us with their possibilities. The modernist view of the self encourages us to see ourselves as incomplete (or, perhaps, even deficient) in mind, behavior, or body. However, the modernist view of self offers us hope: It suggests that, ultimately, we are capable of a significant degree of personal transformation. Atwater (1994) notes, "Americans spend millions of dollars every year in the hope of improving themselves, buying and trying self-help manuals and cassettes and attending workshops, not to mention academic courses in psychology" (p. 165). I would venture to say that the rest of the Western world is not far behind.

However, as we have seen, this model also implies that we are responsible, to a large extent, for achieving this transformation (see Giddens, 1991). To refuse to take up this opportunity to change ourselves is to risk not becoming the people we could be—it is to deny our optimum selves.

Patrolling the Borders of the Self

As the modern self is conceptualized as a distinct entity marked off from others by clear divisions, there is a great deal of attention given to the issue of borders and boundaries within dominant constructions of the self. This is manifest in several spheres. Personality, as the public and private expression of self, is understood to develop within specific expected parameters. Traditional approaches to psychology have viewed the self as developing through stages or phases. The experiences of attachment and separation, and the processes of individuation, are the dominant elements in the development of the self and of identity. Developmental psychologists, in particular, endorse the view that the self grows and develops through identifiable stages (Carlson, 1993). For example, Piaget (1963, 1965, 1969), in his model of cognitive development, explores the relationship between a child's experiences or cognitive abilities and external stimuli. As the child passes through the four stages of cognitive development, she or he learns to differentiate between the self and external objects. With this development comes an understanding of object permanence, which leads to the ability to represent objects or things symbolically.

Erikson's (1968) theory of psychosocial development divides the life span into eight stages ranging from birth to old age. Erikson believed that social relationships and circumstances change throughout the life span, and he articulated the various personal and interpersonal crises that might confront the individual as she or he moves through these stages of development. Underlying the theoretical framework of the life span trajectory is the premise that the ultimate goal of these developmental processes is the achievement of autonomy and self-determination.

Inherent in these theories of stage development is the idea that failure to master the tasks or crises peculiar to each stage may result in a series of problems for the individual. Indeed, the construct of "crisis," as articulated by Erikson and other theorists, may be understood as a "border experience" in which the individual is required to find a route back to "the center" or to move across the border into another domain (McNamee, 1992, p. 188). I explore, in the section on postmodernism, the effects of border crossings, border wars, and border erasures.

First, however, I reflect on the significance of reason to modern life and the construction of the self.

Raising the Barricades

Modernity is founded on the primacy of reason and rationality. Reason offers us security and confidence; it promises mastery, choice, and control. Reason gives us access to the real. As Bauman (1992b) explains, "Reason is first and foremost the art of separating the real from the apparent. . . . Reason is both the umpire and the trademark of the real" (pp. 180-181). Reason erects a boundary around the territory of the real; it excludes and denies the legitimacy, and indeed the existence, of extraneous knowledge. Outside the boundaries of the real lie all that reason does not claim: the irreal. This may be the counterfeit, the fake, the deception—that which dissimulates or pretends. Reason and rationality are the vehicle for probing, examining, and testing that which lies beyond, but which also seeks admittance to, the domain of the real. The knowledge systems of modernity, grounded in the tenets of empiricist science, provide the tools for assessing the status of sensory experience. This involves the search for meaning—the penetration of the world of appearances and the discovery, through interrogation, of the essence of things. This essence is understood to be located below the surface; it is seen to reside in the depth of objects or experiences. As Bauman observes, "Meaning can only be grasped through pursuing the relation between elusive appearance and solid, yet hidden, reality" (pp. 182-183). Furthermore, "Meaning is the hard yet invisible core wrapped tightly in what offers itself to the senses, what can be seen and heard: the signifier. That core can be uncovered and repossessed if the carapace of the signifier is broken" (p. 183). Science, in all its manifestations, is the instrument that makes this quest possible.

Reason and rationality are the central organizing principles of the modern self. Indeed, the birth of the modernist construction of self occurred in direct relation to the ascendancy of reason. The rationalist project of the 17th century, driven in particular by the anxious imaginings of Descartes, provided the basis for the development of the idea of the individuated, contained, and regulated self. Haunted by fears of mergence with the cosmos, Descartes, in his *Meditations,* began the intellectual work of establishing boundaries—of delineating the differences between *here* and *there, inside* and *outside.* The *embedded* consciousness of the Middle Ages receded; arising in its place was the *differentiated* consciousness: an inner self composed of introspection and self-observation, in which knowledge is understood to be the possession of a vertically layered self. The idea of the inwardness of mental life displaced the more archaic, organic view of the relations between humans and the cosmos (Merchant, 1990; Berman, 1981). This was the beginning of the processes of interiorization. These processes reverberated throughout Renaissance culture, affecting all levels of social discourse, shaping the patterns of experience, and setting the terms for modern modes of interaction (see Elias, 1978, 1982; Hatty & Hatty, 1999).

The "dialectics of separation and individuation," which underscore Descartes's *Meditations,* were the product of profound fear and dread at immersion in nature and entrapment within the body (Bordo, 1986, 1987). In the first book of the *Meditations,* Descartes draws the reader into speculation about the continuity between madness and dreams, and questions whether our very existence might not be an illusion. The outcome of this speculation is "the securing of all the boundaries . . . between the 'inner' and the 'outer,' between the subjective and the objective, between self and world" (Bordo, 1986, p. 450). With the establishment of the two distinct ontological categories of *mind* and *body,* and the privileging of the former over the latter, came the centrality of reason, which is "bent on foreclosing, finalizing, completing" (Bauman, 1992b, p. 181). And, of course, bent on assuaging dread and anxiety at the prospect of organic unity with the cosmos. Bordo (1986, 1987) refers to this phenomenon as the 17th-century flight from the feminine. From this affective source emerged the philosophical and scientific culture we inherited with modernity. The prohibitions against commingling—of self with Other, subject with object—still inform the pragmatics of empiricist science. Independence, detachment, impartiality: These are the hallmarks of legitimized knowledge systems. Reason is the architect of these valorized forms of inquiry. As Susan Bordo (1986) so astutely observes, "The new epistemological anxiety is . . . evoked by the memory or suggestion of union. . . . The otherness of nature is now what allows it to be known" (pp. 452-453).

Reason, of course, also attaches itself to masculine subjectivity. This subjectivity coheres in its proximity to the real. The irreal, and all its contents, belongs to the dangerous territory beyond the confines of normalized masculine subjectivity. There reside disturbing emotions, confused thoughts, transports of delight—madness, desire, and the feminine. Madness and its torments are now viewed as the antithesis of reason; the so-called disordered mind, and its corresponding lack of mastery over the body, stands in stark opposition to that modern invention, the rational mind, which is governed by ordered thought processes disposed to autonomous and responsible functioning. It was Foucault who argued that sovereign reason excluded all that threatened it; he noted in *Madness and Civilization* (1967) that "the language of psychiatry, which is a monologue of reason about madness, could be established only on the basis of such a silence" (p. 12).

The modern construct of reason, however, is profoundly gendered. Jane Flax acknowledged over a decade ago that Enlightenment epistemologies reflect what Susan Bordo (1986) describes as the "Cartesian masculinization of thought" (p. 439). Flax (1983) notes, "In Hobbes, Freud and Rousseau . . . reason can only emerge as a secondary process, under the authority and pressure of the patriarchal father. . . . Reason is seen as a triumph over the senses, of the male over the female" (p. 134). Desire, associated with the body and its unpredictable ways, is linked to the sensual. Women, according to Rousseau, evoke desire in men and tempt them away from the path of reason. Furthermore, sexual desire, once aroused, may interfere with rational functioning; self-control may be undermined and irrational actions ensue. Women, therefore, possess the capacity to draw men closer to the outer boundaries of masculine subjectivity, and may even entice them over the edge into the abyss of the irreal. I consider the implications of this border travel in later chapters. Let us now briefly explore the rise of the "sciences of man."

The Human Sciences: The Subject of Crime

Foucault argued in his early work that it was during the modern episteme that man became the subject and object of knowledge. In his book *The Order of Things* (1971), Foucault provided a detailed analysis of the rules and ordering procedures underlying the Renaissance era, the classical era, and the modern era, focusing on the alterations in the sciences of life, labor, and language. In this work, Foucault presented what he called an "archaeology" of the contemporary discourses of Western civilization.

According to Foucault (1971), it was during the modern era (1800–1950) that the knowledges that formed the basis of the human sciences emerged. These new knowledges included criminology, psychology, sociology, and anthropology. Foucault claimed that the rise of the human sciences as fields of scholarly inquiry owed a great deal to the spread of disciplinary technologies. This was exemplified by the Panopticon, the early model for the prison, which was adapted for the hospital, the school, and the factory. Indeed, Foucault nominated the Panopticon, developed by Jeremy Bentham in 1791, as a paradigmatic example of a political technology based on discipline. Foucault viewed the Panopticon as the archetypal expression of disciplinary power: The surveillance of the inmates was ceaseless and all-encompassing. They became objects on permanent display. Foucault (1979) described the cells as being like "small theatres in which each actor is alone, perfectly individualized and constantly visible" (p. 200). The Panopticon, argued Foucault, "is the diagram of a mechanism of power reduced to its ideal form" (p. 205). It was not only a highly efficient structure to ensure the direct control of individuals but also a laboratory in which experiments could be carried out. Constant observation made possible the recording and tabulation of events.

The knowledge that forms the basis of the human sciences was first compiled within these disciplinary sites. Foucault did not regard this as a noble moment in the history of knowledge. He noted, "The birth of the sciences of man [sic] . . . is probably to be found in . . . ignoble archives, where the modern play of coercion over bodies, gestures and behavior had its beginnings" (1979, p. 191).

As we have already seen, the gaze reigned supreme in these sites. Visual surveillance of the highly visible subjects confined or held within the walls of these institutions produced a body of scientific data. As the activities within these sites became more specialized, a vast array of data (or knowledge) was compiled. As the human sciences took shape, they drew their legitimacy and authority from the discourses and practices integral to these sites of power/knowledge.[4] Correspondingly, power/knowledge in the human sciences began to mark out and categorize man, rendering man knowable. According to Foucault (1979), the production of docile and manageable bodies within the network of disciplinary technologies

> called for a technique of overlapping subjection and objectification.
> . . . [This] network constituted one of the armatures of this power/
> knowledge that made the human sciences possible. *Knowable man*
> [italics added] (soul, individuality, consciousness, conduct, whatever
> it is called) is the object-effect of this analytic investment, of this
> domination-observation. (p. 305)

This is not to suggest that the human sciences are the direct outcome of the disciplinary matrix that is the prison, but rather to suggest that they arose out of a common historical legacy and share an investment in the power/knowledge technologies that characterize the prison. The constant compilation of data, the continuous expansion of recordkeeping systems, and the conduct of experimentation in the context of the disciplinary matrix of the prison converged with the emergence of the human sciences.

It is in this sense that the modern individual—observed, objectified, categorized, and analyzed—can be viewed as a historical achievement, the product of the complex strategic developments in disciplinary technologies (see Rose, 1996a, 1996b). Such disciplinary technologies now order and shape everyday social practices in an extension of the biopolitics of coercive institutions (Lyon, 1993;

Dandeker, 1994). The entire society is now invested with disciplinary techniques and strategies designed to regiment and subdue. Deeply imbricated in this disciplinary system is the censure of Otherness—of disease, madness, and social disorder.

Criminology, as the science of moral transgression, had its origins in the Italian school of criminal anthropology. Cesare Lombroso sketched an outline of the "born criminal" in 1876. He claimed to have identified significant anatomical features—twisted faces and large jaws reminiscent of an earlier ancestral type—that distinguished the criminal from his normal counterpart. Lombroso also denoted physiological features that marked the born criminal, including an insensitivity to pain and an instinctive tendency to antisocial behavior. These were identified in an attempt to map out the contours of a preventive science capable of predicting dangerous and criminal behavior. Early French criminologists, like their Italian peers, sought to catalog the diagnostic criteria linked to criminality. The French, however, were more concerned to construct a criminal sociology, and regarded their fellow Italians as excessive in their positivist zeal. Nevertheless, both schools developed secular and scientific rationales for the exclusion of specific groups or classes of people. These rationales legitimized the practices designed to manage perceived political threats to the social order.

Governing Subjectivity

According to Nikolas Rose (1992), the societies of North America and Europe were increasingly driven during the late 19th and early 20th centuries by the desire to govern individuals. Rose claims that while these political and social maneuvers were diverse in shape and form, they were united by a belief in the possibility, and indeed necessity, of managing specific aspects of social organization. Rose notes that in order for these programs to be successful, it was vital to find a way to represent the domain to be governed.

It was under the auspices of the human sciences that vocabularies for the systematic governing of human subjectivity could be formulated. As we have seen, an acquaintance with the work of Foucault reveals the historical origins of these discourses and social practices and, of course, the centrality of power to the formulation of vocabularies for governing the human subject (see Rose, 1996a, 1996b).

We have also seen that it was the human sciences that assisted in the project of delineating the human subject and that provided a language for establishing normality and inducing discipline. Rose (1992) believes that we could view the human sciences as "techniques for the disciplining of human difference: for individualizing humans through classifying them, calibrating their capacities and conducts, inscribing and recording their attributes and deficiencies, and managing and utilizing their individuality and variability" (p. 123).

We might conclude that disciplinary power now operates at the level of the individual. The apparatus of normalization subsumes all varieties of disorder. Distributed across the entire social field, the hegemony of the normative exists in a cooperative relationship to other modalities of power. Disciplinary techniques serve these processes of normalization, inducing the individual to adopt strategies supportive of a generalized normative order. The human sciences legitimize and prescribe the limits of this normative order. Criminology, in particular, is central to this project.

In deconstructing the traditional domain of criminology, Pfohl and Gordon (1987) claim that it is the desire to master Otherness—to empty Nature of her subversive and unpredictable power, to dispel fear and substitute a cruel domination, to objectify—that characterizes the science of criminology. The gaze of the criminologist is a form of mastery: It surveys, fixes, classifies, and disciplines. This is the carceral gaze of the Panopticon (Pfohl & Gordon, 1987). Furthermore, criminology, as the science of Otherness, is a discourse of truth. The criminologist is positioned as the truth-teller: the normalized, legal subject sitting in judgement over other disqualified and illegitimate knowledges.

On the individual level, Western man, the "confessing animal" (Foucault, 1980, p. 60), now possessed the authority to annunciate the truth. The self had become "the locus of truth, the locus of certainty" (Pfohl & Gordon, 1987, p. 242). The criminologist has fashioned an interpretive device to render the Other's confession understandable. The pleasure of criminology, according to Pfohl and Gordon (1987), is to subject the Other—this "unreasonable savage other, dark and unruly" (p. 230)—to the authority of reason.

Below we canvass the impact and effects of the arrival of the postmodern moment, with its profound challenges to modern knowledge systems and its accompanying social and technological manifestations.

From the Modern to the Postmodern

> Modern civilization simultaneously appears both frenzied and decrepit.
>
> —*Peter Beilharz*

> The shock of modernization was that things were never going to be the same again but at least it offered the reassurance that the direction in which things were going to change was, at least in principle, perceptible. . . .
>   The shock of postmodernization is that directionality is totally unclear; the only certainty is continuing uncertainty.
>
> —*Stephan Crook, Jan Pakulski, and Malcolm Waters*

There is no doubt that contemporary Western society is in the grip of pervasive anxiety about the present and about the future—about the present as a result of the rapidly changing social circumstances that enfold us as we slip from the modern[5] to the postmodern[6] epoch, and about the future as a result of the close of one century (and, indeed, one millennium) and the opening of another, replete with the unknown and the unknowable (see Gery, 1996; Nowotny, 1994; Pahl, 1995; Thompson, 1995). Mark Dery (1999) comments,

> The belief that we are history's witnesses to extremes of social fragmentation and moral malaise, that we stand at critical junctures and teeter on the brink of momentous decisions, is part and parcel of the fin-de-siècle; the fin-de-millennium simply turns up the cultural volume tenfold. (p. 31)

What, then, are the effects of the social and technological changes that surround us?

Social commentators now proclaim the transition from the 20th century to the 21st century as a time of profound transformation equivalent in magnitude to the Renaissance. Douglas Rushkoff (1994a), for example, claims that the Renaissance had a technological stimulus—the invention of the Gutenberg Press—that assisted in the dissemination of knowledge. He also claims that the Renaissance was spurred on by the discovery of visual perspective. At the present moment, we have the technological stimulus of the computer and the aesthetic and structural stimulus of the hologram.

Rushkoff (1994b) maintains that the invention of the computer modem and the Internet, as well as the proliferation of satellites and the fiberoptic communications, have radically altered our relationship with the media. The one-way model of communication, in which there was an identifiable viewer or listener, has disappeared. Interactive models of multimedia, accessed and controlled by multitudes, have emerged as the contemporary construction of media. Furthermore, we are now firmly located in the era of repetition, in which the distinction between the original and the copy, between innovation and seriality, has been effaced (Eco, 1990). The modern concept of unique artistry, inspired by creative talent or even genius, has been supplanted by the replicability of postmodern media forms. Electronic reproduction of images guarantees the ceaseless circularity of data, trends, styles, and gestures (Debord, 1990). As Baudrillard (1990b) notes, "Nothing disappears any more through an end or death, but through proliferation, continuity, saturation and transparence" (p. 12). The transience and impermanence of postmodern life is captured by the unlimited replication of images, the demise of the "new," and the perpetual rehearsal of events or experiences. Critical theorist Mark Poster (1995) believes that recent developments in electronic media have so altered our communication practices and so transformed the process of identity construction that we are justified in calling the present a second media age. I will explore this issue further in Chapter 3.

Nicholas Negroponte claims that we are living in the post-information age in which everything is made to order, information is extremely personalized, and the audience is singular. In his recent work, *Being Digital* (1995), Negroponte suggests that digital technology is an empowering force, which has the potential to bring people into greater world harmony. Negroponte acknowledges the negative possibilities of what he calls "being digital," but remains highly optimistic about the future.

Clearly, although some commentators worry about the "digital colonization of the analogue dataspace" (Chesher, 1994), we could conclude that technological and social change can result in both utopian and dystopian tendencies. Dystopian tendencies often receive expression in apocalyptic fears and desires (Sartelle, 1994), manifest perhaps as apocalypse culture (Bertsch, 1994) or as technological/biological revenge (Tenner, 1996).

Best and Kellner (1991) note that the information technology revolution could work either to multiply knowledge (and information) or to overwhelm us with a surfeit of data; it could democratize access to significant sources of information or it could strengthen the control and domination of economic or political elites.

Multiple Selves in the Postmodern Era: Toward Transgressive Knowledge

Together with the build-up of information superhighways we are facing a new phenomenon: loss of orientation. . . . A duplication of sensible reality, into reality and virtuality, is in the making. A stereo-reality of sorts threatens. A total loss of bearings of the individual looms large.

—Paul Virilio

Well, welcome to the 21st century. We are all immigrants to a new territory. Our world is changing so rapidly that we can hardly track the differences, much less cope with them. . . . Without having migrated an inch, we have, nonetheless, traveled further than any generation in history.

—Douglas Rushkoff

How might we define the important features of postmodernism? Although there are varieties of postmodernism—for example, ludic or resistance approaches (see Ebert, 1998)—it is possible to assert that postmodernism, in general, debunks the myths of modernity: the "liberation" of progress; the "advances" of Western civilization; the totalizing narratives surrounding nation, state, society; the linearity of time; and the barriers and markers of geographical space.

Postmodernism rejects the products and processes of the scientific revolution: the primacy of scientific knowledge; the objective, neutral character of scientific method; the division of knowledge into disciplines; and the fragmentation of knowledge. Postmodernism derives from a "sense of the inadequacy of Enlightenment theories of knowledge and traditional rationalist or empiricist methodologies and a shift towards the aesthetic as a means of discovering an alternative to Cartesianism and Kantian Reason" (Waugh, 1992, p. 4). Postmodernism replaces the modernist striving for determinacy, unity, synthesis, and specificity with their opposites—indeterminacy, diversity, difference, and complexity. Frederic Jameson (1991) observes that "the rise of postmodernism is signaled in parallel developments in our culture: diffusion of power, decentering of contexts, and denaturing of the physical" (p. 38).

Distinguished by its disillusionment with the unfulfilled modernist promises of reason and scientific progress, postmodernity repudiates the grand narratives, renounces the truth claims of science, and challenges the traditional arbiters of truth. The prevailing metaphor of postmodernity is "the game," in which the rules are changeable and modernist notions of chance have no place. Modernity, by contrast, is characterized by the dominance of deterministic, orderly Law, which upholds the primacy of "the norm" and denies the legitimacy of chance. The Law floats independently "above scattered individuals," while rules exist only when shared by the games' participants (Baudrillard, 1990a, p. 132). A multitude of games exist in postmodern society. These games subsume all: No one can escape involvement. Yet the game is fluid, malleable, and unpredictable: Contingency is banished in favor of ambiguity; durability is cast out in favor of transience. The "*ephemerality* and *evanescence* of things" becomes apparent (Bauman, 1992b, p. 187) in the embrace of open space-time (Lyotard, 1988).

The critical theorist Mark Poster (1995) reminds us that the postmodern age has been accompanied by an explosion of narrativity led by the revolution in computer technologies. Of course, the question of narrative has been central to a discussion of the postmodern condition (Lyotard, 1986). Literary theory and criticism, historiography, media and cultural studies, and various other social science disciplines have all been affected by the preoccupation with narrative form (see, for example, Lieblich & Josselson, 1994; Polkinghorne, 1988).

As a result of the transformations in knowledge and social experience wrought by postmodernization, subjectivity has come to the fore (see Bradley, 1995; Edge, 1994; Flax, 1993; Haber, 1994; Kolak, 1991; Luntley, 1995; Marsh, 1995; Seidman, 1995). In addition, sustained challenges have been launched by those whose voices have traditionally been silenced—women, indigenous peoples, ethnic and racial minority groups, to name a few. The question of Otherness—whether defined in biological, psychological, cultural, or political terms—is being debated anew. The issue of difference, played out within categories of race, ethnicity, and gender, is integral to discussions about hegemony, social change, and the potential for social transformation (Barker, 1995; Brinker-Gabler, 1994; Hall & du Gray, 1996; San Juan, 1995; Sarup, 1996).

What does this imply for the modern view of self? Nikolas Rose (1996a) states, "The idea of 'the self' has entered a crisis that may well be irreversible" (p. 169). K. J. Gergen (1996) claims that the concept of psychological essentialism is losing its credibility. The cultural significance attached to the idea of psychic interiority is being devalued in the wake of technological change. With the trend toward the demise of psychological essentialism, the conditions sustaining a discourse of the self have also changed. According to Gergen, we now have the proliferation of ontologies; there are now multiple approaches to making sense of existence. No single orthodoxy prevails: Instead, we are presented with a range of vocabularies to describe our experiences of everyday life. Taussig (1993) describes contemporary human ontology in terms of "mimesis"—coming-into-being in the continuous interplay between the copy (that is, the representation) and the copied. We become ourselves by copying and incorporating observed fragments of others' experiences; however, we also become ourselves through the process of differentiation. There is a link, therefore, between mimesis and alterity. Finally, according to Gergen (1996), there is resistance to the idea of consensual cultural goals as a result of the decentering of some power relations and the rise of the voices of the previously marginalized or excluded.

Consequently, it is clear that the once confident, hopeful, and masterful imperial self (Lasch, 1984) is no longer ascendant. The imperial self, with its solid, fixed sense of identity and its constitution as an autonomous subject, has all but disappeared. The personal history, friends, family, and a sense of place, which comprised the core identity of the imperial self, no longer command the focus of attention. Instead, these aspects of self-definition are scattered and divided.

A postmodern analysis reveals that the self is in a state of continuous construction and reconstruction. The self in the postmodern era appears to have no center, and is not autonomous; anti-essentialist readings of the self now prevail. The self may be viewed as a narrative, arising out of discourse and constrained by economic, political, social, and cultural imperatives (Lax, 1992); hence the self may be viewed as a "text," interpreted through its history and "rewritten through recollection" (Freeman, 1993, p. 16). This perspective emphasizes the role of memory in evoking a past history that the individual may use as a guide to the self. The psychologist John Shotter (1993) refers to "linguistically constructed relationships" characterized by "the contingent flow of continuous communicative interaction between human beings" (pp. 2, 7). This approach emphasizes the intertextuality of human communication systems, and exposes as an illusion the modernist view of the individual as self-enclosed and "possessing an inner sovereignty" (p. 43). Following Deleuze and Guattari (1988), Rose (1996b) suggests that we might conceive of the self as an assemblage that alters or metamorphoses as new connections are entered into. In this view, subjectivity is constituted through the linkage of humans and other objects with practices, multiplicities, and forces (Rose, 1996b). (See also the groundbreaking work of Gergen, 1991; Gergen, 1995; McNamee & Gergen, 1992; Shotter & Gergen, 1992; see also Grodin & Lindlof, 1996; Grossley, 1996.)

As we have seen, the self may now be understood as an array of constructed phenomena, loosely encapsulated within the sexed body. However, the social categories of *body* and *gender* are now hotly contested. This has been exacerbated by the arrival of new communication technologies and new forms of social experience, such as virtual reality.

What of the body in this new environment? Clearly, we could argue that the body is always present as a social construct in virtual space. The critical media theorist A. R. Stone (1991) notes that, in virtual systems, there is an interface between the human body (or bodies) and an associated *I* (or *I*'s). There is also a great deal of corporeal play. She observes, however, that such corporeal play in a virtual medium is not new. Stone points, for example, to the conjuring of the body by phone sex workers, especially the ways in which verbal gestures and hints may produce an image of a particular kind of body; she claims that after a verbal engagement with a client over the phone, all sex workers appear to be white, 5′ 4″ tall, with red hair (Stone, 1995b).

However, virtual worlds present the opportunity for a thorough and *interactive* engagement in sexual fantasy. Julian Dibbell (1999) describes how he invented an online persona, called Dr. Bombay, who developed a virtual sexual relationship with another online persona. In his account of their affair, Dibbell calls this passionate virtual union "tinysex."

Stone (1991) suggests that, as a result of technological innovation, the boundaries between subjects, technology, and nature are "undergoing a radical refiguration" (p. 101). The technological restructuring of these boundaries might provide a space in which to reevaluate the categories of sex and gender, redefine the body, and establish new theories of subjectivity (Mazur, 1994).

What are the effects of the new communication technologies on accepted gender categories? Donna Haraway's *Manifesto for Cyborgs* (1989) paved the way for a discussion of the identity issues at stake in the digital age. Judith Butler (1990) notes that the category of *woman* is often viewed as both stable and coherent. However, Butler asks whether this gender system is not an "unwitting regulation and reification of gender relations?" (p. 5). I investigate this further in Chapter 4.

According to Sherry Turkle, Professor of Communications at MIT, the new communication technologies offer significant possibilities for gender redefinition. She has said of the computer, "It can be negotiated with, it can be responded to, it can be psychologized" (1984, p. 118). Both Turkle and Shannon McRae (1994) note that in MUDs (Multi-User Dungeons on the Internet), gender—as a primary marker of identity—is often subverted. Of course, Internet Relay Chat (IRC) also offers unbounded opportunities for self-invention. In text-based virtual worlds, gender becomes "a verb, not a noun, a position to occupy rather than a fixed role, and in many cases, the effect that one individual can have upon another" (McRae, 1994).

In her more recent work, Turkle is concerned with the boundary-challenging potential of computer mediated interactions. In her latest book, *Life on the Screen: Identity in the Age of the Internet* (1995), Turkle maps out the potential of a set of boundary negotiations around identity, gender, and embodiment. In discussing the politics of virtuality, Turkle (1996) asks, "Is the real self always the one in the physical world? . . . Where does real life end and a game begin?" However, she also believes that "virtual personae can be a resource for self-reflection and self-transformation."

Clearly, computer mediated communication challenges our cultural assumptions about gender and embodiment (McAdams, 1996). Lynn Cherny (1994) notes that "virtual reality technology poses particularly obvious challenges to a politics of identity." This is nowhere more evident than in what are called immersive virtual technologies. In immersive virtual reality technologies—as opposed to the text-based versions involved in MUDs, for example—bodies become "flickering signifiers, characterized by their tendency toward unexpected metamorphoses, attenuations, and dispersions" (Hayles, 1993, p. 76; see also Cherny, 1995, Cherny & Weise, 1996).

Indeed, it has been claimed that cyberspace itself is grounded in "a curious form of *disembodiment*" (Wilson, 1995, p. 224). In his recent book, *Digital Sensations* (1999), Ken Hillis asserts that the development of virtual reality is the actualization of the Western desire to escape the confines of the body. We can therefore view the emergence of these technologies as the expression of cultural tendencies toward somatophobia (Hatty & Hatty, 1999).

Boundary Wars

Consistent with the current emphasis on narrativity, I would like to conclude this section with a story. This is a story that illustrates the problematic nature of identity in the 1990s (Stone, 1993, 1995a, 1995b). It illustrates the congruence between psychological and legal understandings of identity, and the divergence between these understandings and postmodern readings driven by cultural and media theory. Consequently, it is a story that reveals the struggles between disciplinary knowledges to assume the authority to define aspects of human experience. It also tells us something about the variable potential of each of these disciplinary knowledges to resonate with contemporary human experience.

As we proceed with the narrative, we should remember that the shift from the modern to the postmodern era involves the erosion of singularity in all its forms. As Stone (1993) explains, "Among the phenomena at the close of the mechanical age which it is useful to note is the pervasive burgeoning of the ontic and epistemic qualities of multiplicity in all their forms. . . ."

This is a story about interpersonal violence and multiple identities. It begins in 1990 with a claim by a Wisconsin woman that she had been sexually assaulted in her car by an acquaintance. However, this was a complaint with a difference. The woman alleged that her assailant had attacked her after carefully drawing out one of her personalities, a naive young woman whom he thought would be willing to have sex with him.

The complainant had been diagnosed some time earlier with Multiple Personality Disorder (MPD). This condition is categorized in the *Diagnostic and Statistical Manual* of the American Psychiatric Association (the *DSM-IV*) as a dissociative disorder, and it involves severe disruption or alteration of identity, memory, or consciousness. It is characterized by the presence of two or more distinct personalities in one person, "each with its own relatively enduring pattern of perceiving, relating to, and interacting with the environment" (Kendall & Hammen, 1995, p. 209). It is a disorder that is being detected at an increasing rate. It is also a disorder that disproportionately affects women.

So what happened in this trial? How did the law respond to this profound challenge to the widely accepted definition of *self* and of *identity*? The defendant's attorney tried two approaches. The first was to suggest that the rape shield law, the legislation that prevented the defense from questioning the victim about her sexual history, did not apply to all of the victim's personalities; hence he wanted to question the victim's other so-called personalities. The judge in the case ruled that this could not be done and that the rape shield law applied to all of the victim's personalities.

The defendant's attorney then moved to his second approach. This was to suggest that MPD had no credibility. To this end, he assembled a "cadre of MPD infidels" (Stone, 1993) who rejected the concept of MPD. One such "infidel," Donald Travers, claimed that MPD has no validity as a diagnostic category. When asked, "How many psychologists actually have patients with MPD?," he replied, "There's a band of very intense believers who have all the sightings, where the rest of us never see any." These sightings were described as the "UFOs of psychiatry" (Stone, 1993).

The victim's attorney responded to this strategic maneuver by putting the victim on the stand. First, of course, he had to ensure that he had the right personality: that is, the one that had experienced the abuse. The attorney asked to speak to Franny. Franny duly materialized, and confirmed that she had been the victim of sexual assault in June, 1990. The presiding judge then swore in Franny, as if swearing in several identities in the one body was an everyday court occurrence.

Franny—a distinct legal subject—proceeded to give her evidence. The defense continued to present evidence that MPD is a sham, a psychological hoax, and that the victim's accounts were duplicitous or fantastic. Surprisingly, perhaps, the trial ended with the conviction of the defendant.

What are some of the important subtexts of this trial? Clearly, the substance of the trial dealt with the cultural meanings attached to bodies and to selves. More specifically, the trial was an exercise in juridical power, an attempt to fix in position a particular view of subjectivity. This fixing was assisted by the enterprise of modern psychology and psychiatry.

Modern psychology and psychiatry confirm the construction of identity as finite and self-enclosed by suggesting that the presence of coexistent selves, not orchestrated by a centralized ego, is pathological. The psychologist Colin Ross notes "The term [multiple personality] suggests that it is necessary to debate whether one person can really have more than one personality, or, put more extremely, whether there can really be more than one person in a single body. Of course there can't . . ." (quoted in Stone, 1993). Indeed, Stone (1993) perceptively argues that the "origin of this 'correct' relationship between body and persona seems to have been contemporaneous with the same cultural moment that gave birth to what we sometimes call the sovereign subject."

Stone also observes, however, that this trial focused on a "fiduciary entity called the person, whose varying modes of existence both support[ed] and problematize[d] the obduracy of individual identity and its refractoriness to deconstruction." Furthermore, the trial captured "the moment of rupture . . . when the seamless surface of reality can be ripped aside" (Stone, 1993); hence we might regard the victim in this trial as a liminal figure, crossing boundaries and disrupting modernist understandings of personhood. The victim's identity did not conform to the dominant construction of subjectivity, in which a single, unified self is attached to or grounded in the body. The appearance of Franny—the personality who directly experienced the victimization—violated the veneer of normative identity, posing a threat to these dominant understandings of the development and maintenance of the singular, unified self.

However, Stone asks whether, at this moment, we should not be searching for more culturally and socially appropriate ways of constructing subjectivity. She is joined in this by Sherry Turkle, who asserts that psychology needs to confront the fact that unitary notions of identity are problematic and illusory. Both Stone and Turkle call for new accounts of subjectivity in which there is an accommodation of nontraumatic (or nonpathological) multiplicity. As we have already seen, Turkle does not regard the multiplication of personae as a sign of pathology, but as a potential liberation in the postmodern, digital age.

Despite these urgings, we need to pay attention to a cultural trend identified by Rose (1996b): the maintenance of the individuated view of the subject in governmental systems at precisely the moment when constructions of the self are not only in crisis, but also subject to reinvention and revision. Rose implies that regulatory regimes integral to social systems such as law, medicine, and health are not only holding fast to this modern view of the self, but are deepening their commitment to surveillance and intervention. Alerting us to these somewhat contradictory developments, he states, "The conceptual dispersion of 'the self' appears to go hand in hand with its 'governmental intensification'" (p. 107).

Below, I draw upon the preceding discussion to articulate important conceptual premises for the arguments developed in this work. I outline these vital "signposts" as a guide to what ensues.

Signposts

This work is premised on the claim that we need to resituate and rework our theoretical understandings of the gender/violence nexus. Specifically, I argue the following:

- It is important to go beyond simple legal definitions of violence and to connect violence to notions of self, boundaries, relatedness, and dependency. We must also locate understandings of violence within particular political, historical, and social moments.
- It is important to employ a feminist epistemological framework that poses a challenge to the Cartesian paradigm: that is, one that overturns the centrality of scientific knowledge to the human project, detaches violence from reason, and admits the affective and corporeal dimensions of the experience of violence.
- It is important to place masculine subjectivity at the core of our inquiries and to explore recent developments in theorizing masculinities.
- It is important to move beyond the description of violence or masculinity as a clutch of actions or social practices, and instead to embrace the significance of the body to both identity and experience.
- It is important to acknowledge the arrival of the postmodern moment and the subsequent transformations in the intellectual and social climate.
- Finally, theorizing about the gender/violence nexus cannot proceed without a recognition of the impact of technological and social change on our understanding of the person, identity, and experience. As we have seen, postmodernism springs from a rejection of Enlightenment theories of knowledge, with their rationalist and empiricist methodologies, and advocates instead context-specific knowledge, heterogeneity, pragmatism, and reflexivity.

It is in this spirit—and with these "signposts"—that we proceed.

Notes

1. Several datasets indicate that sex offenders are generally older than violent offenders, and that they are more likely to be white (Greenfield, 1997). Offenders who have victimized a child are on average five years older than offenders who have committed crimes against adults, and are also more likely to have victimized several children, most of whom are less than 12 years of age (Greenfield, 1996).

2. It is clear from what we have discussed so far that a series of classic Cartesian splits lie at the base of modern ideas about subjectivity. These dualisms are closely associated with dominance and oppression (Plumwood, 1993). This interlocking system of dualisms has been described as follows:

culture	nature
reason	nature
male	female
mind	body (nature)
master	slave
reason	matter (physicality)
reason	emotion (nature)
freedom	necessity (nature)
universal	particular
human nature	(nonhuman)
civilized	primitive (nature)
production	reproduction (nature)
public	private
subject	object
self	other

(Plumwood, 1993, p. 43)

3. It would seem that the therapeutic culture of the self has been extended to the Internet. Media commentator and critic Douglas Rushkoff (1997) recently predicted that the Internet will transform human consciousness from an individual to a collective experience (p. 3). Rushkoff declares, "I believe we are in the midst of a transition—intimated by the Internet—towards more collective thinking, with the individual psyche becoming a component of a larger group mind" (p. 3). The psychologist of the future will be charged with the responsibility of supporting the growth of global community. "At first," notes Rushkoff, "psychologists will be called on to address the panic and paranoia associated with forced cultural intimacy." Collective therapy delivered via the new media will then follow. Finally, the mandate of these psychologists "will be to reduce cultural fear and anxiety associated with the collapse of boundaries and the formation of collective awareness" (p. 3).

4. Foucault, in *The History of Sexuality* (1980), presents us with a number of propositions about power. First, according to Foucault, power relations are unequal and fluid or mobile. Power, then, "is not a commodity, a position, a prize, or a plot; it is the operation of the political technologies throughout the social body" (Dreyfus & Rabinow, 1986, p. 185). The playing out of these "political rituals of power" is what shapes the nonegalitarian relations that characterize society.

Foucault's second proposition states that power does not reside within the subject, either as a property or a possession. Instead, power circulates throughout society, and is conceptualized as both positive and productive. Madan Sarup (1988) summarizes this well when he states,

> Power is not an institution, a structure, or a certain force with which certain people are endowed; it is a name given to a complex strategic relation in a given society. All social relations are power relations. . . . (p. 92)
>
> Furthermore, writes Sarup, Foucault inverts . . . the commonsense view of the relation between power and knowledge. Whereas we might normally regard knowledge as providing us with the power to do things that we could not do without it, Foucault argues that knowledge is a power over others, a power to define others. In his view knowledge ceases to be a liberation and becomes a mode of surveillance, regulation, and discipline. (p. 73)

Power, in Foucault's schema, is multidimensional, operating not only from the top down but also from the bottom up. As power is not an attribute, institutions do not possess it. Power is, nevertheless, productive: It produces a certain kind of subject, for example the obedient schoolchild, the docile patient, or the disciplined prisoner.

Furthermore, power, according to Foucault, is exercised in the context of aims and objectives; it is *intentional* and *instrumental,* and it is to social practices that Foucault turns to comprehend the intentionality of power.

5. Drawing on the work of the social theorists Emile Durkheim, Karl Marx, and Max Weber, the authors Crook, Pakulski, and Waters (1992) identify three outcomes of social change, especially the transition into the phase described as the modern era: differentiation, commodification, and rationalization.

The concept of differentiation emerged in the 19th century as social theorists attempted to make sense of industrial capitalism. Differentiation refers to the specificity in organization, operation, or function within units of the social structure. Such units include the family, the economy, the political system, and organized religion. *Modern* societies are characterized by increasing distance (separation) between these units (or institutions). Also, as noted above, modern societies are distinguished by their trend toward greater internal differentiation or specialization within social institutions.

Commodification is a concept drawn from Marx's analysis of the capitalist mode of production. The process of commodification refers to the translation of social items or experiences into objects that can be bought or sold. This might include human labor, the human body, and, of course, knowledge.

Rationalization comes from the work of Weber, and it refers to the rendering of action as both impersonal and calculable. According to Roger Brubaker (1984), rationalization involves "the depersonalization of social relationships, the refinement of techniques of calculation, the enhancement of the social importance of specialized knowledge, and the extension of technically rational control over both natural and social processes" (p. 2). Weber viewed rationalization as critical to the transformation of four areas: law, administration, ethics, and production.

Crook, Pakulski, and Waters (1992) claim that

> differentiation, commodification and rationalization . . . define the transformation of premodern into modern systems as well as the central internal processes of modern societies. The three processes are closely related: modern social systems have a high or complex level of differentiation and are equally characterized by progressive commodification and rationalization. (p. 10)

It is this process of modernization that permitted the development of the scientific enterprise as we know it today.

6. The claim that we are now living in a postmodern era is often sustained by reference to three features of contemporary life: the demise of the grand master narratives of rationality and progress; the collapse of the distinction between highbrow and lowbrow (or popular) culture; and the proliferation of simulated images in the age of mass-mediated communications.

References

American Psychological Association. (1994). *Diagnostic and statistical manual of mental disorders* (4th ed.). Washington, DC: Author.

Atwater, E. (1994). *Psychology for the living: Adjustment, growth, and behavior today.* Englewood Cliffs, NJ: Prentice Hall.

Barker, S. (Ed.). (1995) *Signs of change: Premodern–modern–postmodern.* Albany: State University of New York Press.

Baudrillard, J. (1990a) *Seduction.* (B. Singer, Trans.). London: Macmillan.

Baudrillard, J. (1990b). *La transparence du mal.* Paris: Galilee.

Bauman, Z. (1992a). *Intimations of modernity.* London: Routledge.

Bauman, Z. (1992b). *Mortality, immortality and other life strategies.* Cambridge, MA: Polity.

Beilharz, P. (1994). *Postmodern socialism.* Melbourne, Australia: Melbourne University Press.

Benhabib, S. (1990). Epistemologies of postmodernism: A rejoinder to Jean-François Lyotard. In L. J. Nicholson (Ed.), *Feminism/Postmodernism* (pp. 107-130). New York: Routledge.

Benjamin, J. (1998). *Shadow of the other: Intersubjectivity and gender in psychology.* London: Routledge.

Berman, M. (1981). *The re-enchantment of the world.* Ithaca, NY: Cornell University Press.

Bertsch, C. (1994). Incredibly strange culture and the end of the world as we know it. *Bad Subjects.* Retrieved May 16, 1996 from the World Wide Web: http://english-www.hss.cmu.edu/bs/.

Best, S., & Kellner, D. (1991). *Postmodern theory: Critical interrogations.* London: Macmillan.

Bilchik, S. (1995). Introduction. In H. N. Snyder & M. Sickmund, *Juvenile offenders and victims: A focus on violence* (pp. 1-4). Washington, DC: Department of Justice, Office of Juvenile Justice and Delinquency Prevention.

Bordo, S. (1986). The Cartesian masculinization of thought. *Signs, 11*(3), 439-456.

Bordo, S. (1987). *The flight to objectivity: Essays on Cartesianism and culture.* Albany, NY: State University of New York Press.

Bradley, H. (1995). *Fractured identities: The dynamics of inequality in post-industrial capitalist societies.* Cambridge, MA: Polity.

Brady, T. V. (1996). *Measuring what matters.* Washington, DC: U.S. Department of Justice, National Institute of Justice.

Brinker-Gabler, G. (Ed.). (1994). *Encountering the other(s): Studies in literature, history, and culture.* Albany, NY: State University of New York Press.

Brubaker, R. (1984). *The limits of rationality: An essay on the social and moral thought of Max Weber.* London: Allen and Unwin.

Burkitt, I. (1991). *Social selves.* London: Sage.

Butler, J. (1990). *Gender trouble: Feminism and the subversion of identity.* New York: Routledge.

Butts, J. A., & Snyder, H. N. (1997). *The youngest delinquents: Offenders under age 15.* Washington, DC: Department of Justice, Office of Juvenile Justice and Delinquency Prevention.

Callahan, D. (1993). *The troubled dream of life: Living with mortality.* New York: Simon & Schuster.

Carlson, N. R. (1993). *Psychology: The science of behavior.* Boston: Allyn & Bacon.

Cherny, L. (1994). 'Objectifying' the body in the disclosure of object-oriented MUD. Retrieved May 19, 1996 from the World Wide Web: http://bhasha.stanford.edu/~chern/charley.txt.

Cherny, L. (1995). The MUD register: Conversational modes of action in a text-based virtual reality. Retrieved November 7, 1999 from the World Wide Web: http://portal.research.bell-labs.com/orgs/ssr/people/cherny/diss-overview.html.

Cherny, L., & Weise, E. R. (Eds.). (1996). *Wired women: Gender and new realities in cyberspace.* Seattle, WA: Seal.

Chesher, C. (1994). Colonizing virtual reality: Construction of the discourse of virtual reality, 1984–1992. *Cultronix, 1*(1), 1-27. Retrieved May 19, 1996 from the World Wide Web: http://english-server.hss.cmu.edu/cultronix/04.

Craven, D. (1996). *Female victims of violence crime.* Washington, DC: Department of Justice, Bureau of Justice Statistics.

Crook, S., Pakulski, J., & Waters, M. (1992). *Postmodernisation: Change in advanced society.* London: Sage.

Dandeker, C. (1994). *Surveillance, power and modernity.* Cambridge, MA: Polity.

Debord, G. (1990). *Comments on the society of the spectacle.* (M. Imrie, Trans.). London: Verso.

Deleuze, G., & Guattari, F. (1988). *A thousand plateaus.* (B. Massumi, Trans.). London: Athlone.

Dery, M. (1999). *The pyrotechnic insanitarium: American culture on the brink.* New York: Grove.

Dibbell, J. (1999). *My tiny life: Crime and passion in a virtual world.* New York: Henry Holt.

Dreyfus, R., & Rabinow, P. (1986). *Michel Foucault: Beyond structuralism and hermeneutics.* Brighton, England: Harvester.

Ebert, T. L. (1998). *Ludic feminism and after.* Ann Arbor, MI: University of Michigan Press.

Eco, U. (1990). *The limits of interpretation.* Bloomington, IN: Indiana University Press.

Edge, H. L. (1994). *A constructive postmodern perspective on commentary: From atomism to idolism.* Lewistch, the Netherlands: E. Mellen.

Elias, N. (1978). *The history of manners.* New York: Pantheon.

Elias, N. (1982). *State foundation and civilization.* Oxford, UK: Basil Blackwell.

Erikson, E. H. (1968). *Identity: Youth and crisis.* New York: Norton.

Flax, J. (1983). Political philosophy and the patriarchal unconscious: A psychoanalytic perspective on epistemology and metaphysics. In S. Harding & M. B. Hintikka (Eds.), *Discovering reality* (pp. 132-154). London: D. Reidel.

Flax, J. (1993). *Disputed subjects: Essays on psychoanalysis, politics, and philosophy.* New York: Routledge.

Foucault, M. (1967). *Madness and civilization: A history of insanity in the age of reason.* (R. Howard, Trans.). New York: Pantheon.

Foucault, M. (1971). *The order of things: An archaeology of the human sciences.* New York: Pantheon.

Foucault, M. (1979). *Discipline and punish.* London: Allen Lane.

Foucault, M. (1980). *The history of sexuality, Vol. 1.* (R. Hurley, Trans.). New York: Vintage.

Freeman, M. (1993). *Rewriting the self: History, memory, and narrative.* New York: Routledge.

Geertz, C. (1975). From the native's point of view: On the nature of anthropological understanding. *American Scientist, 63*: 47-53.

Gergen, K. J. (1991). *The saturated self: Dilemmas of identity in contemporary life.* New York: Basic Books.

Gergen, K. J. (1996). Technology and the self: From the essential to the sublime. In D. Grodin & T. R. Lindlof (Eds.), *Constructing the self in a mediated world* (pp. 58-74). Thousand Oaks, CA: Sage.

Gergen, K. J. (1997). The ordinary, the original and the believable in psychology's construction of the person. Retrieved November 16, 1997 from the World Wide Web: http.://www.swathmore.edu/SocSci/kgergen1/.

Gergen, M. (1995). Postmodern, post-Cartesian positionings on the subject of psychology. *Theory and Psychology, 5*(3), 361-368.

Gery, J. (1996). *Nuclear annihilation and contemporary American poetry: Ways of nothingness.* Gainesville, FL: University Press of Florida.

Giddens, A. (1991). *Modernity and self-identity.* Cambridge, MA: Polity.

Gilman, S. L. (1988). *Disease and representation: Images of them from madness to AIDS.* Ithaca, NY: Cornell University Press.

Greenfield, L. A. (1996). *Child victimizers: Violent offenders and their victims.* Washington, DC: Department of Justice, Bureau of Justice Statistics.

Greenfield, L. A. (1997). *Sex offenses and offenders.* Washington, DC: Department of Justice, Bureau of Justice Statistics.

Grodin, D., & Lindlof, T. R. (Eds.). (1996). *Constructing the self in a mediated world.* Thousand Oaks, CA: Sage.

Grossley, N. (1996). *Intersubjectivity: The fabric of social becoming.* London: Sage.

Grosz, E. (1995). *Space, time, and perversion: Essays on the politics of bodies.* New York: Routledge.

Haber, H. F. (1994). *Beyond postmodern politics: Selves, community, and the politics of difference.* London: Routledge.

Hall, S., & du Gray, P. (1996). *Questions of cultural identity.* London: Sage.

Haraway, D. (1989). A manifesto for cyborgs: Science, technology, and socialist feminism in the 1980s. In E. Weed (Ed.), *Coming to terms* (pp. 173-214). New York: Routledge.

Hatty, S. E. (1992). Women, dependence and the law. In P. Easteal (Ed.), *Women and the law* (pp. 36-48). Canberra, Australia: Australian Institute of Criminology.

Hatty, S. E., & Hatty, J. (1999). *The disordered body: Epidemic disease and cultural transformation.* Albany, NY: State University of New York Press.

Hayles, N. K. (1993). Virtual bodies and flickering signifiers. *October, 66,* 69-91.

Hillis, K. (1999). *Digital sensations.* Minneapolis, MN: University of Minnesota Press.

Jameson, F. (1991). *Postmodernism.* Durham, NC: Duke University Press.

Kant, I. (1959). *Foundations of the metaphysics of morals.* Indianapolis, IN: Bobbs-Merrill.

Kelley, B. T., Huizinga, D., Thornberry, T. P., & Loeber, R. (1997). *Epidemiology of serious violence.* Washington, DC: Department of Justice, Office of Juvenile Justice and Delinquency Prevention.

Kendall, P. C., & Hammen, C. (1995). *Abnormal psychology.* Boston: Houghton Mifflin.

Kolak, D. (1991). *Self and identity: Contemporary philosophical issues.* New York: Macmillan.

Kristiansen, C. M. (1994, July). *Recovered memories of child abuse: Fact, fantasy, or fancy?* Invited address to the Annual Convention of the Canadian Psychological Association, British Columbia, Canada.

Lasch, C. (1984). *The minimal self: Psychic survival in troubled times.* New York: Norton.

Lax, W. D. (1992). Postmodern thinking in a clinical practice. In S. McNamee & K. J. Gergen (Eds.), *Therapy as social construction* (pp. 69-85). London: Sage.

Lieblich, A., & Josselson, R. (Eds.). (1994). *Exploring identity and gender: The narrative study of lives.* Newbury Park, CA: Sage.

Loftus, E. F. (1993). The reality of repressed memories. *American Psychologist, 48*(5), 518-537.

Loftus, E. F. (1994). The repressed memory controversy. *American Psychologist, 49*(2), 443-444.

Luntley, M. (1995). *Reason, truth, and self: The postmodern reconditioned.* London: Routledge.

Lyon, D. (1993). *The electronic eye: The rise of surveillance society.* Cambridge, MA: Polity.

Lyotard, J. F. (1986). *The postmodern condition: A report on knowledge.* Minneapolis, MN: University of Minnesota Press.

Lyotard, J. F. (1988). *Peregrinations.* New York: Columbia University Press.

Marsh, J. L. (1995). *Critique, action and liberation.* Albany: State University of New York Press.

Mascuch, M. (1996). *Origins of the individualist self: Autobiography of self-identity in England, 1591–1791.* Stanford, CA: Stanford University Press.

Matsumoto, D. (1994). *People: Psychology from a cultural perspective.* Pacific Grove, CA: Brooks/Cole.

Mazur, T. (1994). Working out the cyberbody: Sex and gender construction text-based virtual space. Retrieved May 17, 1996 from the World Wide Web: http://www.wdenver.edu/~mryder/itc_data/postmodern.html.

McAdams, D. P. (1993). *The stories we live by: Personal myths and the making of the self*. New York: William Morrow.

McAdams, M. (1996, March). Gender without bodies. *CMC Magazine.* Retrieved November 7, 1999 from the World Wide Web: http://www.december.com/cmc/mag/1996/mar/mcada2.html.

McCartney, B. (1997, September-October). Promise makers. *Policy Review, 85.* Retrieved June 5, 1998 from the World Wide Web: http://www.esva.net/~bam/pk.htm.

McGuckin, F. (1998). *Violence in American society*. New York: H. W. Wilson.

McNamee, S. (1992). Reconstructing identity: The communal construction. In S. McNamee & K. J. Gergen (Eds.), *Therapy as social construction* (pp. 186-199). London: Sage.

McNamee, S., & Gergen, K. J. (Eds.). (1992). *Therapy as social construction*. London: Sage.

McRae, S. (1994). Coming apart at the seams: Sex, text, and the virtual body. Retrieved August 4, 1996 from the World Wide Web: http://humanities.ucsb.edu/shuttle/gender.html.

Merchant, C. (1990). *The death of nature: Women, ecology, and the scientific revolution*. San Francisco, CA: Harper.

Negroponte, N. (1995). *Being digital*. New York: Knopf.

Nowotny, H. (1994). *Time: The modern and postmodern experience*. Cambridge, MA: Polity.

Pahl, R. (1995). *After success: Fin-de-siècle anxiety and identity*. Cambridge, MA: Polity.

Pateman, C. (1989). *The disorder of women: Democracy, feminism, and political theory*. Cambridge, MA: Polity.

Pfohl, S., & Gordon, A. (1987). Criminological displacements: A sociological deconstruction. In A. Kroker & M. Kroker (Eds.), *Body invaders* (pp. 224-254). New York: Routledge.

Phelan, P. (1997). *Mourning sex: Performing public memories*. New York: Routledge.

Piaget, J. (1963). *The child's conception of space*. London: Routledge.

Piaget, J. (1965). *The child's conception of number*. New York: Norton.

Piaget, J. (1969). *The child's conception of the world*. Totowa, NJ: Littlefield, Adams.

Pitch, T. (1995). *Limited responsibilities*. New York: Routledge.

Plumwood, V. (1993). *Feminism and the mastery of nature*. London: Routledge.

Polkinghorne, J. (1988). *Narrative knowing and the human sciences*. Albany, NY: State University of New York Press.

Poster, M. (1995). *The second media age*. Cambridge, MA: Polity.

Rand, M. R. (1997). *Criminal victimization and the United States, 1994*. Washington, DC: Department of Justice, Bureau of Justice Statistics.

Rand, M. R., Lynch, J. P., & Cantor, D. (1997). *Criminal victimization, 1973–1995*. Washington, DC: Department of Justice, Bureau of Justice Statistics.

Rose, N. (1991). *Governing the soul: The shaping of the private self*. London: Routledge.

Rose, N. (1992). Individualizing psychology. In J. Shotter & K. J. Gergen (Eds.), *Texts of identity* (pp. 119-132). London: Sage.

Rose, N. (1996a). *Inventing ourselves: Psychology, power, and personhood*. Cambridge, UK: Cambridge University Press.

Rose, N. (1996b). Power and subjectivity. In C. F. Graumann & K. J. Gergen (Eds.), *Historical dimensions of psychological discourse* (pp. 103-124). Cambridge, UK: Cambridge University Press.

Rushkoff, D. (1994a). *Cyberia: Life in the trenches of hyperspace.* San Francisco, CA: Harper.

Rushkoff, D. (1994b). *Media virus: Hidden agendas in popular culture.* New York: Ballantine.

Rushkoff, D. (1996). *Playing the future.* San Francisco, CA: HarperCollins.

Rushkoff, D. (1997, June 21-22). Cures for a new age of anxiety. *Weekend Australian,* p. 3.

Sampson, E. E. (1993). *Celebrating the other: A dialogic account of human nature.* Boulder, CO: Westview.

San Juan, E. (1995). *Hegemony and strategies of transgression: Essays in cultural studies and comparative literature.* Albany, NY: State University of New York Press.

Sartelle, J. (1994). Introduction. *Bad Subjects.* Retrieved July 4, 1996 from the World Wide Web: http://english-www.hss.cmu.edu/65.

Sarup, M. (1988). *An introductory guide to post-structuralism and postmodernism.* New York: Harvester Wheatsheaf.

Sarup, M. (1996). *Identity, culture, and the postmodern world.* Athens, GA: University of Georgia Press.

Seidman, S. (Ed.). (1995). *The postmodern turn.* Cambridge, UK: Cambridge University Press.

Shotter, J., & Gergen, K. J. (Eds.). (1992). *Texts of identity.* London: Sage.

Shotter, J. (1993). Conversational realities: Constructing life through language. Thousand Oaks, CA: Sage.

Simons, H. W., & Billig, M. (Eds.). (1994). *After postmodernism: Reconstructing ideology critique.* Newbury Park, CA: Sage.

Smith, D. M., & Zahn, M. (Eds.). (1999). *Homicide: A sourcebook of social research.* Thousand Oaks, CA: Sage.

Snyder, H., Sickmund, M., & Poe-Yamagata, E. (1996). *Juvenile offenders and victims: 1996 update on violence.* Washington, DC: Office of Juvenile Justice and Delinquency Prevention.

Steedman, C. (1995). *Strange dislocations: Childhood and the idea of human interiority, 1780–1930.* Cambridge, MA: Harvard University Press.

Stone, A. R. (1991). Will the real body please stand up? Boundary stories about virtual cultures. In M. Benedikt (Ed.), *Cyberspace: First steps* (pp. 81-118). Cambridge, MA: MIT Press.

Stone, A. R. (1993). Violation and virtuality: Two cases of physical and psychological boundary transgression and their implications. Retrieved October 14, 1996 from the World Wide Web: http://www.actlab.utexas.edu/~sandy/violation-and-virtuality.

Stone, A. R. (1995a). Identity in Oshkosh. In J. Halberstam & I. Livingston (Eds.), *Posthuman bodies* (pp. 23-37). Bloomington, IN: Indiana University Press.

Stone, A. R. (1995b) *The war of desire and technology at the close of the mechanical age.* Cambridge, MA: MIT Press.

Taussig, M. (1993). *Mimesis and alterity: A particular history of the senses.* New York: Routledge.

Taylor, C. (1989). *Sources of self: The making of the modern identity.* Cambridge, UK: Cambridge University Press.

Tenner, E. (1996). *Why things bite back: Technology and the revenge of unintended consequences.* New York: Knopf.

Thompson, J. B. (1995). *The media and modernity.* Cambridge, MA: Polity.

Toomey, M. (1992). The price of masculinity based on violence. *Education Digest, 58*(4), 44-46.

Travis, J., Chaiken, J., & Auchter, B. (1996). *Domestic and sexual violence data collection.* Washington, DC: Department of Justice, National Institute of Justice.

Turkle, S. (1984). *The second self: Computers and the human spirit*. New York: Simon & Schuster.

Turkle, S. (1995). *Life on the screen: Identity in the age of the internet*. New York: Simon & Schuster.

Turkle, S. (1996). Interview with Sherry Turkle. *Salon: Fin de siècle*. Retrieved March 21, 2000 from the World Wide Web: http://www.salon.com/12nov1995/departments/howard.html.

U.S. Department of Justice, Office of Juvenile Justice and Delinquency Prevention. (1994). *Comprehensive strategy for serious, violent, and chronic offenders*. Washington, DC: Author.

Virilio, P. (1995). Speed and information: Cyberspace alarm! *C Theory: Theory, Technology, and Culture, 18*(3), 1-6. Retrieved April 7, 1996 from the World Wide Web: http://www.ctheory.com.

Waugh, P. (1992). Introduction. *Postmodernism* (pp. 1-13). London: Arnold.

Wilson, P. L. (1995). Boundary violations. In S. Aronowitz & B. Martinsons (Eds.), *Technoscience and cyberculture* (pp. 220-236). New York: Routledge.

Yapko, M. D. (1994). *Suggestions of abuse: True and false memories of childhood sexual abuse*. New York: Simon & Schuster.

2

Bodily Harm

Violence and the Cultural Imagination

My power. So powerful. And the guns and these magazines filled
with bullets, I could go bang, bang, bang.

—*Martin Bryant, convicted mass murderer*

Before, with his long, unruly blond locks, he had an individuality, an
image. . . . But with the crew cut . . . he had become just another
man. He could have been anybody on the street. A neighbor. A work
colleague. He had become Everyman.

—*Matt Condon, journalist,*
describing Martin Bryant at his trial

On the 28th April, 1996, Martin Bryant rose early and packed a
sports bag full of weapons—three military style, semi-automatic fire-
arms, including an Armalite ARIS.223 calibre rifle, large quantities of
ammunition, handcuffs, a hunting knife, and rope. He drove to a local
guesthouse and shot the two elderly inhabitants. Bryant then traveled
a short distance to the historic tourist site of Port Arthur in Tasmania,
Australia.

Port Arthur was originally a brutal penal establishment founded in
1830 to house the most intransigent and difficult of convicts. Known
in the 19th century as "the abode of misery" or the Earthly Hell, the
Port had an extremely harsh regime. It relied on physical violence and
severe psychological deprivation: Prisoners were forbidden to make

eye contact with others, and were forced to wear a hooded mask to enforce this. Violence, in the form of floggings, beatings, and whippings, was endemic. Escape was well-nigh impossible. The site has long been thought to be haunted by the souls of those who were tortured and died there. Now marketed as a tourist destination, complete with ghost tours and evening visits to the dissection room, Port Arthur continues to assume a vivid significance in Australia's painful past. For Martin Bryant, there could be no more appropriate killing ground.

Around lunch time on April 28th, 1996, Martin Bryant calmly entered the Broad Arrow Cafe at Port Arthur, ate lunch, then produced a weapon and proceeded to shoot 22 people in 15 seconds. Twelve of these people were killed, and 10 were injured. Bryant moved methodically between the tables in the cafe, aiming directly at the diners' heads and pulling the trigger. He continued shooting, and within two minutes, Bryant killed 8 more people. One victim remembers him saying, "No one gets away from me."

Outside the cafe, Bryant pursued tourists and shot them in the back. Many of the visitors to the site thought the shootings in the cafe were some sort of tourist reenactment—a bringing to life of earlier convict horrors. Some realized too late that this was, in fact, not entertainment but real life.

Bryant was convicted in November, 1996, of the murder of 35 people, the attempted murder of 20 others, and 17 additional charges relating to unlawful wounding, aggravated assault, grievous bodily harm, and arson. Bryant was sentenced to 35 life terms, one for each count of murder, and another 37 terms, each for a duration of 21 years. As Australia does not have capital punishment, his file was marked, "Never to be released."

In sentencing Bryant, Justice William Cox stated,

> It is difficult to imagine a more chilling catalog of crime. . . . The prisoner, having had a murderous plan in contemplation and active preparation for some time, deliberately killed two persons against whom he held a grudge. . . . [He] then embarked on a trail of devastation that took the lives of a further 33 other human beings.

Despite psychiatric testimony at his trial that suggested Martin Bryant suffered from Asperger's Syndrome, the media was saturated with speculation about the reasons for Bryant's aberrant behavior. These speculations covered the range of theoretical possibilities: Some suggested that the cult of the individual was to blame; others invoked biology, and in a strange doubling, referred to Bryant as a "natural born killer." Other commentators alluded to the role of socialization in the production of the violent male. Here, in a reiteration of the principles of linear causality, was evidence of the pathologization thesis, the availability-of-weapons thesis, and the media-violence thesis. Each was a search for an explanation. This search was rendered more urgent by Martin Bryant's refusal to account publicly for his actions.

Although Bryant's crimes did lead to a major review of gun ownership legislation in Australia, Bryant himself remains an enigmatic figure. Described by his mother as "a monster," the fair-haired, blue-eyed Bryant is popularly understood as intellectually and emotionally immature: a figure of pathos, not power. He is seen as a young man nursing the cumulative hurt of repeated episodes of ridicule and rejection, a young man of wealth and privilege who destroyed for no apparent reason. A rare and opaque specimen.

This chapter reviews the various ways in which we construct and define violence, including both understandings integral to social institutions, such as the law, and definitions developed to take account of the perspectives of victims and survivors of violence. I consider the range of theoretical explanations for aggression and violence in society, acknowledging, as I proceed, the ideological content of these explanations. I then insert these definitions, constructions, and explanations in the wider sphere of cultural politics, posing questions about the primacy of particular violent formations. This leads to an analysis both of the contemporary popular and politico-legal responses to the rise of specific configurations of violent behavior, and of the remarkable persistence of gendered modes of violence.

Naming the Limits:
Aggression, Conflict, and Violence

How do we define violence? And how do we distinguish violence from conflict or aggression?

Aggression is often defined in behavioral or affective terms. It is thought to range from acts of assault and threats of abuse to emotional outbursts. Silverberg and Gray (1992) define aggression as "the initiating toward some other(s) of an act that is higher on the violence scale than the previous act in a given interaction sequence, i.e., a readiness to initiate acts at higher levels of violence" (p. 3). In a more straightforward rendition, Gottfredson and Hirschi (1993) state that "the idea of aggression connotes unprovoked, senseless, or unjustifiable violence or threat of violence" (p. 52).

Conflict has been defined as "incompatibility of interests, goals, values, needs, expectations, and/or social cosmologies (or ideologies)" (Van Der Dennen, 1990, p. 2). Furthermore, conflict can be viewed as an objective or subjective phenomenon, or as functional or dysfunctional in its effects. Nevertheless, Van Der Dennen (1990) asserts that conflict exists at all levels of organic existence, and is "pervasive, persistent, ubiquitous" (p. 1).

Violence has been defined as the infliction of "emotional, psychological, sexual, physical and/or material damage" (Stanko, 1994, p. xiv). Hearn (1996b) defines violence as "that which violates or causes violation, and is usually performed by a violator upon the violated" (p. 42). Moreover, violence may be sexual, physical, verbal, cognitive, emotional, or representational. Violence may also include the "creation of conditions of violence, potential violence, threat and/ or neglect . . . [and] can be dramatic, subtle, occasional or continuous" (Hearn, 1996a, p. 43).

Legal definitions of violence are somewhat more restrictive than those outlined above. These definitions are premised on the use of intentional physical force applied to another person, contrary to that person's will. The degree of physical force may vary, and may range from minimal (e.g., nonconsensual touching) to severe (e.g., fatal injury). Offences that fall under this broad banner include assault, at one end of the spectrum, and homicide, at the other.

Physical acts are generally viewed as the paradigmatic case of violence in society, both in law and in everyday accounts (see Hearn, 1996a). In the Western tradition of liberal legalism, violence is understood to be a corporeal experience, involving the collision of bodies, the extension of touch (painful or injurious) into spaces and places where it is not welcome. Violence, then, involves the crossing of boundaries relating to personal space and, in particular, the transgression of bodily boundaries—of skin, of muscle, of visceral tissue— by hands, fists, feet, or weapons. This construction of violence resonates with the legal privileging of the body perimeters as the defining characteristic of personhood: the body as the *boundary* marking off one person from another. Consequently, in the doctrine of liberal legalism that dominates Western legal systems, it is the body that articulates the limits of personhood and that circumscribes the range of others' behavior. A gesture can, therefore, be translated into a criminal offense when it connects with or invades this physical boundary. Ironically, although the law recognizes a variety of physical incursions as criminal offenses, it does so to promote the idea that the rational subject is enclosed within a material container, and so denies the importance of the body to personhood.

Legal definitions of violent behavior are under constant challenge and revision as the law responds to shifting political and social circumstances.[1] Michael Allen (1996) relates how United Kingdom laws on assault have undergone recent and dramatic change: The definition of assault has been stretched to incorporate psychological harm and the effects of the accused's actions. This has redirected the emphasis away from the conduct of the accused, and has placed in doubt the previous legal requirement that the victim must apprehend immediate personal violence. The case that catalyzed the change in U.K. laws concerned incidents of telephone harassment. The question before the court turned on whether or not such actions could be construed, in legal terms, as an assault. The Court of Appeal affirmed the appellant's conviction of assault occasioning actual bodily harm. The harm suffered by the three victims included physical manifestations of stress and anxiety—dizziness, sweating, heart palpitations, and so on. Allen regards this judgment as highly controversial, because it has produced a definition of violence that diverges from that which exists in common law.

The other end of the violence spectrum, involving various forms of homicide, is less subject to legal modification. Homicide, as the mode of interpersonal violence that marks the boundaries of the human condition, articulating in law the limits of reason/unreason and setting down the psychological parameters for *mens rea* (guilty mind), continues to be defined as the unlawful taking of another's life. It is the *methods* or *means* used to achieve this purpose that are subject to redefinition at law. For example, we now have an understanding of the ways in which individuals, infected with particular contagious viruses, can be held responsible for harming others in specific circumstances. There are now laws in many jurisdictions that criminalize unsafe sexual conduct on the part of HIV-positive individuals.

Violence is not the province only of law. There are many groups in society that have an investment in contesting the meanings and interpretations of violence. There have been many attempts to redefine the individual experience of violence. Women's advocates have sought to admit the psychic and social aspects of violence to the dominant legal and theoretical constructions of violence (see Fawcett, Featherstone, Hearn, & Toft, 1996; Hatty 1987, 1992a, 1992b; Nicolson & Sanghui, 1993; Wells, 1994). At the same time, some researchers and activists have raised objections to contemporary approaches to defining and describing the patterns of violence in society (see Gelles & Loseke, 1993; Krista, 1994; Letellier, 1994; Lucal, 1995; McNeely & Robinson-Simpson, 1987), and to current strategies of response (see Hamberger & Potente, 1994). Other researchers point to the qualitative differences between the received categories of violence. Jeffrey Fagan (1996), in a recent report on the criminalization of domestic violence, notes that domestic violence differs from other forms of violence in several important respects. He argues that the emotional ties between assailants and victims, the private and recurring nature of the violence, the prevalence of domestic violence compared with other crimes, and the often irrational and rage-driven outbursts associated with domestic violence make the logic of deterrence largely irrelevant. For these reasons, the effective legal control of domestic violence is difficult (Fagan, 1996).

There have also been attempts to open up the definition of violence to include a focus on collectivities and corporations (see, for example, Hearn, 1996b). This has relied on an acknowledgment of the role of the state, its instrumentalities, and multinational and local corporations in the production and perpetuation of harms. Other discussions have examined types of harms, arguing that they are directed not only at individuals, but also at groups and, of course, the social and natural environment. Violence, from this perspective, is often viewed as the prerogative of the nation-state and of governments. The maintenance of public order and the protection of national security and international interests are seen to hinge on the use of institutionalized and routinized violence. Some of this violence is legitimate (that is, consistent with the legal mandate), and some is illegitimate (especially unauthorized covert actions in foreign jurisdictions or excessive force utilized by criminal justice professionals). We could nominate here the brutal policing of ethnic and minority groups that has been reported in many Western nations, including the United States. We could also nominate the systematic violation of marginal groups, such as homeless youth, by police, security guards, and vigilante squads in some countries.

While these attacks on the young homeless are a feature of street life for many in the West (see Hatty, Davis, & Burke, 1996), they are a predictable and terrifying experience for large numbers of young people in Third World countries. In Thailand, for example, children may be assaulted and beaten in the course of their work in the ever growing trade in recreational child sex. In South American nations such as Brazil and Colombia, street children are assassinated by professional hitmen, police officers (both on- and off-duty), and citizen "justice-

makers" (see Higgins, 1993). A climate of terror pervades the populace of these nations; certain groups of people are literally viewed as
expendable, and the killing of these people is spoken of as a "social
cleansing" (Buchanan, 1994). Such metaphors of pollution obscure
the fact that the state itself may become an instrument of torture or
may intimidate its citizens through fear. Taussig (1984) describes the
processes whereby state instrumentalities terrorize the citizenry of
Colombia by dispensing arbitrary and extreme violence in public
places. Within this "space of death" (Taussig, 1984), individuals may
simply disappear and power is made manifest as "unfettered, undis-
guised force" (Marcus, 1991, p. 129). It is worth noting that state-
based torture is now carried out on an ever increasing scale, despite its
denunciation by the United Nations (Millett, 1994).

Mass violence, occurring through warfare, civil strife, or the creation of life-threatening conditions (Gellert, 1995), is also a 20th-
century phenomenon. Genocide, defined as "the systematic, planned
annihilation of a racial, political, or cultural group" (Gellert, 1995,
p. 997), was undertaken by at least 40 nations during the last century.
Social conditions conducive to genocidal campaigns include national-
ist tendencies to invade or rule others; explicit expressions of national,
ethnic, or racial superiority by one group at the expense of others; and
the denigration and subjugation of minority groups (Straub, 1989).

An exhaustive and painful exploration of genocide has recently
occurred in Australia. A national inquiry conducted by Australia's
Human Rights and Equal Opportunity Commission (HREOC) examined the history, effects, and appropriate responses to the widespread
practice of forcibly removing indigenous children from their families
and their cultural context. The commission heard testimony, either
oral or written, from 535 indigenous people. Much of this testimony
was redolent with grief, sadness, and pronounced feelings of loss. One
respondent keenly captured the pain of abduction and separation:

> We may go home, but we cannot relive our childhoods. We may
> reunite with our mothers, fathers, sisters, brothers, aunties, uncles,
> communities, but we cannot relive the 20, 30, 40 years that we spent
> without their love and care, and they cannot undo the grief and
> mourning they felt when we were separated from them. We can go
> home to ourselves as Aboriginals, but this does not erase the attacks
> inflicted on our hearts, minds, bodies and souls, by caretakers who
> thought their mission was to eliminate us as Aboriginals.

The commission heard that the "stolen children" suffered from a
lack of knowledge about their own culture, genealogy, and language,

and felt an alienation caused by a lack of spiritual connection to their tribal country. The children were told that aboriginal culture was worthless, a remnant of an earlier evolutionary stage, and that they themselves must adopt Anglo-Celtic ways of knowing and seeing. Aside from these assaults on culture and kin, the children suffered direct attacks. They were paid insufficient wages or received no remuneration at all. They were housed in harsh and punitive institutions. And they were sexually assaulted and beaten by those who had responsibility for their welfare.

One indigenous woman told how everyday life at the home camp became infused with danger and extreme fear. She said,

> During the raids on the camps it was not unusual for people to be shot—shot in the arm or the leg. You can understand the terror that we lived in, the fright—not knowing when someone will come unawares and do whatever they were doing—either disrupting our family life, camp life, or shooting at us.

Several people spoke of the violence meted out in the institutions:

> There was no food, nothing. . . . Sometimes at night we'd cry with hunger.

> They were very cruel to us, very cruel. . . . I remember once, I must have been 8 or 9, and I was locked in the old morgue. The adults who worked there would tell us of the things that happened in there, so you can imagine what I went through. I screamed all night, but no one came to get me.

> I've seen girls naked, strapped to chairs and whipped. We've all been through the locking up period, locked in dark rooms.

The intergenerational effects of forcible removal are tangible. Many spoke to the HREOC of their lack of parenting skills, their inability to form close emotional ties, their unresolved grief and trauma, the depression associated with such removal, and the very high rates of self-harm. Violence within families was also common. One parent, a member of the "stolen generation," commented, "There's things in my life that I haven't dealt with and I've passed them on to my children. Gone to pieces. . . . Somehow I'm passing down negativity to my kids."

On the question of indigenous identity, and a place in which to begin the healing, it was noted by one respondent that going home is fundamental to healing the effects of separation. Going home means finding out who you are as an Aboriginal: where you come from, who your people are, where your belonging place is, what your identity is. Going home is fundamental to the healing process of those who were taken away as well as those who were left behind.

Furthermore, the report noted that

just as there are many homes, there are many journeys home. Each one of [the stolen children] will have a different journey from anyone else. The journey home is mostly ongoing and in some ways never completed. It is a process of discovery and recovery, it is a process of (re)building relationships which have been disrupted, or broken or never allowed to begin because of separation.

As we can already see, the naming of actions as "violence" is inherently political.[2] Penny Green (1994) claims that the state, with its powerful vested interests, selectively labels its own actions and those of its opponents. She states,

Violence which defends the status quo, or violence which ensures the continuing conditions required by the capitalist economy to thrive does not carry with it the pejorative connotations of criminal "violence." These connotations are reserved for people and activities which undermine the conditions upon which the established order relies. (p. 33)

Furthermore, Green alleges that such selective naming generates a climate of anxiety in which the community is riven by internal tensions, and fails to turn its attention to a critique of the existing inequities and injustices:

By creating public straw-enemies (terrorists, serial killers, drug traffickers, striking miners, etc.) and shrouding them with the attire of violence, widespread fear may be engendered and the state's monopoly over the use of violence to "protect" the victim population is reinforced. In this process public attention is deflected from the sources of real violence in our society, and the brutality of an economic system based on profit and inequality is obscured. (p. 38)

This forces us to question directly how culture contributes to the production and dissemination of violence. How might cultural institutions, industries, and everyday practices make certain types of violent actions or processes both possible and inevitable? How might the culture in which we live exert an influence that forcefully shapes our lived reality? What are the constraints that operate on the frameworks we employ to make sense of human subjectivity and human action? Which alternative visions are excluded and denied? Whose voices are silenced, and which discourses prevail? We are reminded, perhaps, in our attempts to answer these questions, of the sporadic and sustained violence of the nation-state, the workplace, the school, the family and the church. We may also be reminded of the pervasiveness of racialized and gendered violence, and of the bleak and chilling impact of the "deadly words" of violent rhetoric (see Feder, 1997; Rosga, 1997). Violence, as a cultural construct, is a site of both struggle and resistance. Contesting and negotiating the definition and meaning of violence is a continuing project.

Indeed, it is possible to suggest that our contemporary definitions and constructions of violence are often essentialist and monolithic. Different types of violence are viewed as related, as erupting from the same motivational wellspring. Acts of violence occurring over a life-span are viewed as events in a linear sequence, with memory being the vehicle that enables individuals to extend or diversify their violent repertoire. However, violence is "incidentalized," viewed as both an incident and incidental (Hearn, 1996a, p. 34). If we were to search for other ways of approaching violence we might find it more appropriate to speak of a multiplicity of violent forms and a plurality of violent practices. We might inject greater subtlety into our understandings of violence, basing them on an appreciation of the nuances of context. Rather than assuming that individual defects in character or abnormal motives are critical determinants of violence, we might place more emphasis on the social and political crosscurrents of violence. This might entail the abandonment of our current prescriptive and rigid taxonomies of violence, and the promotion of a more context-driven interpretation to legitimize a range of meanings. Let us explore what this might mean.

Taking physical behavior as our starting point, and assuming the above conditions, we could propose that it is the appreciation of the differences wrought by various violent practices that is of primary significance. For example, we accept as evident that to kill with a gun is a qualitatively different act than to kill with a knife. This is so for both the assailant and the victim. The geographical distance between the killer that the victim, the possible verbal and nonverbal communications, the apprehension of imminent danger by the victim, the degree of pain inflicted on the victim, the contact between bodies and spilling or merging of bodily fluids, and the speed of death all vary according to the modality of the violence. To take another example, we can say that to punch an individual with whom one is intimate is not the same act (or experience) as punching a stranger; the affect, the perceived rationale, and the impact of the crime will vary markedly between the two circumstances. Nevertheless, although the qualitative difference between these acts will remain constant, the meaning varies according to context and may not be replicated in a future episode of violence. These actions may assume an alternative meaning or significance if enacted in another temporal, social, or political context. Violence, then, can be regarded as both intersubjective and context-dependent—as the behavioral bridge that inexorably links two or more people, but whose meaning and significance may vary both within and between subjects. This is not to imply that the responsibility, moral or legal, for violence is necessarily shared, but that the experience of violence is about process or flow, rather than circumscribed acts or stasis. I explore this in more detail in Chapter 6.

Furthermore, we need in general to distinguish between aggression, violence, and conflict. To aggress is to injure or destroy through some form of violence. Violence is the expression—the physical manifestation—of aggression. Conflict, unlike aggression or its literal companion, violence, always implies mutuality, a dispute occurring *between* two or more parties. Below, we consider how we explain the linked constructs of aggression and violence.

Explaining Aggression and Violence

What are the various explanations for aggression and violence? Below, I canvass some of the major schools of thought, including sociobiology, psychology, and sociology. This review is not intended to be exhaustive, but rather to give the flavor of the various and often incompatible readings of violence in society.

Biological, physiological, and evolutionary perspectives on violent behavior have their origins in scientific discourse about animals and humans. Genetic and hormonal approaches have contributed significantly to the body of theoretical knowledge about violence, and have proven increasingly popular as explanations of both socially acceptable and deviant human conduct (Mariani, 1995). We could think here, for example, of the ill-fated biocriminology of the Violence Initiative sponsored by the National Institute of Mental Health.[3]

Genetic studies of violent behavior have examined, in the main, heritability and crime. Typically, this has involved research on monozygotic (identical) and dizygotic (nonidentical) twins in an attempt to tease out the varying influences of genetics and the environment. This has generated conflicting outcomes; differences in methodology and problems with the definition and measurement of the variables under study have undermined the reliability and validity of the results (see Turner, 1994).

Neural and physiological factors have also been implicated in the genesis of violent behavior. Although genes were thought to influence aggression or violence by acting on the central nervous system, now physiology rather than genetics is thought to control aggression. According to this new view, low arousal may be associated with the absence of a fear response to a high-risk situation, and this may be associated with the suppression of pituitary hormones that increase the likelihood of avoidance behaviors. Other biochemical factors, such as differences in serotonin levels, are thought to be linked to aggression as well (see Turner, 1994). Furthermore, studies have also shown a relationship between traumatic brain injury and subsequent verbal and physical aggression (Warnken, Rosenbaum, Fletcher, Hoge, & Adelman, 1994). Indeed, Rosenbaum, Hoge, Adelman, Warnken, Fletcher, and Kane (1994) found that males with head injuries were six times more likely than their noninjured counterparts to engage in aggressive behavior toward their female partners.

However, hormones, with their important role in fetal and adolescent development, are most prominently featured in biological explanations of aggressive or violent behavior. Androgens, particularly testosterone, have been extensively studied. Research on humans and primates has sought to determine the role played by such hormones in violent and criminal behavior (see Archer, 1991). Again, methodological problems have led to equivocal results, leading at least one critic to conclude that variations in aggression or violence cannot be accounted for by genetic or hormonal factors alone (Turner, 1994). Nevertheless, clinical reports of aberrant behaviors continue to suggest that physiological factors may play a critical role in the production of certain extreme forms of violence. The consumption of anabolic steroids by athletes, for example, has been the topic of much medical and legal debate. Psychiatric evidence of symptomatology, including heightened irritability, grandiosity, paranoid delusions, hallucinations, and impulsivity culminating in episodes of violence, is not uncommon among heavy steroid users (see, for example, Pope & Katz, 1990).

Evolutionary approaches to violence emphasize the intense competition between males for access to reproductive females. This competition may not necessarily assume the form of violent confrontation, but it may include competition within the social and political arena, especially competition that enhances reproductive opportunities. Consequently, resources other than physical strength and prowess may inform the struggle between males. Intrasexual competition between males of many species, including *Homo sapiens,* is viewed as integral to evolutionary processes (Wilson & Daly, 1985). Competitive and perhaps dangerous risk-taking is therefore posited as an "evolved aspect of masculine psychology" (Wilson & Daly, 1985, p. 66). This assertion is based on a recognition of the importance of sexual selection to evolution; it does not, however, imply that men's violence is genetically determined. It does, nevertheless, imply that violence performs a useful function: It is a means to defend and protect the self, and to subdue, expel, or eradicate a reproductive competitor. Violence, then, cannot be dismissed as pathological. Daly and Wilson (1994) assert, "Dangerous acts are adaptive choices if positive fitness consequences offset the possible negative consequences" (p. 268).

Violence against women is also explained by reference to men's reproductive interests. Sexual infidelity, abandonment of the relationship, or conflicts over parental investment in raising offspring can be catalysts to violence. Male sexual jealousy propels the violent response (Daly, Wilson, & Weghorst, 1982), which is a tool wielded to control the behavior of a (potential) reproductive partner (Daly & Wilson, 1988a, 1988b, 1989, 1990). Young men are disproportionately at risk of being caught up in violent events, either as perpetrators or victims. This risk-prone behavior derives, according to Daly and Wilson (1994), from selection pressures that operated in the remote past. Young men were expected to demonstrate continuing competitive success in order to sustain their position in the group and to maintain access to their chosen mate. Failure to achieve this could result in ostracism within the community and the long-term denial of reproductive opportunities. Daly and Wilson (1994) call this the *young male syndrome* (see also Wilson & Daly, 1985).

An evolutionary approach must account for the variation in the levels of violence against women reported in different societies and for the uneven use of violence in a society at any particular time. Smuts (1992) believes that situational factors are central to an explanation of this conundrum. Employing an evolutionary framework,

Smuts proposes several hypotheses regarding these varying patterns of violence. She claims that violence against women is more prevalent when alliances between women are weak and alliances between men are valued and strong, and when women lack support from their family of origin. Women's exposure to violence increases when relationships between males are less egalitarian and when men's control of material and social resources increases. Although these sociobiological perspectives on aggression and violence remain contentious (Segerstrale, 1990), they continue, for many, to possess significant explanatory power.

Sociological and psychological perspectives on aggression and violence encompass a number of diverse theoretical positions. Social structural accounts emphasize the ways in which the organization of society generates the conditions conducive to violence (Hatty, Davis, & Burke, 1996). This relates to the distribution of power in society and frequently contains reference to gender. For example, Jeff Hearn (1996a) notes, "When violence is understood as fundamental to gender, and power is recognized as adhering to all social relationships, then a different kind of social theory is required: one that simultaneously deals with differences, conflict, and forms of violent contact" (p. 35). Feminist accounts of violence against women are, in general, premised on the insertion of power at the center of the explanatory discourse (see Caputi, 1987, 1989; Dobash & Dobash, 1979, 1992; Kelly, 1988; Stanko, 1985; Yllö & Bograd, 1988).

Psychocultural accounts of aggression and violence locate the source of the explanation at the level of the actors themselves (Ross, 1992). These accounts concentrate on the effects of socialization, and on the beliefs, cognitions, and personality characteristics of both violent individuals and their victims (Petersen & Davies, 1997). Below, I consider various applications of this perspective.

Social learning theory (Bandura, 1973, 1977, 1986) deals with the triadic relationship between environment, behavior, and cognitive attributes. Stith and Farley (1993), for example, tested a predictive model of severe relationship violence utilizing social learning theory. They found that observing marital violence as a child had only an indirect effect on later relationship violence. It had a direct effect, however, on the perpetrator's approval of this violence. Furthermore, involvement in marital violence, emerging out of the matrix of everyday experiences, instilled poor self-concept and low self-esteem in the violent male.

The frustration-aggression theory proposed by Berkowitz (1969) originally held that increases in frustration can lead to displays of aggressive behavior. A revision of this theory proposed that aversive events that instigate negative affect can produce aggressive behavior (Berkowitz, 1989). This theory broadens the earlier hypothesis: Aversive events are thought to include psychological and physical pain, in addition to the blocking of goals. This contrasts the social interactionist perspective, which emphasizes the importance of transactions between individuals and which does not suggest a direct connection between negative affect and aggression (see Felson, 1992).

Personality trait approaches to aggression and violence search for typical or defining characteristics that distinguish, on a statistically significant basis, between violent and nonviolent individuals (see Barnett, Fagan, & Booker, 1991; Maiuro, Cahn, Vitaliano, Wagner, & Zegree, 1988). This approach often generates profiles of assaultive or aggressive individuals. Meaningful profiles of the male likely to engage in partner violence, however, have proven elusive (Hamberger & Hastings, 1986, 1991), which raises doubts about the validity and utility of typologies of assaultive men (see Gondolf, 1988; Hastings & Hamberger, 1988). Critics of the personality trait approach point to the fact that such research is based mainly on detected or volunteer samples and, therefore, may not yield representative results (Tolman & Bennett, 1990). Furthermore, this research cannot provide an explanation for the link between personality traits and behavior (see Bersani, Chen, Pendleton, & Denton, 1992).

There has also been significant interest in the contribution of language and discourse to theories about aggression and violence. Hans Toch (1993) points to the importance of public or official accounts of violent actions, especially those provided by the perpetrator. The formulation of these accounts, according to Toch, is a means to provide either an *excuse* or a *justification* for the violence. An excuse is an admission regarding the violent acts, but not an admission of responsibility for those acts. A justification is an admission of responsibility, but also a denial of the condemnatory nature of the violent acts. Public accounts of violence, generally prepared for audiences that adjudicate, such as authority figures or powerful institutions, are intended to lessen the likelihood of punishment or the severity of the sanction. Private accounts, in contrast, are designed for consumption by peers or intimates in contexts characterized by shared social values, with interactions based on loyalty and comradeship. Public or private accounts may discount the level of violence or its effects. They may also invite empathy with the circumstances surrounding the violence and with the violent actor himself, while encouraging relative distance between the audience and the victim of violence.

Toch also draws a distinction between the ways in which violence itself is conceived. Toch notes that violence may be understood as *good* or *bad*; good violence is deployed for a just cause. It may redress a loss; it may avenge an incident of bad violence; or it may restore order and balance to the social system. Violence is viewed as good if there is consensus regarding the worthiness of the goals underlying it and the appropriateness of the means used to achieve these objectives. Narratives about this good violence are stories about commendable violence. Toch labels these narratives "war stories." Such stories mythologize violence within the group, romanticize the actors and their behaviors, engage in self-congratulation, and reinforce reputations for bravery in dealing with the avowed enemy.

Of course, talk about violence communicates profound messages about gender in society. Men's accounts of violence within the family, especially violence against a female partner, may minimize, excuse, deny, or justify the use of violence (see Hearn, 1998). Men may exclude certain behaviors from the definition of violence—verbal or sexual abuse, for example—thereby slicing away large parts of the violent experience (see Goodman, Koss, Fitzgerald, Russo, & Kerta, 1993; Koss, Goodman, Browne, Fitzgerald, Keita, & Russo, 1994). Men may absent themselves from the consequences of their actions by constructing self-portraits based on restraint and self-control under "normal" circumstances. Men may also employ particular rhetorical devices to reinforce the contours of their version of reality—of their entitlement to use violence and of their interpretation of the woman and her presumed attitudes or behavior. In analyzing the statements of violent men, Adams, Towns, and Gavey (1995) found evidence of culturally pervasive discourses of male dominance, including a discourse of natural entitlement. These discourses were the resources that individual men depended on to rationalize their behavior. The specific texts of men's speech about violence revealed a number of themes; for example, they demonstrated a reliance on ambiguity, a strategic maneuver intended to confuse those beyond the relationship and to attack the woman's sense of certainty. Men's speech also contained global statements that served as indicators of omniscient thoughts. These were often statements about "the way things are in the world," authoritative statements dispelling the legitimacy of another point of view. All of these speech acts prepare the ground for violence, support the man's use of violence, and psychologically destablize the victim of the abuse. Consequently, narratives about violence, and the discourses that underpin these narratives, are central to the patterning of violence in society.

Anne Campbell (1993) argues that there are clear gender differences in the meanings ascribed by men and women to aggression and violence. Men view aggressive or violent acts as a means to assert or maintain control over others. These violent acts are an attempt to reaffirm a positive self-concept, enhance self-esteem, and reclaim interpersonal power. They are also an attempt to pacify and tame the "disruptive and frightening forces in the world around them" (Campbell, 1993, p. 1). Women, in contrast, view aggressive or violent acts as a failure of self-control, as the literal expression of overwhelming anger and frustration leading to guilt and self-recrimination. Campbell asserts that we acquire gendered social representations about aggression as we develop. These representations are socially conditioned ideas about the entitlement to aggression, the form aggression might assume, and the meanings we might attribute to it. Campbell notes that, by adulthood, these social representations describe parallel but divergent ideas about aggression, which leads to serious misunderstandings and misinterpretations: Men and women have great difficulty in finding common ground on the issues (see also Campbell & Muncer, 1994).

Below, I consider the interpretations and responses to violence evident in the contemporary cultural landscape. It is unmistakable in this discussion that certain theoretical explanations of violent conduct possess more potency than others; these are the explanations that direct social policy and that mould our everyday experiences.

New Dangers, New Safeguards

Fin de siècle America . . . has created and commodified "ambient fear"—a kind of total fear that saturates day-to-day living, prodding and silently antagonizing, but never speaking its own name. This anxiety manifests itself symptomatically as a cultural fascination with monsters—a fixation that is born of the twin desire to name that which is difficult to apprehend, and to domesticize (and therefore disempower) that which threatens.

—*Jeffrey Jerome Cohen*

The decency and civility of our society has been fractured. Women are terrified, men are feeling feeble. . . . [W]e just want to stop the killing.

—*Denis Glennon, father of Ciara, murdered*
by an unknown serial killer

Today, public concern about mass killings is widespread, but during the 1980s acts of serial violence tended to stir community ire and fear. It was during this decade, according to Philip Jenkins (1994), that serial homicide became defined as a major social problem. Jenkins argues that the threat of serial murder loomed large in the public imagination in the mid-1980s. The news and entertainment media showcased the violent acts undertaken by individuals such as Charles Starkweather, Ted Bundy, David Berkowitz, and John Wayne Gacy. The stereotype of the serial killer as the white male who preferred to kill young women or young gay men began to form. Furthermore, serial killers were seen to be different, lacking the normal psychic apparatus that constrains an individual or attaches one human being to another. In his book *Serial Killers* (1988), Joel Norris informs us that these offenders "belong to a newly identified class of criminals . . . motiveless killers, recreational killers, spree killers, or lust murderers whose numbers are increasing at an alarming rate" (p. 15). Not surprisingly, these transgressive figures became the object of intense official scrutiny and popular speculation (see, for example, Cameron & Frazer, 1987; Egger, 1990; Hickey, 1991; Holmes & DeBurger, 1988; Keppel, 1989; Leyton, 1986a, 1986b; Linedecker, 1987; O'Brien, 1985; Ressler & Schachtman, 1992, 1997).

These killers bore the mark of difference: They executed their crimes at the margins of human society; they extended the limits of human cruelty, crossing borders into forbidden territory and entering new behavioral domains. Their excursions beyond the bounds of socially acceptable behavior seemed to hint at the possible breakdown of the existing cultural order. It was claimed that "male serial killers represent the darkest, most sinister side of human existence" (Hickey, 1991, p. 128). Disturbed and violated from within, society was gripped by new levels of fear, a fear of annihilation by something not quite human, something monstrous. This is especially the case for serial killers like Jeffrey Dahmer, a man who confounded societal understandings of normalcy by dismembering and devouring his victims. The fact that Dahmer was also gay was deeply unsettling; this bizarre mix of cannibalism and homosexuality served to underscore Dahmer's monstrousness.

The political climate of the 1980s and 90s supported the development of a retributivist approach to crime and justice. The stereotype of the sexually deviant serial killer nurtured the growth of this increasingly punitive perspective on violent offenders. Novels, true-crime books, magazines, and academic works seemed to concur on the size and scope of the problem, and on the urgency for greater efforts at law enforcement. Philip Jenkins (1994) argues that such sentiments provided the ideal political context for the Federal Bureau of Investigation's Behavioral Sciences Unit (BSU) in the U.S. Department of Justice to expand its purview and to influence the public and the upper echelons of government on issues of crime and punishment. He claims that the exaggeration of the problem of serial killing in the United States served the ideological interests of the BSU and other social control agencies. Jenkins concludes that the social problem of serial homicide was contrived out of sensationalized material, appropriated by political groups, and seized upon by a fearful and vengeful public.

Of course, retributive justice models have not always been in ascendance. Foucault (1978) demonstrates that in the 19th century the law was witness to the medicalization of crime, madness, and the dangerous individual. Criminal psychiatry began to define itself as a "pathology of the monstrous" (Foucault, 1978, p. 5). The crimes observed by the psychiatrists were "against nature," "without reason," and unintelligible (Foucault, 1978, p. 5). The medico-legal term invoked to describe this condition was *monomania,* and it called up a specific idea of the dangerous individual as anonymous and unpredictable— invisible before the crime and undifferentiated from his peers: Everyman.

Medico-legal knowledge of the dangerous individual provided the ground for the evolution of the clinical model of dangerousness, the first conceptual approach to the management of dangerous offenders in civil society (Petrunik, 1994). This model assumed the existence of an individual pathology that diminished legal responsibility, and it suggested that treatment rather than punishment was the appropriate response. The clinical model was displaced in many jurisdictions by the justice model (Petrunik, 1994), which advocated an increased emphasis on the offender's rights, due process, and a minimal intrusion on the offender's long-term prospects. The severity of the current offence and the offender's criminal history were paramount in sentencing. Central to the justice model was accountability for criminal behavior by those not deemed insane.

The most recent approach to conceptualizing and managing dangerousness is the community protection model. Emerging in the 1980s, this model drew on the heightened public fear about sensationalized and bizarre killings, and it led to legislative and procedural change. The interests of the so-called general community were promoted with these changes: The focus on public safety, victim's rights, and revised understandings of punishment has led to increased recourse to indeterminate confinement, post-sentence detention, and public notification of offender release. As we see below, this model continues to hold sway. Consequently, it is worth looking at the legislative maneuvers undertaken under the auspices of this model to uncover the implicit or explicit conceptions of violent behaviors encoded within it.

On an explicit level, it would appear that adult male sexuality underpins the construction of dangerousness in the community protection model. A plethora of recent legislation deals with what might be defined as sexual psychopaths and their insidious relatives, sexually violent predators. Sexual psychopaths are often defined against traditional psychiatric criteria of psychopathology; that is, they are viewed as affected by a mental illness that predisposes them to commit sexual offenses, which constitute a menace to the health and safety of others. Typically, such psychopathology is understood to affect the individual's emotional or volitional, rather than intellectual, capacities. The countless laws now dealing with sexually violent predators often take detected sexual transgression as their starting point. In the state of Washington, for example, a sexually violent predator has been defined as a person convicted or charged with a crime of sexual violence who suffers from an abnormality of mind or personality that makes it likely the person will engage in predatory acts of sexual violence if he or she is not confined in a secure facility. The statute in California, likewise, refers to convictions for sexually violent offenses against two or more victims and to the presence of a diagnosed mental disorder.

The express purpose of these laws is to render visible and to control the behavior of the multiple and repeat sex offenders who are judged to be disproportionately responsible for the volume of detected or reported sex offenses. These laws emphasize the danger of recidivism posed by child sex offenders and by mentally disordered offenders. The thrust of the legislation is to expose the geographical movements of convicted sex offenders and other problematic individuals to the gaze of law enforcement officials and members of the local community. Sexually violent predator laws seek to protect the public, first, by introducing indeterminate detention (e.g., civil commitment on release from prison) and, sometimes, mandatory treatment; second, by requiring that released sex offenders be registered with local authorities; and, third, by providing for varying degrees of public access to this registered data.

Civil commitment has proven to be especially controversial in this new regime. Legislatures and the court system have oscillated between diametrically opposed perspectives on the civil commitment of sex offenders. According to Janus (1996), the U.S. Supreme Court has veered towards a therapeutic jurisprudence, which places mental disorder at the core of the debate about the limits of civil commitment. In doing so, the court has rejected the jurisprudence of prevention—a series of legal strategies adopted to protect the public against future harm. In this latter calculus, mental disorder becomes irrelevant; the state's interest in the preventing violence outweighs the individual's interest in the circumstance of liberty. The jurisprudence of prevention approach is linked historically to traditional models of public health, in which there is a strong appeal to the idea of contagion and a clear reliance on the practices of quarantine. If such models are extended to law, they absolve the state of the need to prove the existence of mental illness to justify civil commitment. However, as I have noted, the U.S. Supreme Court has rejected the jurisprudence of prevention position, holding that mental disorder is a constitutional requirement for civil commitment.

It could be argued that the pursuit of civil commitment as a means of reducing sexual violence is seriously flawed. Janus (1996) maintains,

> Criminal proceedings focus on what the defendant did, and the intent with which the defendant acted. In contrast, in sex offender commitment cases, the respondent is treated as an object to be examined and evaluated. . . . The language of commitment is the language of determinism, not free agency. It is the language of classification—objectifying and demeaning. (p. 16)

Furthermore, in addition to the problematics of predicting dangerousness, there are definitional dilemmas surrounding mental disorders generally (see Quinsey, 1995; Schopp & Sturgis, 1995; Wakefield, 1992).

Laws concerning sexually violent predators may be regarded as a political and legal response to the public's strident and incessant assertion of the right both to know about the potential dangers posed by those in their midst and to find protection from those individuals. A violent incident in 1994 provided the catalyst for many of these legal reforms. In 1994 in New Jersey, seven-year-old Megan Kanka was kidnapped, sexually assaulted, and murdered by convicted sex offender Jesse Timmendequas. The killing of young Megan Kanka galvanized the nation.

In October, 1994, three months after Megan Kanka's death, New Jersey passed the legislation familiarly called Megan's Law (N.J.S.A.

2C: 7-1 to 7-11), which requires convicted sex offenders to register with law enforcement officials, and sets in place a mechanism to alert the public, if necessary, to prevent or resolve incidents of sexual abuse or to attend to cases of missing persons. Under this law, offenders are categorized according to the seriousness of the offense, their offense history, the characteristics of the offender, and community support. If offenders are classified as high risk, the prosecutor is required to notify all members of the public likely to come into contact with the offender. Information provided can include the offender's physical description, address, place of employment or schooling, and the license plate number of the offender's vehicle. Although the phrase "sexually violent predator" is not employed as a descriptive category in the legislation, reference is made to offenders who commit non-sexual "predatory acts" on children and to the mentally ill who might "prey on others."

In 1994, the Jacob Wetterling Crimes Against Children and Sexually Violent Offender Registration Act (§170101 of the Violent Crime Control and Law Enforcement Act of 1994), commonly called the Wetterling Act, was also passed. This federal act requires the state-wide registration of two classes of offenders: those convicted of a criminal offense, in particular a sexually violent offense, against a victim who is a minor; and those defined as sexually violent predators. By the close of 1996, all 50 states had passed legislation requiring the registration of sex offenders (see Finn, 1997).

The Wetterling Act defined a sexually violent predator as "a person who has been convicted of a sexually violent offense and who suffers from a mental abnormality or personality disorder that makes that person likely to engage in predatory sexually violent offenses" (§170101[a][3][C]). The act defines a mental abnormality as a condition "involving a disposition to commit criminal sexual acts" that make the person "a menace" to others. The act offers no definition of personality disorder; consequently, states are free either to rely on standard diagnostic criteria, such as that contained in the fourth edition of the *Diagnostic and Statistical Manual of Mental Disorders*, commonly called the *DSM-IV* (APA 1994), or to devise their own criteria (§170101[a][3][D]).

Interestingly, the act defines a predatory act as one "directed at a stranger or at a person with whom a relationship has been established or promoted for the primary purpose of victimization" (§170101[a][3][E]). This construction of predation is noteworthy for its emphasis on public, rather than private, relationships—for its focus on strangers, albeit manipulative and devious strangers, rather than destructive and dangerous fathers, stepfathers, uncles, or other kin. The legislation deepens the presumed divide between the benevolent, safe, and (re)productive sexual behaviors supposedly enacted by men in a domestic or familial setting and the malevolent, dangerous, and damaging sexual behaviors enacted by a minority of apparently perverse, strange, and frightening men in the public arena. This dichotomy is both false and misleading. Clearly, the push to recognize the reality of men's violent behavior in the home still meets resistance.

A 1996 amendment to the Wetterling Act requires states to establish registries of sex offenders and to inform the public about violent sex offenders released from prison or released on parole. According to the Department of Justice (1997), the federal Megan's Law effectively negates the privacy provisions attached to registration data under the Wetterling Act and strengthens the language relevant to the release of· information provisions. The amendment sets down the principle that "information must be released to members of the public as necessary to protect the public from registered offenders" (Department of Justice, 1997, p. 16189). This release of information is based on the concept of specific risk assessments of registered offenders.

At a ceremony arranged to coincide with the signing of Megan's Law in May, 1996, President Clinton relied on frontier rhetoric to communicate his message. He declared,

> Today, America warns: If you dare to prey on our children, the law will follow you wherever you go, state to state, town to town.
>
> Today, America circles the wagons around our children. Megan's Law will protect tens of millions of families from the dread of what they do not know. It will give more peace of mind to our parents.

Such sentiments clearly imply that sex offenders—even sexually violent predators—are akin to "marauding Indians" or stealthy wolves, watching and waiting for an opportunity to abduct and harm America's most vulnerable and innocent individuals. Yet we might ask the question: Who constitutes this America that threatens to hunt down the enemy? We might also ask: What are we to do about the institutionalized and routinized abuse of children in families, schools, churches, and recreational groups? Clinton's pronouncement is silent on these transgressions; it assumes, instead, the existence of an identifiable and visible Other. This Other does not resemble the law-abiding and socially responsible citizen. He lurks on the margins with a disordered mind and a twisted heart, waiting to pounce on his frail quarry. He is at best barely human, and at worst some kind of savage, untamed beast.

This splitting of the forms of masculinity into the respectable and the dangerous mirrors the way in which masculinity is constructed in legal doctrine. Collier (1995) notes that the law distinguishes between intrafamilial and extrafamilial masculinities. The former are presumed to be nonthreatening, and the latter are presumed to be potentially destructive. This distinction reflects the dualisms that underpin gender relations: public/private, work/home, and dangerous/safe. The attribution of danger to the public domain has its origins in the 19th century, when anxiety about working-class males, loosed from the moral bonds of dominant society, reached exaggerated proportions (Collier, 1995).[4] The family man was legally defined in opposition to the so-called dangerous classes. This respectable family man is the quintessential legal subject: reasonable, responsible, and economically successful. However, to suggest that intrafamilial masculinity is antithetical to crime and violence is to subscribe to toxic ideologies about gender and society. It is to relegate the monstrous to the zone beyond the family, outside the domestic.

Indeed, we might argue that the clutch of laws passed since the killing of Megan Kanka in 1994 contains a new "pathology of the monstrous" (Foucault, 1978, p. 5). What is the significance of this shift? We know that monsters surface at a time of cultural crisis, when existing structures and categories are beginning to tremble (Cohen, 1996a). The instability of these systems of order sets the groundwork for the possible collapse of borders. The failure of the borders to hold—to contain and separate that which should not mingle—unleashes the potential for border crossings, for entry into taboo terrain. Furthermore, monsters undo binary oppositions. They are "disturbing hybrids," who "resist attempts to include them in any systematic structuration" (Cohen, 1996a, p. 3). This is what renders the monster culturally and socially dangerous. Through engagement with monsters, writ large on cinema or television screens, we seek to allay our anxieties about the category crisis that threatens to imperil our ontological experience.

What kinds of category crises confront us today? What kinds of border crossings are implied? To answer these questions, we need to inspect the nature and character of contemporary monsters. I have argued in this chapter that the male and the male body are now, through specific readings, culturally produced as monstrous. The monstrous figure is the male who misdirects his sexuality, who desires prepubescent children, and who refuses to fit within the gendered, heterosexual order, with its norms of family, domesticity, and productive labor. The serious violent predator—the "sex monster"—is a figure of excess (Braidotti, 1994), of unrestrained and unregulated public desire. As Warner (1994) notes, "Alongside the warrior, the figure of the sex criminal has deep roots in the cultural formation of masculinity" (p. 23; see also Caputi, 1987, 1989; Smith, 1989).

The predatory pedophile and the roving serial or mass killer have emerged to haunt society. These cultural creations, and their living manifestations, disturb the borders between the categories of adult/child and pleasure/pain. I believe it is also possible to argue that such monstrous aberrations distort the categorical distinctions between different kinds of masculinities. They both represent and signify a profound category crisis around gender, especially the proper constitution of masculinity.

The new pathology implicated in the sexually violent predator laws, embedded in the criteria of abnormality developed by the psychiatric profession, conjures into being a malevolent and foreboding figure of religious dimensions. Indeed, Rosi Braidotti (1994) declares, "The monster is the bodily incarnation of difference from the basic human norm; it is a deviant, and a-nomaly; it is abnormal" (p. 78). Although these new laws have been subject to extensive and ongoing litigation regarding their constitutionality (see Janus, 1996), this rational challenge to the laws' integrity will not erase the predatory male figure from the public imagination. Janus (1996) cites the following legal reading of one such figure within the proceedings of the Minnesota Court of Appeal, 1995:

> The trial court cited testimony that Toulou [the defendant] was like a wild, predatory animal, which will strike when it is hungry and when prey is available unless deterred by other larger predators. The court found that Toulou is "totally dependent on external forces to conform to society's mores," and that a "removal of those external controls, however, will predictably result in [Toulou] acting on his impulses." (p. 40)

This figure serves to distract the culture from the grimy and seedy activities of ordinary men: The latter are displaced by the specter of sexualized evil. Society is cleaved by violence—a terrible violence laden with abnormal intent, born of difference, and directed at the youngest and most defenseless members of the community.

The articulation of these boundaries between self and Other, between ordinary men and predators, shifts the social and legal frame. Within this schema, essential human qualities, accorded to all citizens under liberal democratic systems, are allocated to some and denied to others. Justice models based on exclusion and extermination become possible under these circumstances. Violence, coursing through the veins of the body politic like a poison, segregates and segments society. Citizens are possessed by fear—fear of neighbors, fear of strangers, fear of the unknown (see Massumi, 1993). It is a new fear of proximity, a rereading of social distance and physical space. Knowledge about Others forearms and forewarns; visibility protects from the ever present threat of uncontrolled male sexual impulses.

Fatal Outcomes:
Ordinary Men and Extraordinary Violence

> I inhabit a culture which is not simply sexist but occasionally lethal for women.
>
> —*Joan Smith*

A balmy summer evening. A beach party. A large group of teenagers celebrating a 16-year-old's birthday. A rape. A murder. A 14-year-old girl dead in the sand, a bloodied rock lying beside her head. These are the circumstances in which Leigh Leigh, a young Australian woman, died in November 1989. Her murder, in a small town on the east coast, sparked outrage. How could a teenage girl meet with such savage violence at a beach party? The beach—the quintessential space of pleasure and indulgence in the Australian psyche—is usually a safe place. And teenagers gathering together for a birthday party are not generally viewed as a threat to each other. In the story of Leigh Leigh's brutal death, however, lie the dark secrets nestled at the core of contemporary masculinity, especially the nascent strivings of adolescent masculinity. For some, violence enacted in company is the social glue that knits together the community of young males. It valorizes the masculine identity of each boy, positioning individuals within a hierarchized order and emphasizing the difference between the genders. Within this system of domination and submission, coercive sex—rape—may become a form of institutionalized recreation for young males, an explicit gesture of group membership.

Lethal violence against women is the ultimate cultural statement about the presumed social value of females. The young males at the tragic beach party told investigating police that one particular young man, now serving a 20-year jail sentence for Leigh Leigh's murder, announced to his mates that he was going to get her drunk so that all the boys could have intercourse with her. That night Leigh did indeed consume more alcohol than was usual for her. Returning to the party very distressed, she claimed that she had been raped by one boy. She was spat on and pushed to the ground by other males at the party. She stumbled, crying, into the distance and was followed by 18-year-old Matthew Webster, the convicted killer. A virgin before the party, Leigh Leigh suffered multiple, severe genital injuries during the course of the evening. There was also evidence that she was repeatedly hit with a large rock thrown from different directions, implying that there was more than one boy involved in Leigh's murder. Despite this, community silence descended on the events. In the week following the crime, only two sets of parents volunteered to assist the police with their inquiries. Leigh Leigh's mother, Robyn Leigh, claimed that she had to leave town due to the harassment she received when trying to piece together the events that had culminated in her daughter's murder. In a subsequent judicial appeal regarding the criminal compensation paid to Leigh's mother and sister, the presiding judge asserted that he had serious doubts about the integrity of the original police investigation. The partygoers revealed little to the police; the parents of these teenagers were uncooperative; and the police themselves neglected to scrutinize thoroughly the statements and the evidence. They also failed to lay charges against a number of young people who admitted committing crimes, including sexual assault, at the party. It is, indeed, remarkable that such serious violence should encounter such a resistant response. It indicates the extent to which men's violence against women, including that committed by young, suburban males living at home and attending school, is normative: an everyday occurrence.

What distinguished the violence directed at Leigh Leigh from the routine applications of abuse in an everyday context was the severity of the violence. In other respects, the behavior of the boys, their parents, the wider community, and the police was ordinary. Connell

(1996) is correct in stating that masculinities are deeply implicated in many forms of violence. Below, I survey the typical scenarios of masculine violence revealed through homicide reports.

Homicide, according to Ken Polk (1994), can be classified in terms of the relationship between the victim and the offender. In his research, Polk divided homicide into several categories: homicides characterized by sexual intimacy, homicides characterized by family intimacy, confrontational homicides, homicides originating in other crimes, conflict resolution homicides, and mass killings. These categories incorporated most forms of homicide.

Masculine possessiveness of a female partner was a staple theme in homicides between sexual intimates. These killings constituted 19% of the homicides studied by Polk. Two-thirds were planned, and many were preceded by intentionally abusive behaviors, such as stalking. Histories of violence lay behind many of these murders. About one-third of the killers alleged infidelity on the part of their female partner. This was often dismissed as delusional thinking by those who knew the victim. In 20% of the cases in which a male killed his female partner, he also ended his own life. Most of these events appeared to be murder-suicides.

Many homicides are the product of confrontational struggles between men (Polk, 1994). Such homicides tend to occur in public places, frequently in and around licensed premises. Polk alludes to the significance of individual reputation and personal honor in these homicides. Many offenders (and their victims) are working class, and the violence often involves alcohol or other drugs. The killing is not planned but may evolve out of a fight between two or more males. Offenders and victims are generally strangers or distant acquaintances. Typically, one male will issue a public challenge to the masculine reputation of another male. This may involve a small gesture or comment; however, the presence of an audience and the involvement of alcohol inflame the situation. The violence often escalates through stages until the final violent act. (On the relationship between violence and public alcohol consumption, see Homel, Tomsen, & Thommeny, 1992; Tomsen, Homel, &Thommeny, 1991.)

Referring to these masculine confrontations, Stanko and Hobdell (1993) state,

> Part of men's knowledge involves anticipating and/or avoiding masculine character contests, even if they choose actively to initiate them. Vulnerability to attack [stems] . . . from situations where the (later) victim did not start the fight himself or where the "rules"

changed; for example, with the opponent pulling out a knife.
(p. 405)

Polk (1994) also notes that confrontational homicides may result from racially motivated attacks or acts of collective violence aimed at members of minority ethnic groups. These attacks typically occur in public thoroughfares.

Other categories of homicide studied by Polk include lethal violence inflicted during the course of another crime, such as burglary, armed robbery, or drug dealing. Needless to say, weapons, especially guns, are often involved. This violence, which may result in the death of the offender or of his intended victim, occurs mostly between strangers. Such excessive force may be viewed as integral to the high-risk activities of property offenders. Included under the rubric of homicide originating in other crime are professional killings, police killings, and deaths in custody.

Polk also describes a category of homicide dedicated to conflict resolution or problem solving. Accounting for about 10% of the homicides studied, these killings frequently took place between those who had known each other for some time and who had shared resources of some kind. Conflict between the individuals had grown to unmanageable proportions, and one person elected to settle the conflict by violent means. In general, these homicides involved males living on the edge of respectability. Socially marginal males were more likely to choose to dispose of problematic individuals than were their more conventional counterparts. Take the case of Rhino, as reported by Polk (1994). Rhino had been for some time "a source of trouble for his friends" (p. 119). He had been accused by his friend, Perry, of breaking into Perry's sister's house, stealing a stereo and video, and perhaps some pills. Rhino apparently threatened Perry and struck one of Perry's children. A wild argument ensued. This was followed by a session of "serious drinking." Later, one of the people attending the session suggested to Perry that they should "kill the scumbag." After more drinking, the two paid a visit to Rhino's truck. They woke Rhino, and proceeded to stab him several times. They buried his body in a shallow grave, later exhuming it, removing the head, and dropping the headless body down a mineshaft.

Such killings, occurring against a background of provocation and inebriation, suggest that responses to a challenge to masculine authority can come in many forms and lead to many outcomes. Below, I examine some of these variations and consider the implications for the wider sphere of gender politics.

Defending the Indefensible:
Rationales for Murder

Is it that ordinary people think that truth is to be defined in terms of the coherence of a story? Or is it that they take the coherence of a story to be one of the tests of truth? Indeed, do they think that the more coherence we see in a story the more likely it is to be true?

—*Ian E. Morley*

Of the many people I have interviewed over the years relating to various offences the most cunning, the most manipulative people in their story-giving are pedophiles.

—*Said Morgan, "Killer cop"*

In New South Wales, Australia, three murder cases recently ended with acquittals. These acquittals sparked strong community concern and a broad fear that these verdicts signaled that it is now legally acceptable to kill another person, that such action will not necessarily result in judicial sanction. These acquittals also throw light on the intersection between gender, violence, and the law; they provide a unique insight into the manner in which masculinities and femininities, saturated with ideas about reason and emotion, are constantly being reaffirmed in law.

One case concerned a young pregnant woman, Belinda Lowe, who admitted killing a drunken flatmate who had punched her in the abdomen. She pleaded self-defense, and was acquitted by the jury within four hours. At her trial, Lowe's apprehension of imminent harm and her feelings of panic were paramount in the legal argument for her defense. Her status as mother-to-be, protecting not only herself but also her unborn child, was undoubtedly a vital aspect of the crime narrative presented to the jury (see Pennington & Hastie, 1993). Lowe emerged as a figure of moral virtue and psychological strength.

The second case concerned a young man who had, at his father's behest, shot and killed his former stepmother's new partner. Dean Waters's defense of diminished responsibility, arising from exposure to his father's brutality and violence, was successful. Waters was portrayed in court as a man who had been deprived of his individuality and lost his will to assert himself. We can easily recognize these characteristics as synonymous with extreme forms of femininity. Waters was able to derive benefit from the contentious but groundbreaking legal argument of battered woman syndrome (Walker, 1984, 1989a, 1989b, 1991, 1994). Waters did not appear a totally feminized figure in court proceedings, however. Despite the suggestion of (induced) psychopathology, he emerged as a credible and sympathetic figure in large part because of his history as a successful boxer. This counterbalanced Waters's temporary loss of rationality and free will; his aggressive and competitive actions as a boxer provided ample evidence of his essential masculinity.

The third case concerned a young man who shot an alleged child sex abuser at close range. Said Morgan, who was then a police officer, had obtained the victim's address from the confidential data available on the police computer system, and he had used his police revolver to shoot the victim. His trial occurred in the midst of public anxiety about child sexual abuse and pedophilia, and the apparent failure of the criminal justice system to detect, prosecute, or deliver appropriate punishments to convicted abusers. Morgan made much of his role as protector in a traditional family of Middle Eastern background. He told the jury that he acted to protect the safety of three young girls in his own extended family who had alleged abuse. Disavowing revenge as a motive, Morgan stated, "I did not kill the man to right a wrong. . . . I was not the jury. I was not the executioner. I was there as the protector" (quoted in Woodley, 1997, p. 20). Morgan relied, furthermore, on masculine metaphorics to promote his case. In graphically depicting the alleged abuse of the six-year-old, he told the jury, "The pain she would have had to be experiencing while these assaults were taking place—I liken to a fight between a heavyweight and a flyweight boxer. You know the result before they get into the ring" (quoted in the *Weekend Australian*, 1997, p. 26). Morgan's attorneys had already attempted to plead provocation, but this was rejected by the judge. They then attempted a variation of the self-defense plea. This presented the jury with three choices: to convict of murder, to convict of manslaughter on the grounds of diminished responsibility, or to acquit on the grounds of an extended plea of self-defense. The jury took less than 45 minutes to acquit Morgan. The decision effectively widened the scope of self-defense plea by accepting as valid not only pleas based on the imminent threat to oneself, but also those based on a future threat to others.

Said Morgan developed for the court a cogent masculine identity, situated within ideas about the patriarchal family and entitlement to violence, and a believable and legally defensible narrative to describe his actions. Morgan, portrayed as a conventional, morally driven public figure of justice pushed beyond the limits of tolerance by the details of the alleged assaults and the appeals of a female relative, is viewed by many as a rational, compassionate, and principled man. To these observers, his lethal interventions in the justice process are understandable and even laudable.

We can contrast this against the mass killer, Martin Bryant, with whom I opened this chapter. Bryant is viewed as an incoherent, inarticulate, inappropriate figure who failed to provide a public explanation for his episode of slaughter. He appeared to have no justifiable moral cause, and offered no understandable account of his actions. We know him as a narcissistic, immature, and emotionally and intellectually undeveloped individual. The law, as a social instrument, can neither make sense of nor support the version of violent masculinity represented by Martin Bryant.[5]

Notes

1. Violence, of course, has increasingly come to constitute the measure of crime itself. The significant penal reforms of the 19th century witness the rise of violence as the central arbiter of criminality (see Foucault, 1977). The incorporation of violence within the core conceptions of crime initiated the great sociopolitical divisions we now experience between the convicted and the unconvicted. These penal reforms arguably placed the criminal beyond the boundaries of the human community, suggesting at the same time that the (violent) criminal is less than human.

2. The political nature of labeling an action "violence" is clearly indicated by the production of the UNESCO-sponsored position on violence, entitled *The Seville Statement on Violence*. This statement, issued in 1986 and adopted by UNESCO in 1989, sets down several propositions on violence. In summary, they are as follows:

> 1. It is scientifically incorrect to say that we have inherited a tendency to make war from our animal ancestors.
>
> 2. It is scientifically incorrect to say that war or other violent behavior is genetically programmed into our human nature.
>
> 3. It is scientifically incorrect to say that in the course of human evolution there has been a selection for aggressive behavior more than for other kinds of behavior.
>
> 4. It is scientifically incorrect to say that humans have a "violent brain."
>
> 5. It is scientifically incorrect to say that war is caused by "instinct" or any single motivation.

See Silverberg and Gray (1992) for the full text of the statement and a critique of its contents (pp. 1-2).

3. One of the most controversial statements on this subject was issued in the 1990s by Frederick Goodwin, a neuropsychiatrist who was, at the time, Director of the National Institute of Mental Health. Goodwin said, in 1992,

> If you look, for example, at male monkeys, especially in the wild, roughly half of them survive to adulthood. The other half die by violence. That is the

natural way of it for males, to knock each other off and, in fact, there are some interesting evolutionary implications of that because the same hyperaggressive monkeys who kill each other are also hypersexual, so they copulate more and therefore they reproduce more to offset the fact that half of them are dying.

Now, one could say that if some of the loss of social structure in this society, and particularly within the high impact inner-city areas, has removed some of the civilizing evolutionary things that we have built up, . . . [then] maybe it isn't just [a] careless use of the word when people call certain areas of certain cities jungles, that we may have gone back to what might be more natural, without all of the social controls that we have imposed upon ourselves as a civilization over thousands of years in our own evolution. (quoted in Mariani, 1995, pp. 137-138)

This conflation of the simian male with the youthful African American male sparked a vociferous outcry. The implied convergence between blackness and a reversion to the "primitive" state of Nature was profoundly offensive to many groups and individuals.

4. Ruth Harris (1991) deduced, from her study of French attitudes and practices in the 19th century, that court representations of working-class males accused of alcohol-related violent crimes stressed the inability of these men to take up the duties of citizenship or fatherhood. The latter implied the transference of responsibility for paternal care from the individual to the state—the establishment of the convention of *in loco parentis*. Furthermore, the most dishonorable and criminally disposed men of the working class were viewed as utterly savage and barbaric, akin to Lombroso's notion of the born criminal. This was especially the case in urban areas where "the image of savagery was applied most consistently to the urban *apaches,* whose 'tribal' ritual underscored a sense of ferocity and menace" (Harris, 1991, pp. 327-328). Working-class men, who disavowed crime and remained gainfully employed, were viewed as childlike and hence morally deficient. This vision of childishness was not the sentimentalized version reserved for "innocent children," but a much bleaker view based on the potential for ill temper and violence.

5. To introduce a sense of proportion here, we need to consider the circumstances of many victimized women who kill. For these women, there is often no vocabulary and no meaningful framework in which to speak about what has transpired (see, also, Stewart, Dobbin, & Gatowski, 1996). As Terry Threadgold (1996) has acknowledged, there "are issues of semantics and narrative, of the need for textual analysis and for the telling of different stories, stories lived from different positions of embodiment." These are the stories whose telling is prohibited in public forums, and that are frequently erased from memory and relegated to the space of silence. Yet these stories are deeply revealing about our cultural codes, our regimes of value, and the processes of Othering.

References

Adams, P. J., Towns, A., & Gavey, N. (1995). Dominance and submission: The rhetoric men use to discuss their violence towards women. *Discourse and Society, 6*(3), 387-406.

Allen, M. J. (1996). Look who's stalking: Seeking a solution to the problem of stalking. *Web Journal of Current Legal Issues, 4.* Retrieved August 24, 1998 from the World Wide Web: http://webjcli.ncl.ac.uk/1996/issue4/allen4.html.

American Psychological Association. (1994). *Diagnostic and statistical manual of mental disorders* (4th ed.) Washington, DC: Author.

Archer, J. (1991). The influence of testosterone on human aggression. *British Journal of Psychology, 82,* 1-28.

Bandura, A. (1973). *Aggression: A social learning analysis.* Englewood Cliffs, NJ: Prentice Hall.

Bandura, A. (1977). *Social learning theory.* Englewood Cliffs, NJ: Prentice Hall.

Bandura, A. (1986). *Social foundations of thought and action: A social cognitive theory.* Englewood Cliffs, NJ: Prentice Hall.

Barnett, O. W., Fagan, R. W., & Booker, J. M. (1991). Hostility and stress as mediators of aggression in violent men. *Journal of Family Violence, 6*(3), 217-241.

Berkowitz, L. (Ed.). (1969). *Roots of aggression: A re-examination of the frustration-aggression hypothesis.* New York: Atherton.

Berkowitz, L. (1989). Frustration-aggression hypothesis: Examination and reformulation. *Psychological Bulletin, 106,* 59-73.

Bersani, C. A., Chen, H. T., Pendleton, B. F., & Denton, R. (1992). Personality traits of convicted male batterers. *Journal of Family Violence, 7*(2), 123-134.

Braidotti, R. (1994). *Nomadic subjects.* New York: Columbia University Press.

Buchanan, E. (1994). The disposables: Social cleaning in Colombia. *News and current affairs.* London: BBC Television.

Cameron, D., & Frazer, E. (1987). *The lust to kill.* New York: New York University Press.

Campbell, A. (1993). *Men, women, aggression.* New York: Basic Books.

Campbell, A., & Muncer, S. (1994). Men and the meaning of violence. In J. Archer (Ed.), *Male violence* (pp. 332-351). London: Routledge.

Caputi, J. (1987). *The age of sex crime.* London: Woman's Press.

Caputi, J. (1989). The sexual politics of murder. *Gender and Society, 3*(4), 437-456.

Clinton, W. J. (1996, May). [Press statement on the signing of Megan's law.] Washington, DC: The White House, Office of the Press Secretary.

Cohen, J. J. (1996a) Monster culture (Seven theses). In J. J. Cohen (Ed.), *Monster theory: Reading culture* (pp. 3-25). Minneapolis, MN: University of Minnesota Press.

Cohen, J. J. (1996b). Preface: In a time of monsters. In J. J. Cohen (Ed.), *Monster theory: Reading culture* (pp. vii-xiii). Minneapolis, MN: University of Minnesota Press.

Collier, R. (1995). *Masculinity, law and the family.* London: Routledge.

Connell, R. (1996, December). Politics of changing men, *Australian Humanities Review.* Retrieved October 15, 1999 from the World Wide Web: http://www.lib.latrobe.edu.au/AHR.

Daly, M., & Wilson, M. (1988a). Evolutionary social psychology and family homicide. *Science, 242,* 519-524.

Daly, M., & Wilson, M. (1988b). *Homicide.* New York: Aldine de Gruyter.

Daly, M., & Wilson, M. (1989). Homicide and cultural evolution. *Ethology and Sociobiology, 10,* 99-100.

Daly, M., & Wilson, M. (1990). Killing the competition: Female/female and male/male homicide. *Human Nature, 1,* 81-107.

Daly, M., & Wilson, M. (1994). Evolutionary psychology of male violence. In J. Archer (Ed.), *Male violence* (pp. 253-288). London: Routledge.

Daly, M., Wilson, M., & Weghorst, S. J. (1982). Male sexual jealousy. *Ethology and Sociobiology, 3,* 11-27.

Department of Justice. (1997). Proposed guidelines for *Megan's law* and *The Jacob Wetterling crimes against children and sexually violent offender registration act. Federal Register, 62*(65), 16180-16189.

Dobash, R. E., & Dobash, R. (1979). *Violence against wives.* New York: Free Press.

Dobash, R. E., & Dobash, R. P. (1992) *Women, violence, and social change.* New York: Routledge.

Egger, S. A. (1990). *Serial murder: An elusive phenomenon.* New York: Praeger.

Fagan, J. (1996). *The criminalization of domestic violence: Promises and limits.* Washington, DC: U.S. Department of Justice, National Institute of Justice.

Fawcett, B., Featherstone, B., Hearn, J., & Toft, C. (Eds.). (1996). *Violence and gender relations: Theories and interventions.* London: Sage.

Feder, E. K. (1997, March). The discursive prediction of the dangerous individual. Paper presented at the Cultural Violence Conference, Washington, DC.

Felson, R. B. (1992). "Kick'em when they're down:" Explanation of the relationship between stress and interpersonal aggression and violence. *Sociobiology Quarterly, 33*(1), 1-16.

Finn, P. (1997). *Sex offender community notification.* Washington, DC: U.S. Department of Justice, National Institute of Justice.

Foucault, M. (1977). *Discipline and punish: The birth of the prison.* New York: Penguin.

Foucault, M. (1978). About the concept of the "dangerous individual" in the 19th-century legal psychiatry. *International Journal of Law and Psychiatry, 1,* 4-11.

Gellert, G. A. (1995). Humanitarian responses to when mass violence is perpetuated against vulnerable populations. *British Medical Journal, 311,* 995-1001.

Gelles, R., & Loseke, D. R. (Eds.). (1993). *Current controversies on family violence.* Newbury Park, CA: Sage.

Gondolf, E. W. (1988). Who are those guys? Toward a behavioral typology of batterers. *Violence and Victims, 3*(3), 187-203.

Goodman, L. A., Koss, M. P., Fitzgerald, L. F., Russo, N. F., & Kerta, G. P. (1993). Male violence against women. *American Psychologist, 48*(10), 1054-1058.

Gottfredson, M. R., & Hirschi, T. (1993). A control theory interpretation of psychological research on aggression. In R. B. Felson & J. T. Tedeschi (Eds.), *Aggression and violence: Social interactionist perspectives* (pp. 47-68). Washington, DC: American Psychological Association.

Green, P. (1994). State violence. In E. A. Stanko (Ed.), *Perspectives on violence* (pp. 30-39). London: Quartet.

Hamberger, L. K., & Hastings, J. E. (1986). Personality correlates of men who abuse their partners: A cross-validation study. *Journal of Family Violence, 1*(4), 323-341.

Hamberger, L. K., & Hastings, J. E., (1991). Personality correlates of men who batter and nonviolent men: Some continuities and discontinuities. *Journal of Family Violence, 6*(2), 131-147.

Hamberger, L. K., & Potente, T. (1994). Counseling heterosexual women arrested for domestic violence: Implications for theory and practice. *Violence and Victims, 9*(2), 125-137.

Harris, R. (1991). *Murders and madness: Medicine, law and society in le Fin de Siècle.* Oxford, UK: Clarendon.

Hastings, J. E., & Hamberger, L. K. (1988). Personality characteristics of spouse abuse: A controlled comparison. *Violence and Victims, 3*(1), 31-47.

Hatty, S. E. (Ed.). (1987). *National conference on domestic violence* (Vols. 1-2). Canberra, Australia: Australian Institute of Criminology.

Hatty, S. E. (1992a). The continuum of unsafety: Violence against women. *Proceedings of the local domestic violence committees' conference* (pp. 62-74). Sydney, Australia: New Ministry for Education.

Hatty, S. E. (1992b). The social structural context of violence. In T. Jagenberg & P. D'Alston (Eds.), *Four dimensional social space: Class, gender, ethnicity and nature* (pp. 49-67). Sydney, Australia: Harper Educational.

Hatty, S. E., Davis, N., & Burke, S. (1996). Victimization of homeless youth: Public and private regimes of control. In M. Schwartz & D. Milovanovic (Eds.), *Gender, race and crime* (pp. 78-94). New York: Garland.

Hearn J. (1996a) Men's violence to known women: Historical, everyday, and theoretical constructions by men. In B. Fawcett, B. Featherstone, J. Hearn, & C. Toft (Eds.), *Violence and gender relations* (pp. 22-38). London: Sage.

Hearn, J. (1996b). The organization(s) of violence: Men, gender relations, organization and violence. In B. Fawcett, B. Featherstone, J. Hearn, & C. Toft (Eds.), *Violence and gender relations* (pp. 39-60). London: Sage.

Hearn, J. (1998). *The violence of men: How men talk about and how agencies respond to men's violence to women.* Thousand Oaks, CA: Sage.

Hickey, E. W. (1991). *Serial murderers and their victims.* Pacific Grove, CA: Brooks/ Cole.

Higgins, M. (July, 1993). Lost childhoods: Assassinations of youth in democratizing Brazil. Presented at the American Sociological Conference, San Francisco, CA.

Holmes, R. M. & DeBurger, T. (1988). *Serial murder.* Newbury Park, CA: Sage.

Homel, R., Tomsen, S., & Thommeny, J. (1992). Public drinking and violence: Not just an alcohol problem. *Journal of Drug Issues, 22*(3), 679-697.

Human Rights and Equal Opportunity Commission. (1997). *Bringing them home: Report of the national inquiry to the separation of aboriginal and Torres Strait islander children from their families.* Retrieved May 19, 1998 from the World Wide Web: http://www.hreoc.gov.au/publications/index/html.

Janus, E. S. (1996). Preventing sexual violence: Setting principled constitutional boundaries on sex offender commitments. *Indiana Law Journal, 72*(1), 12-24.

Jenkins, P. (1994). *Using murder: The social construction of serial homicide.* New York: Aldine de Gruyer.

Kelly, L. (1988). *Surviving sexual violence.* Minneapolis, MN: Minnesota Press.

Keppel, R. D. (1989). *Serial murder: Future implications for police investigations.* Cincinnati, OH: Anderson.

Koss, M. P., Goodman, L. A., Browne, A., Fitzgerald, L. F., Keita, G. P., & Russo, N. F. (1994). *No safe haven.* Washington, DC: American Psychological Association.

Krista, A. (1994). *Deadlier than the male: Violence and aggression in women.* New York: HarperCollins.

Letellier, P. (1994). Gay and bisexual male domestic violence victimization: Challenge to feminist theory and responses to violence. *Violence and Victims, 9*(2), 95-106.

Leyton, E. (1986a). *Compulsive killers: The story of modern multiple murder.* New York: New York University Press.

Leyton, E. (1986b) *Hunting humans.* Toronto: McClelland & Stewart.

Linedecker, C. L. (1987). *Thrill killers.* New York: Paperjacks.

Lucal, B. (1995). The problem with "battered husbands." *Deviant Behavior, 16,* 92-112.

Maiuro, R. D., Cahn, T. S., Vitaliano, P. P., Wagner, B. C., & Zegree, J. B. (1988). Anger, hostility and depression in domestically violent versus generally assaultive men and nonviolent control subjects. *Journal of Consulting and Clinical Psychology, 56*(1), 17-23.

Marcus, J. (1991). Under the eye of the law. *Journal for Social Justice Studies, 4,* 117-132.

Mariani, P. (1995). Law-and-order science. In M. Berger, B. Wallis, & S. Watson (Eds.), *Constructing masculinity* (pp. 135-156). New York: Routledge.

Massumi, B. (1993). *The politics of everyday fear.* Minneapolis, MN: University of Minnesota Press.

McNeely, R. L., & Robinson-Simpson, G. (1987). The truth about domestic violence: A falsely framed issue. *Social Work, 32*(6), 485-490.

Millet, K. (1994). *The politics of cruelty: An essay on the literature of political imprisonment.* New York: Norton.

Morley, I. E. (1996). Narratives, anchored narratives and the interface between law and psychology: A commentary on Jackson (1996). *Legal and Criminological Psychology, 1*(2), 271-286.

Nicolson, D., & Sanghui, R. (1993). Battered women and provocation?: The implications of *R. v. Ahluwalia. Criminal Law Review, 10,* 728-739.

Norris, J. (1988). *Serial killers.* New York: Doubleday.

O'Brien, D. (1985). *Two of a kind: The Hillside Stranglers.* New York: New American Library.

Pennington, N., & Hastie, R. (1993). A theory of explanation- based decision making. In G. A. Klien, J. Orasanu, C. E. Calderwood, & C. E. Zsambok (Eds.), *Decision making in action: Models and methods* (pp. 188-201). Norwood, NJ: Ablex.

Petersen, A., & Davies, D. (1997). Psychology and the social construction of sex differences in theories of aggression. *Journal of Gender Studies, 69*(3), 309-320.

Petrunik, M. W. (1994). *Models of dangerousness: A cross-jurisdictional review of dangerous legislation and practice.* Ottawa, Canada: University of Ottawa.

Polk, K. (1994). *When men kill: Scenarios of masculine violence.* Melbourne, Australia: Cambridge University Press.

Pope, H. G., & Katz, D. L. (1990). Homicide and near homicide by anabolic steroid users. *Journal of Clinical Psychology, 51*(1), 28-31.

Quinsey, V. L. (1995). The prediction and explanation of criminal violence. *International Journal of Law and Psychiatry, 18,* 115-132.

Ressler, R., & Schachtman, E. (1992). *Whoever fights monsters.* New York: St. Martin's.

Ressler, R., & Schachtman, E. (1997). *I have lived the monster.* New York: St Martin's.

Rosenbaum, A., Hoge, S. K., Adelman, S. A., Warnken, W. J., Fletcher, K. E., & Kane, R. L. (1994). Head injury in partner-abusive men. *Journal of Cognitive and Clinical Psychology, 62*(6), 1187-1193.

Rosga, A. J. (1997, March). *Deadly words.* Paper presented at the Cultural Violence Conference, Washington, DC.

Ross, M. H. (1992). Social structure, psychocultural dispositions and violent conflict: Extensions from a cross-cultural study. In J. Silverberg & J. P. Gray (Eds.), *Aggression and peacefulness in humans and other primates* (pp. 271-294). New York: Oxford University Press.

Schopp, R. F., & Sturgis, B. J. (1995). Sexual predators and legal mental illness for civil commitment. *Behavioral Sciences and the Law, 13,* 428-447.

Segerstrale, U. (1990). The sociobiology of conflict and conflict about sociobiology: Science and morals in the larger debate. In J. Van Der Dennen & V. Falger (Eds.), *Sociobiology and Conflict* (pp. 273-284). London: Chapman & Hall.

Silverberg, J., & Gray, J. P. (1992). Violence and peacefulness as behavioral potentialities of primates. In J. Silverberg & J. P. Gray (Eds.), *Aggression and peacefulness in humans and other primates* (pp. 1-34). New York: Oxford University Press.

Smith, J. (1989). *Misoygnies.* London: Faber & Faber.

Smuts, B. (1992). Male aggression against women: An evolutionary perspective. *Human Nature, 3*(1), 1-44.

Stanko, E. A. (1985). *Intimate intrusions.* New York: Routledge, Chapman, & Hall.

Stanko, E. A. (1994). Introduction. *Perspectives on violence* (Vol. 1, pp. xiii-xx). London: Quartet.

Stanko, E. A., & Hobdell, K. (1993). Assault on men: Masculinity and male victimization. *British Journal of Criminology, 33*(3), 400-415.

Stewart, M. W., Dobbin, S. A., & Gatowski, S. I. (1996). "Real rapes" and "real victims": The shared reliance on common cultural definitions of rape. *Feminist Legal Studies, 4*(2), 159-177.

Stith, S. M., & Farley, S. C. (1993). A predictive model of male spousal violence. *Journal of Family Violence, 8*(2), 183-201.

Straub, E. K. (1989). *The roots of evil: The origins of genocide and other group violence.* Cambridge, UK: Cambridge University Press.

Taussig, M. (1984). Culture of terror—space of death. *Journal for Social Justice Studies, 26*(3), 467-497.

Threadgold, T. (1996). Cultural studies, feminist values: Strange bedfellows or sisters in crime? *Australian Humanities Review.* Retrieved June 14, 1997 from the World Wide Web: http://www.lib.latrobe.edu.au/AHR.

Toch, H. (1993). Good violence and bad violence: Self-presentation of aggression thought accounts and war stories. In R. B. Felson & J. T. Tedeschi (Eds.), *Aggresson and violence* (pp. 193-208). Washington, DC: American Psychological Association.

Tolman, R. M., & Bennett, L. W. (1990). A review of quantitative research on men who batter. *Journal of Interpersonal Violence, 5*(1), 87-118.

Tomsen, S., Homel, R., & Thommeny, J. (1991). The causes of public violence: Situational "versus" other factors in drinking related assaults. In D. Chappell, P. Graboskey, & H. Strang (Eds.), *Australian violence: Contemporary perspectives* (pp. 177-193). Canberra, Australia: Australian Institute of Criminology.

Turner, A. K. (1994). Genetic and hormonal influences on male violence. In J. Archer (Ed.), *Male violence* (pp. 253-288). London: Routledge.

Van Der Dennen, J. (1990). Introduction. In J. Van Der Dennen & V. Falger (Eds.), *Solutions and conflict* (pp. 1-22). London: Chapman & Hall.

Wakefield, J. C. (1992). Disorders as harmful dysfunction: A conceptual critique of DSM-III-R's definition of mental disorder. *Psychological Review, 99*(2), 223-247.

Walker, L. (1984). *Battered woman syndrome.* New York: Springer.

Walker, L. (1989a). Psychology and violence against women. *American Psychologist, 44,* 695-702.

Walker, L. (1989b). *Terrifying love: Why battered women kill and how society responds.* New York: Harper & Row.

Walker, L. (1991). Post-traumatic stress disorder in women: Diagnosis and treatment of battered woman syndrome. *Professional Psychology: Research and Practice, 21*(5), 344-353.

Walker, L. (1994). *The abused woman and survivor therapy: A practical guide for the psychotherapist.* Washington, DC: American Psychological Association.

Warner, M. (1994). *Managing monsters: Six myths of our time.* London: Vintage.

Warnken, W. J., Rosenbaum, A., Fletcher, K. E., Hoge, S. K., & Adelman, S. A. (1994). Head injured males: A population at risk for relationship aggression. *Violence and Victim, 9*(2), 153-166.

Weekend Australian. (1997, August 2-3). p. 26.

Wells, C. (1994). Battered women syndrome and defenses to homicide: Where now? *Legal Studies, 14,* 260-282.

Wilson, M., & Daly, M. (1985). Competitiveness, risk taking and violence: The young man syndrome. *Ethology and Sociobiology, 1*(1), 59-73.

Woodley, K. (1997, August 19). Killer cop. *The Bulletin,* pp. 13-20.

Yllö, K., & Bograd, M. (Eds.). (1988). *Feminist perspectives on wife abuse.* Newbury Park, CA: Sage.

3

Of Excess, Lack, and Displacement

Reel Violence

Grace (to Mickey):   You're a vampire, or the devil, or a monster, or cyborg, or something like that. But you're not human.
—Natural Born Killers (1994)

The masculinist descent to the primitive has resurfaced in another guise—the return of the monster as hyper-masculine beast. . . . In *Wolf*, Jack Nicholson's transformation reconnects his character, a somewhat stuffily effete book editor, with a fierce, heroic, and sensual nature that civilized discourse had all but completely sapped. (Even his vision gets sharper.) But for James Spader, his rival, that same descent brings out a deeper cruelty, less concealed by social convention. Nicholson uses his descent to elevate his manhood while Spader uses his as an invitation to unchecked depravity. Nicholson becomes a passionate lover, Spader becomes a rapist.
—Michael Kimmel

P ublic fear and concern about serial killers, bizarre violence, and urban crime rose significantly in the 1980s. As we saw in Chapter 2, this translated into a raft of dangerous offender legislation that continues to depict violent criminals as predators. The increased media attention to violent crimes, especially extraordinary crimes, has inflated the level of community fear and reshaped the public perception of offenders. The confluence of these factors has led to a correspondence between imagined and felt reality: Media portrayals validate laws (and law enforcement), and vice versa, in an escalating cycle of emotion and reaction.

The language of representation has enthusiastically embraced the motif of (sexual) predation, and has perpetuated and extended this within media coverage. As a consequence, the discussion of serial killing has not abated, but rather continues to feed on itself producing ever more anxious responses. Today, serial killers are hunted everywhere; law enforcement officials instruct the public that the killer could be located anywhere, suggesting that the entire continent is his "killing field" and the entire population is at risk of harm. The FBI led the media coverage of the search for Rafael Resendez-Ramirez in 1999 in this way. Described as highly mobile and in possession of many manufactured identities, Ramirez was defined as the antithesis of the law-abiding, normalized citizen. The Hispanic Ramirez was portrayed as an elusive figure, slipping across state lines and shedding aliases as he traveled. The fear of attack was thus not localized in one region or one state, but was experienced on a national level.

Another contemporary site of spectacular panic involves youth access to visual materials—film videos and video games (see Cerulo, 1998; Levine, 1996). In the wake of the 1999 school shootings in Littleton, Colorado, the U.S. legislature attempted to impose controls on the film and entertainment industry. The Colorado incident, driven by the apparently apocalyptic and alienated desires of two young men, seared the public consciousness. It suggested to a populace greedy for answers that there is a potent relationship between visual violence and gun violence. Indeed, so convincing did this relationship seem that the parents of three students killed in a prior school shooting in Kentucky filed a $130 million lawsuit against two Internet sites, several computer game companies, and Time Warner and Polygram, makers and distributors of the film *The Basketball Diaries* (1995), which contains a dream sequence in which the main character shoots a teacher and some of his classmates. The irony of this situation is that sections of the population are both attracted to and repulsed by the depiction of graphic violence (see Dudley, 1999).

The preoccupation with extreme violence is clearly evident in recently produced films, where we often encounter the predatory male who is, in many instances, synonymous with the serial killer. It might be argued that these films afford the audience the opportunity to assume a short-lived psychological proximity to the predatory male, and that such proximity might yield a sense of control, a body of knowledge, and a catalog of signs that can guide both individuals and society. Consequently, films such as *The Silence of the Lambs* (1991), *Seven* (1995), *Copycat* (1995), and *American Psycho* (2000) may be read, in part, as a cinematic response to the contemporary groundswell of fear and anxiety about victimization and public safety that has been particularly evident since the 1980s.

This chapter explores the ways in which multitudes of social and psychic boundaries are now being breached. I examine how representations of violence have become more extreme and confrontational in the last thirty years, exploring the possibility that this may be expressive of the prevailing mood in Western society. I also explore how these postmodern desires and fears draw on constructions of identity that suggest that the self is no longer a unified entity, but a raft of fragmented elements. Furthermore, I investigate how cinematic violence is both implicated in this process of self-disintegration and reflective of it, looking particularly at the overt and covert violence in the horror film, the often bloody violence in the recent films depicting the crime-ridden underworld, and the television portrayal of real crime and violence. First, however, I probe the significance of our temporal context for current renderings of violence.

Millennial Violence:
Loss of the Center

Various social commentators claim that many Western societies experience a heightened sense of uncertainty and apprehension at the turn of both the century and the millennium. Gerrard (1996) acknowledges this, stating,

> Violence . . . is an image bred in the bone for the way we live as we approach the end of the millennium; it feeds off the lurching fears we have about our society. And as such it crosses the boundary between fantasy and fact. (p. 88)

We may also be witnessing the emergence of new modes of violence, or violence deployed in new forms. Simon Chesterman (1998) describes this as

> violence that is unrecognizably sterilized or distorted to serve other ends. Violence justified by reference to a consensus reducible to a single voice. Violence that derives meaning only from representation, which perfect representation emerges as the ordering principle of a world rendered pure by the disavowal of reality beyond the borders of the image.

I return to a discussion of the transgression of the accepted boundaries between fantasy and fact a little later. Let us first focus on how violence is integrated into media, especially film.

Violence is encoded in popular films in various ways. In examining the techniques used, Newman (1998) divides violence into instrumental (or goal-directed) violence and expressive (or emotion-driven) violence, and defines violence as a series of events that culminate in injury to persons or damage to property. He specifies ten cinematic rationales for the use of instrumental violence in films and eleven for expressive violence, arguing that these justifications for the inclusion of violence in popular films are employed in a range of genres: westerns, crime dramas, and futuristic films, to name a few.

Violence is encoded in popular movies, not only by use of the rationales enumerated by Newman, but also via a range of techniques, such as shocking the viewer, drawing the viewer into the violence, employing innovative or particularly harmful forms of violence, setting up contests between opponents, and exposing hidden or secret aspects of experience. An example of this last method is the body-revelations technique so integral to horror movies. In this technique, the viewer is shown severed body parts or internal organs in lurid detail. Newman (1998) claims that such impulses to peer inside the body parallel, albeit in a much more diluted form, the compulsive desire of some violent individuals to dissect and dismember their victims. Curiosity about the body's internal structure and function is high in society, but access to knowledge is restricted to a select few, for example, surgeons (Newman, 1998).

Violence is central to the narrative frames of contemporary cinema and justified by recourse to the devices of character and context. Indeed, cinematic violence is now a major medium of entertainment. So pronounced is this trend toward movie violence that Nigel Andrews (1996) believes that "Violence as variety show" characterizes late 20th-century American cinema (p. 145; see also Bok, 1998). Young (1996) speaks of the "trauma of the visible" and the social and psychological limits set on the representability of violence. Young is, here, referring to the technologizing of the image in real-life trials, and the fissure of anxiety opened up by what lies beyond the image. Writing of the killing of toddler James Bulger in Britain in 1993 by two 10-year-old boys, Young notes that the videotape of the boys abducting young James from the shopping center is the only visual record of the crime. This is traumatic because it invites us to consider what happened to James beyond the frame; this challenges the boundaries of our tolerance for imagined disorder.

One recent film, condemned for its immoral and depraved content and, of course, its violence, is *Crash* (1996). Directed by the Canadian David Cronenberg, the film won the prestigious Jury Prize at the 1996 Cannes Film Festival. The film generated controversy in Britain, a nation recently in the throes of an ongoing debate about the link between screen violence and real-life violence (see Dewe-Matthews, 1996; Walker, 1996). The film addresses the extreme and somewhat strange sexual possibilities that exist in an age of high technology in which the car is an erotic object and speed itself is a sexual experience.

The film tells of a couple, described by the director as the "archetypal post-nuclear, post-technology couple" (Fine Line Features, 1996), who have constructed an emotionally barren and adulterous relationship. Following a collision with another car, the male protagonist, James Ballard, experiences a reawakening of sexuality and vitality. Ballard, in conjunction with the female victim of the car crash, Dr. Helen Remington, begins a series of odd and often shocking sexual couplings. In this cocktail of primal urges and conventional pleasures, sex and violent death collide. The allure of the flirtation with danger and death leads the protagonists to restage famous, fatal car crashes. The disabled and scarred bodies of the protagonists and the crushed carcasses of the cars fuel their appetites for risk and danger. The yearning for more intense experiences propels the characters deeper into this erotic space of injury and death.

The violence in the film is not only the literal spectacle of the car crashes, but also the social and individual desire (often repressed and denied) for the vicarious thrill afforded by the sight of a car crash or its aftermath.[1] Furthermore, the film embodies a postmodern interpretation of selfhood and identity. Consequently, the injuries sustained by the characters in the car crashes could represent, both literally and figuratively, a relinquishing of omnipotence and a splintering of identity. Aspects of self (and body) are lost or abandoned at the crash site or shortly thereafter, and the sexual encounters that follow may be viewed as an attempt to recuperate the loss. David Cronenberg said of the film, "It does violence to people's understanding of human relationships, it does violence to people's understanding of eroticism. If people find it disturbing, I think that's where the disturbing element is" (Fine Line Features, 1996).

Until the 1960s, films contained sanitized violence; however, since this time, screen violence has become more explicit and unnerving (French, 1996). *The Wild Bunch* (1969), a film made by Sam Peckinpah, has been identified as the turning point for the portrayal of violence in cinema. Undoubtedly, this is an early example of what Michael Medved (1996) calls the "blood-soaked imagery of American entertainment" (p. 27). This film graphically recorded bullets as they the enter into and exit from flesh in slow motion; the camera lingers as the bullet travels through the body and bursts out, carrying its cargo of blood and viscera (see Jacobs, 1996). Martin Amis (1996) wryly observes of this period,

> In the cinema, if not elsewhere, violence started getting violent in 1966. . . . And I was delighted to see it, all this violence. I found it voluptuous, intense, and (even then) disquietingly humorous; it felt subversive and counter-cultural. Violence had arrived. (p. 12)

Contemporary cinema has extended the conventions of violence established in earlier films. Now, depictions of violence may function, ironically, as commentaries on screen violence, and the audience may require multiple opportunities for catharsis (Self, 1996). At the same time, some films now manipulate the audience's point of view of the audience to such a degree that we are compelled to abandon our emotional and psychic detachment and become complicit with the violence on screen.

Will Self (1996) describes how the use of mixed media and radical changes in point of view achieves this effect in the film *Henry: Portrait of a Serial Killer* (1986). The film depicts a family being raped and murdered, and it then shows the killers watching the video they had shot of the crime. The film cuts between the filmmaker's point of view, the killers' point of view when videotaping, and their point of view when watching their ghastly video. The disjunction between reality and representation has been superseded in the film; the audience no longer has access to a stable narrative position. The authorial voice of the film—its center—keeps shifting, preventing the audience from forming comfortable identifications or assuming a nonthreatening viewing position.

Another instance in which the authorial voice of a film destabilizes the viewer is Kathryn Bigelow's *Strange Days* (1996). In this film, the viewer is encouraged to identify with a woman's terror as she is sexually assaulted. Joan Kelly (1996) maintains that such an identification is both a novel and very alarming experience for the male viewer, who is accustomed to experiencing a distinct separation between watching violence and participating in a victim's suffering.

In the next section, I look more closely at the relationship between the shifts and changes involved in the information revolution and constructions of identity. I also consider the process of seeing, its link to affect, and the impact of this process on representations of difference. This will assist us in our understanding of the visualization of violence in contemporary America.

Images, Emotions, Politics

> The spectacle is not a collection of images, but a social relation among people, mediated by images.
>
> —*Guy Debord*

> The postmodern is a cinematic age; it knows itself through the reflections that flow from the camera's eye.
>
> —*Norman Denzin*

We are, according to Mark Poster (1995), sliding from one media age into another. We are moving from the first media age, with its emphasis on the unidirectional broadcast model, in which a small number of media outlets disseminate information to a large number of consumers, to the second media age. This second age is characterized by a multidirectional exchange of information. Media are decentralized, and digital technologies enable a new "configuration of communication relations" (Poster, 1995, p. 3), which largely negates the distinctions between producers, distributors, and consumers (see Castells, 1996). The second media age is one of mass suggestibility, in which image and reality vacillate in an unpredictable relationship. As Martin Amis (1996) testifies, "This is now perhaps the most vulnerable area in the common mind. There is a hole in the credulity layer, and it is getting wider" (p. 18).

Poster (1995) claims that the communication technologies of the second media age, including the democratic and subversive possibilities afforded by the Internet, are changing the ways in which subjectivity is constituted:

> If modern society may be said to foster an individual who is rational, autonomous, centered, and stable (the "reasonable man" of the law, the educated citizen . . .), then perhaps a postmodern society is emerging which nurtures forms of identity different from, even opposite to, those of modernity. (p. 24)

In this construction of identity, electronic images are viewed as pivotal (see Kroker, 1993; Virilio, 1991). Why is the image so significant? The privileging of the visual in the Western imagination is the legacy of a Cartesian world-view, in which vision is constituted as a conduit to knowledge and in which the body as a source of wisdom is sub-jugated to the mind—and the "mind's eye" (Hatty, 1996). As Rosi Braidotti (1994) notes "to *see* is the primary act of knowledge and *the gaze* the basis of all epistemic awareness" (p. 80).

Ron Burnett (1995) argues that we need to rethink the simplistic causal models of knowledge that conflate vision and understanding. Instead, we need to situate the visual within the context of gender, class, and race. We need to appreciate that seeing (and listening) are embodied processes that create and recreate the political, cultural and personal meanings we invoke to make sense of lived experience. Fur-thermore, according to Burnett, we need to appreciate that vision is not necessarily a rational process, but is one that involves the eruption into consciousness of a plethora of associations and interpretations. Thought and vision are thus interdependent, and feeling and seeing penetrate each other and disturb our desire to control what we see. Donna Haraway (1991) refers to the relationship between vision and subjectivity as follows:

> The knowing self is partial in all its guises, never finished, whole, simply there and original; it is always constructed and stitched to-gether imperfectly, and *therefore* able to join with another, to see to-gether without claiming to be another. (p. 193)

Images, thus, do not determine what we see; seeing is a complicated process born of our memory, our experience, our consciousness, and the politics of our location in culture. Images may distort, negate, clar-ify, or enhance our interpretive frameworks. As Burnett states, "The image in and of itself does not name what it depicts. It merely sets in place a process of potential identity. The visible in an image is there-fore merely a fragment of what is signified" (p. 71).

Images are, of course, integral to processes of representation. Representations of individuals or particular groups in society rely on cultural categories or stereotypes, and use the conventions or codes embedded in the dominant cultural forms of presentation. These cul-tural forms lend themselves to a number of different, and sometimes competing, readings; for example, specific representations of women, portraying them as vindictive or malevolent, may not always be read in that way by the viewer. This is an aspect of what John Hartley (1992) calls the politics of pictures.

However, we need to remember that representations relate to other representations in a circular loop; any given image is linked referentially to other images. Representations also exist in tension with lived experience; images assist in the defining and categorizing of others, and can delimit and inhibit specific individuals or groups. This is particularly the case for those viewed as different and perhaps threatening, and hence subject to surveillance (Foucault, 1977). We could think here of the extensive and often negative imagery developed to represent HIV-positive individuals, and the efforts made to counteract this (see Dyer, 1993; Gilman, 1988; Watney, 1995).[2]

The representation of social groups as different is, of course, an expression of the binary system of oppositions that characterizes masculinist societies. As I have already argued, the first sign of difference in this system is femaleness. As we have seen, women—and women's bodies, in particular—have traditionally been marked as inferior, abnormal, and strange in Western society. Modern science has developed several classification systems to rationalize the existence of these bodily differences. One of these systems, the so-called science of teratology, is defined as the study of monsters. Geoffrey Saint-Hilare devised a taxonomy of the monstrous in the 19th century. He described the monstrous in terms of *"excess, lack or displacement of organs"* (Braidotti, 1994, p. 78). I explore the significance of this description a little later. First, we need to focus more clearly on this notion of the monstrous.

When we encounter the monstrous we inevitably experience a potent reaction: a strange mixture of fascination and horror (Braidotti, 1994). Horror is inexorably linked to physical and psychological violence; the twin feelings of attraction and repulsion are a catalyst to a violence of displacement and annihilation. I examine next how this urge to represent the monstrous—to produce images of horror—has been manifest in 20th-century American cinema. I then discuss how this urge is linked to the representation of violence.

The Abject Imagination:
The Horror Film

The central thematic tension in horror is the clash between reason, which is repressive, and unreason, which is repressed and therefore eruptive.

—*Roger Horrocks*

Horror takes many forms in contemporary film (Crane, 1994; Grant, 1996a, 1996b; Skal, 1998). It can dwell on the realm of nature and human experience, as well as on the unknown and perhaps unknowable that exists beyond the social and natural worlds that we inhabit. It is not surprising that Joseph Grixti (1989) refers to the narrative of horror as essentially a tale about fear and uncertainty.

Horror has an interesting history in 20th-century cinema. Early films were preoccupied with the supernatural. Films were populated by werewolves, vampires, and Egyptian mummies. These creatures "from the other side" posed a threat to human existence; sometimes this threat emanated from within, as characters become possessed or transformed, and sometimes the threat emanated from outside human society, as people attempted to fend off an attack.

According to Andrew Tudor (1989), horror film derives from the two traditions of horror fiction. The first of these deals with secure horror, in which there is an external threat in narrative, a clearly defined set of oppositions, and an absence of anxiety and doubt, and in which human action is meaningful. This first tradition is generally represented in the cinema of the 1930s, 1940s, and 1950s. The second tradition in horror fiction deals with paranoid horror. Here, the narrative is open and tensions are unresolved, anxiety and doubt are pervasive, the threat is internal and impending, and human action is futile. This interpretation of horror can be found in films made from the 1970s until today. (The late 1950s and 1960s constitute a transitional period, bridging the two horror traditions.)

Furthermore, Tudor (1989) identifies two different kinds of supernatural threats present in horror films: those that are autonomous and unrelated to human actions, and those that are dependent on human endeavors. In the latter category, manipulation of natural forces through the magical arts is central to the narrative. Examples of this theme include *White Zombie* (1932), *Cat People* (1942), *I Walked With A Zombie* (1943), and *Dead of Night* (1945). Many early films also focused on external threats so profound that "the fabric of an everyday world [is] ripped apart by a malevolent and obtrusive power" (Tudor, 1989, p. 160). In films such as *Nosferatu* (1921), *Dracula* (1931), and *The Mummy* (1932), a supernatural domain coexistent with the natural order sets the scene for the intrusion of the supernatural into the natural. It is only in later films that the supernatural realm is portrayed as displacing or obliterating the natural realm. Although some of the early films—for example, *Nosferatu*—prefigure the theme of radical invasion of the natural realm, they do not contain the paranoiac elements of later films such as *The Shining* (1980).

Tudor also identifies two kinds of science-oriented horror traditions that featured prominently in the films of the 1930s and 1940s. The first of these was the idea of science as a route to knowledge and power—often detached from ethics or values. Examples include *Frankenstein* (1931) and *The Invisible Man* (1933). The second was the idea of science as a means to evil ends; here, science was seen as trespassing on the sanctity of natural processes, thereby risking disorder and mayhem.

Later, these themes gave way to a more apocalyptic vision involving a focus on such unarticulated effects of human engagement with natural forces as atomic energy. Following the 1950s, these apocalyptic views mutated into an emphasis on disease and bodily breakdown or decay. See, for example, *Invasion of the Body Snatchers* (1956), *I Married a Monster From Outer Space* (1958), *The Most Dangerous Man Alive* (1961), and *It's Alive* (1975).

Despite these historical variations in the depiction of horror images, Skal (1993) concedes that "very little about the underlying structure of horror images really changes, though our cultural uses for them are as shape-changing as Dracula himself" (p. 23).

What is the meaning and significance of horror? What is its relationship to the monstrous? Noel Carroll (1990) argues that we may distinguish between art-horror and real-life or natural horror. The latter refers to disasters and catastrophes that are part of human experience. Art-horror refers specifically to the various forms of entertainment produced by culture industries. Central to art-horror is the monster, which elicits fear, disgust, or revulsion in the viewer or reader. These emotive reactions are based on the recognition that the monster is both threatening and impure. Impurity or "dirt" is associated with objects that are ambiguous and cannot easily be categorized, or that transgress boundaries that mark out the social or natural order (see Douglas, 1992). Such objects are regarded as interstitial—interposed *between* opposed categories—or as liminal—relegated to the edges or the margins, the shadow zones far from the center. Consequently, the monster represents *risk*—of danger and of pollution.

Carroll (1990) suggests that monsters can be grouped into a typology and that five processes generate the variety of monsters we encounter in the entertainment media. The first of these processes is fusion, which begets a monster comprised of stable characteristics drawn together from categorically distinct elements; a vampire or a zombie would, for example, be a fusion figure. The second process of monster generation is fission. Here, contradictory elements are dispersed across a number of different but related identities: for example,

Doppelgängers (doubles) or Dr. Jekyll and Mr. Hyde. The third process is magnification, in which living entities judged to be dangerous or impure (certain insects, such as flies) assume giant proportions. The fourth process, massification, groups repellent creatures together into marauding armies that threaten humans. The fifth process is horrific metonymy, in which a central protagonist, who appears normal, is surrounded by objects or beings that induce a phobic reaction.

These processes of monster creation combine with changing social circumstances to produce images of horror. Ruptures in cultural arrangements, upheavals in social institutions, and radical shifts in social practices beget a new set of monsters. Such disturbances in social understandings and expectations often revolve around gender and sexuality (see Badley, 1995; Benshoff, 1997; Grant, 1996a; Pinedo, 1997). Speaking of the manifestation of the anxiety, dread, and disgust that accompanies this deviation from the norm, Marina Warner (1994) observes that today "popular culture teems with monsters, with robots, cyborgs and aliens, fiends, mutants, vampires and replicants" (pp. 17-18). Why should this be so? Warner lists the current social (or external) catalysts to horror:

> Millennial turmoil, the disintegration of so many familiar political blocks and the appearance of new national borders, ferocious civil wars, global catastrophes from famine to AIDS, threats to ecological disasters—of another Chernobyl, of larger holes in the ozone—all these dangers feed fantasies of the monstrous. (pp. 17-18)

Each time period, of course, produces its own monstrous imagery. Horror films in the 1920s were sprinkled with pictorial references to castration, especially the films made by the director Tod Browning. Prominent among these films was *Freaks* (1931), which foregrounds physical difference and mutilation, and which, according to Skal (1993), reflected the deeply felt anxiety over reproduction in an age of financial and environmental disaster (see also Hawkins, 1996). So, in the 1920s, art-horror mimicked real-life or natural horror, as is so often the case.

Horror films of the 1940s explored the bestial undercurrents of masculine existence. "Devolved animal-men" (Skal, 1993, p. 216), often equipped with wolflike traits, strode across the screens of postwar America. During the 1950s, the threat of mass destruction loomed large, and the cinematic monsters grew in proportion to this fear. Films such as *It Came From Beneath the Sea* (1955), *Them!* (1954), and *The Beginning of the End* (1957) effectively captured this mood of angst and foreboding. Of course, the Japanese represented their own fears and desires in films such as *Godzilla,* made in 1954.

The 1960s ushered in a new flurry of fears, and themes of altered or aberrant reproduction came to the fore. In *Village of the Damned* (1960), sex was uncoupled from procreation. A subsequent rash of films featured strange and malevolent fetuses: for example, *Rosemary's Baby* (1968). Films such as *Eraserhead* (1976) and *Alien* (1979) included bizarre and distorted interpretations of birth and reproduction. These films bear out Skal's (1993) assertion that "all monsters are expressions or symbols of some kind of birth process" (p. 287). Furthermore, as the body is frequently the site of contemporary horror, it is predictable that horror movies should be so preoccupied by the shapeshifting nature of pregnancy and birth.

During the 1970s and 1980s, children themselves came to be defined as monstrous. Skal (1993) notes,

> Embryonic imagery, by the 1980s and 90s, was as firmly established as the walking corpse as a method to elicit horror. Generation, it seemed, was as repulsive as decay. To the modern, technologically identified mind, it was no longer death that frightened, but a whole spectrum of biological phenomena. (p. 305)

Nowhere is this more evident than in the films of the Canadian filmmaker David Cronenberg. His films, according to Hogan (1986), describe an "*organic* horror" located "*within* the victim's body" (p. 277). Testa (1996) refers to the "intimate 'body-horror'" associated with Cronenberg's films and their reliance on "disgusting and excessive images of the body and sexuality, especially female sexuality." *The Brood* (1979), for example, shows a female character externalizing her rage through the production of malformed creatures that hang in a sac attached to her abdomen. In one scene, this female character, Nola, bites open this sac and removes the misshapen contents, complete with bloody placenta, and proceeds to lick it. So disgusting is this performance that Nola is murdered by her husband: After reeling back in horror, he strangles her.[3]

Roger Horrocks (1995) is undoubtedly correct in asserting that horror is a conservative film genre, based on masculinist fears of dissolution and the collapse of the boundaries that divide not just sexes and bodies, but life and death. "Under order lies disorder: the disorder terrifies and fascinates us, while the order irritates us," he says (p. 84). Of course, this order of which Horrocks speaks is both the masculinist social order from which women (as disorderly influence) have traditionally been excluded (see, for example, Pateman, 1989), and the masculinist fantasy of the "clean and proper" body possessed by men (see, for example, Hatty & Hatty, 1999). The horror film genre explores, through visualization, the affective experience of boundary transgression, in which the impure contaminates the pure and distinctions between inside/outside, self/other, and male/female threaten to dissolve.

The horror film also touches on the consequences of the disintegration of masculine identity by focusing on the exploits of the murderous male (see Clover, 1993; Derry, 1987). Often defined within the narrative as "mad"—that is, psychotic—these men are "monsters brought forth by the sleep of reason, not by its attraction" (Tudor, 1989, p. 185). These madmen terrorize, rape, assault, and kill as a consequence of an inner, uncontrollable compulsion. Here, normality and reason are abandoned, and the audience witnesses the rampages of the violent, monstrous male. Many films have articulated this theme, ranging from the classic *Psycho* (1960) to such films as *Halloween* (1978) and *Seven* (1995).[4] Andrew Tudor (1989) comments that "horror movie psychosis is deep-rooted human malevolence made manifest" (p. 183).

Some critics fix the origins of these films in the shrinking sense of self available in an overregulated society. However, Shor (1995) insists that a gendered interpretation of the social imaginary is the conceptual foundation of this subgenre. Consequently, films such as *The Shining* (1980), starring Jack Nicholson, delve into the problematics of male power in society. In this film, the male protagonist "slips into madness and regression," which releases "a monstrous schizophrenic masculine other that stalks both his wife and child" (Shor, 1995).

The film *The Silence of the Lambs* (1991) catalogs and explores the quintessential characteristics of the psychotic male. Expressive of the contemporary crisis of masculine identity (see Halberstam, 1991), the serial killer Buffalo Bill strips the skin off the bodies of his female victims and wears it as clothing. According to Niesel (1994a), this is reminiscent of the practices of taxidermy, in which the body of the dead animal is evacuated and the skin becomes a kind of substitute identity. This inverts the usual relations portrayed in the horror film: "The rupture between inside and outside exploited in the act of taxidermy is a trope often used in horror films, which consistently try to jolt audiences by showing insides coming out" (Niesel, 1994a). Niesel further argues that the taxidermic impulse, displayed so fully in *The Silence of the Lambs*,[5] is "the most literal expression of male violence," and "an extreme response to the lack of center of masculine subjectivity." (See also Horrocks, 1995.)

This masculine violence is clearly associated in the film's narrative of the visual. Hannibal Lecter describes serial killers as covetous by nature, and frames this assertion in terms of objectification and looking at another. Indeed, the film assembles a great many references to the visual; for example, the FBI is shown as immersed in the culture of photography—what Niesel calls the "aesthetics of objectification." The correspondence in ideology and method between those hunting the serial killers and the killer himself is deeply ironic. Both fetishize the surface of the victim's body, displacing the excess of viscera, bone, and (reproductive) organs, and substituting in their place, lack.

Instrumental Violence:
Descent into the Criminal Underworld

Young Woman: I love you, Pumpkin.

Young Man: I love you, Honey Bunny.

> *And with that, Pumpkin and Honey Bunny grab their weapons, stand up and rob the restaurant. Pumpkin's robbery persona is that of the in-control professional. Honey Bunny's is that of the psychopathic, hair-triggered, loose cannon.*

Pumpkin (yelling to all):   Everybody be cool, this is a robbery!

Honey Bunny: Any of you fuckin' pricks move and I'll execute every motherfuckin' last one of you.

—*Pulp Fiction (1994)*

This is how the film *Pulp Fiction* (1994) begins. The film consists of three stories that culminate in one integrated story. We begin by seeing the disconnected fragments of the narrative: Two young bandits attempt to hold up the customers of a cheap diner; an aging boxer hopes to engage in a final lucrative, rigged fight; and two hitmen go about their tawdry work. At the center of these splintered stories are Marcellus Wallace and his beautiful but bored wife, Mia. Marcellus, muscular, threatening, and powerful, sounds like "a cross between a gangster and a king" (Tarantino, 1994, p. 34). He commands the action of the film, and the narrative revolves around his sinister influence.

The film is a blend of droll humor, sardonic wit, and brutal, messy violence. Individuals are reduced to grease spots, bodies are torn to shreds by bullets, and cars are turned into "portable slaughterhouses" (Tarantino, 1994, p. 159). The film is littered with the trivia of popular culture, with many visual and linguistic allusions to television shows, films, and fast food restaurants. It draws its inspiration from its namesake, the genre of pulp fiction, which Palmer (1994) has described as follows:

> Like the dime novels that preceded them, pulp magazines offered the sensational, the lurid, the exciting. They also promoted, quite consciously, a wish fulfillment that was energized by the breaking of laws and taboos, by the admission of the licit and uncanny into the everyday, by the discovery of exciting transgression in an otherwise dull existence. (p. 34)

In this urban tale of vice, temptation, and redemption, Tarantino weaves a narrative that questions the masculinist culture of violence even as it exploits it. This is, however, a movie in which morality does matter: There are references to good and evil (in Biblical terms) throughout the film, and one of the central figures, Jules, a hitman, has a spiritual revelation. He talks of "divine intervention" (Tarantino, 1994, p. 139), and declares that he wishes to turn his back on "the tyranny of evil men" (p. 187).

Pulp Fiction also explores the sexual and violent overtones of needle culture. Vincent, Jules's partner, has a penchant for high-grade heroin, and is shown injecting it in the film. This incident is linked with a brief conversation about body piercing, in which the dealer's wife informs Vincent that her body is pierced in sixteen places. She is emphatic that all these piercings have been done with a needle. Vincent seems intrigued by this personal revelation, and his fascination in this scene complements the underside of his own sexual fantasy life, revealed when he admits to Mia that thoughts about dominance and submission have crossed his mind.

Indeed, the sexual aspect of penetration/violation is an idea taken up with a vengeance in the film. At one stage, Butch, the fading boxer, and Marcellus, are tethered in a dungeon below a pawnshop, held captive by two hillbilly sodomites. At another point, Butch is given his father's watch, which was hidden in the rectums of two men during wartime—an act that had preserved the "boy's birthright" (Tarantino, 1994, p. 86). Not surprisingly, the watch turns out to be of great significance to Butch and of great importance to the plot. This particular scene depends for much of its humor and effect on the masculine code of loyalty and honor constructed around and maintained by violence—a code explored and exploited throughout the film.

In this cinematic extension of pulp fiction conventions, Tarantino touched a nerve in contemporary culture. The film permits the audience to flirt with the lurid and sensational aspects of life in a place far from the fatigue and ennui of everyday routines; the film focuses on crime from the perspective of those who commit it, and the audience enjoys an empathy with some of the characters at least some of the time. *Pulp Fiction*, like pulp fiction itself, foregrounds "the conflict between individual desire and the law" (Palmer, 1994, p. 35).

Tarantino's earlier film, *Reservoir Dogs* (1992), was also situated in the underworld. Like its successor, the film unfolds in a sequence of amusing, anxiety-provoking, and brutal scenes, and invokes the language and mannerisms of an imagined criminal milieu. Characters are revealed to the audience in a nonlinear and fragmented fashion, and the central tale (about a jewelry robbery gone wrong) provides a showcase for the violent unraveling of the relationships between the offenders. Tied together by anonymity, and infiltrated by an undercover cop, the robbers taunt and tear at each other in a desperate search for the "dog" they fear will betray them.

Violence is endemic to the narrative of the film, invading both dialogue and action. Violence and psychosis, however, are explicitly disassociated in the film; the one character who uses violence indiscriminately is sanctioned severely by the other characters, and is labeled "unstable" and a "sick fuckin' maniac."

However, there is no real distinction drawn between the values or practices of the criminals and the police. There is no clear moral divide portrayed here. The criminal men are shown as interesting and even likeable characters. They are, in the end, scared, terrified, brave, and tender. One of the criminals, a Mr. White, exclaims,

> Without medical attention, this man won't live through the night. That bullet in his belly is my fault. Now while that might not mean jack shit to you, it means a helluva lot to me. And I'm not gonna just sit around and watch him die. (Tarantino, 1990)

These men identify themselves as professionals. This implies adherence to a code of conduct and a hierarchy of values. Mr. White instructs his colleagues,

What you're supposed to do is act like a fuckin' professional. A psychopath is not a professional. You can't work with a psychopath, 'cause ya don't know what those sick arseholes are gonna do next. (Tarantino, 1990)

The language of the film transgresses the linguistic norms of mainstream society. (Even the scriptwriter's directions are couched in the same hard-boiled language used by the protagonists.) Profanity is the thick cord binding the characters together; the racist and sexist terminology, the crude discussion of sexuality (spliced, at times, with astute sociological observations) is the stuff of masculinist interaction. It establishes the parameters of their social world and lubricates the communication between the characters. It is the shared discourse of exclusion.

The film is stark, intense, and disturbing; it presents episodes of extreme violence without moral condemnation of criminal behavior, and the tensions within the narrative are not easily resolved with a happy conclusion. We are simply left to ponder the bad luck of the robbers, even if the cruelty and the violence sicken us. The film is, finally, both tragic and comic.

Tarantino's more recent film, *Jackie Brown* (1997), adapts Elmore Leonard's novel *Rum Punch* (1998), shifting the geographic location and character register of the novel: Instead of Miami, the film is set in Los Angeles, and instead of a blond heroine, it features an African American lead. The film is grounded in a complicated plot involving gunrunning, money laundering, and double-dealing. It is full of raunchy language and dry humor. The lead is played by Pam Grier, a screen icon from the 1970s who acted in a range of popular films characterized by both effrontery and charm. Unlike many other female stars in the blaxploitation films of the era (see James, 1995; Martinez, Martinez, & Chavez, 1998), Grier was known for her vivacious and indomitable characters. In the film *Jackie Brown,* Grier plays Jackie Brown, a flight attendant who is trapped between the Federal Police and an unscrupulous hustler. This is a more subtle and less violent film than Tarantino's earlier efforts; it showcases Grier's acting skills and revives interest in the courageous and gutsy female characters typical of her earlier performances.

Although many of Tarantino's movies have been well received, not all pop culture films dealing with violence have met with such a reception. Oliver Stone's polemical piece, *Natural Born Killers* (1994), has generated fierce argument: Many claim that the violence is gratuitous and excessive; others claim that the moral message of the film is simplistic or that the filmmaking techniques employed are seductive (Niesel, 1994b). Shot in the style of an extended music video clip, the film traces the murderous journey of its two young protagonists—Mickey and Mallory—as they lurch from one violent encounter to the next. Constructed as a satire, the film catalogs many deaths, including the killing of Mallory's parents.

In portraying the carnage caused by two young serial-killers-in-love, director Oliver Stone implicates family relationships and media sensationalism in multiple murder. The film is intended as a critique of American family life and the increasingly punitive responses to crime that typify American politics. Stone therefore included a segment in the film that seeks to explain Mallory's murderous rage. Staged as a cheap sitcom, this segment reveals Mallory's father to be a leering and repulsive character who grabs at her body while abusing and berating his family.

Stone also suggests that the media, especially television, are largely responsible for our contemporary attitudes toward violence and even the proliferation of violence itself. In a series of surreal scenes, the killers are transformed from anonymous offenders to highly visible public figures. Stone draws on a number of television genres to articulate his claim that both the entertainment and the news media glorify detected violence and encourage and incite the commission of further violence.

Venturing into the arena of tabloid news, Stone depicts Mickey and Mallory as killer-celebrities appearing on a show called, tellingly, *American Maniacs*. Wayne Gale, the windy host, does a profile of the murderous duo based on interviews, reenactments, and lively dramatizations. Stone here seems to be pointing to the slippage between the real and the hyperreal in tabloid television: the manufacture and dissemination of entertaining images for their own sake, divorced to a large degree from the circumstances of everyday life.[6] Stone also appears to be pointing to the hypocritical and absurd attitudes toward violence, and to the commodification of violence implied in the placement of Mickey and Mallory on the covers of *Esquire* and *Newsweek*. At the same time, the heroization and sexualization of the killer-celebrities is evident in the placards held by teenagers outside the court in which Mickey and Mallory appear. One young woman holds a placard that reads, "Murder Me Mallory." This young woman seems to want to participate (albeit in a perverse fashion) in the escalating cycle of infamy and violence.

Commenting on the film in an online interview, Oliver Stone (1994) said,

I think Americans have a schizophrenic relationship to violence. One the one hand, they condemn it and [are] appalled by it and on the other they are attracted to it and watch a lot of it. The local news shows are the worst offenders in this area. They offer up real life violence on a 24-hour basis. . . .

My point was to show the American landscape in the 1990s as reflected in the media . . . [and] make my audience think about the consequences of this social and cultural violence.

Referring specifically to the media, Stone went on to say that the press "can create mass hysteria. Can create war. Can demonize any individual it seeks to demonize. And obviously distort the truth."

Oliver Stone's flawed but provocative film is clearly a powerful indictment of the role of the media in postmodern America, especially of its capacity to construct a reality that is misleading, confused, and perhaps dangerous.

Reality TV: Perverse Appetites for Violence

Mass-mediated visual culture occupies the "objective" space of dreamwork and imagination. . . . [W]hat constitutes popular or mass culture has become technologically mediated so that television is not merely a manipulator of popular culture, but it is also the decisive element in the construction of imaginary life and is appropriated as popular culture.

—Greg Barak

In providing formats for thinking, speaking, organizing, and controlling, mass media technologies do not stand apart from social reality and social relations but are integral to them. Mass media technologies not only make dramatic cultural representations of reality, they participate in the construction of reality and of particular configurations for social relations.

—Richard Ericson

It is now widely accepted that a large proportion of the American population receives information about crime and the criminal justice system from the media. This is not a new phenomenon; Surette (1992) has shown that our contemporary ideas, impressions, and beliefs about crime and social disorder were first established during the late

19th century. Indeed, crime and justice themes were popular in the entertainment media at that time.

Today, the population continues to derive its so-called knowledge about crime, offenders, law, and criminal justice from mass-mediated entertainment (see Spring, 1992; Surette, 1992). Television shows commonly feature violent resolutions to lawbreaking, and frequently represent offenders in a negative fashion (McNeely, 1995). Furthermore, the entertainment media is now preoccupied with the figure of the predator criminal—the individual driven by irrational, malevolent desires, and replete with a more vengeful and animal-like character (Barak, 1996). Consistent with the role of the mass media to articulate and perpetuate aspects of order—which Ericson (1991) defines as "morality, procedure, and hierarchy" (p. 242)—these portraits of predatory criminals validate individualistic explanations of deviant behavior. They also suggest that the vast majority of the population (especially males) do not resemble these violent "monsters."

However, in the programming commonly called *reality television* we often find the most titillating and perturbing depictions of violent crime and punishment. Described by Erik Nelson, one of the creators of reality TV shows, as the "idiot stepchildren" of television, such shows have occupied a vital niche in American television programming for over ten years. These programs capture the underbelly of public and private life, and expose the extreme experiences of law enforcement officials and offenders. They include weekly shows such as *Busted on the Job, RedHanded,* and *World's Wildest Police Videos,* and such special shows as *When Good Pets Go Bad.*

To achieve its effects, reality television relies on media looping, which is the practice of rebroadcasting images in new contexts. These new contexts might involve the recycling of images from other television genres: transferring images from a newscast to a game or talk show, for example. Peter Manning (1998) claims that such "media representation and looping laminate realities or layer them and interweave types of experience in a single visual experience" (p. 28). He also notes that the specific production techniques employed to simulate reality in such shows as *Rescue 911, True Stories of the Highway Patrol,* and *Cops* use "close-up pictures of police work taken by a handheld camera, and 'live' footage to convey verisimilitude" (p. 29).

The viewer, of course, is not a passive recipient of mediated images, but is required to engage in cognitive work to transform these images into an acceptable rendition of reality. According to Manning, six rules govern this cognitive effort: the *veridicality rule,* or the assumption that television accurately mirrors social experience; the *sampling rule,* or the assumption that a selection of displayed images is both nonrandom and purposeful; the *ordering and sequencing rule,* or the assumption that images, once broadcast, will be repeated in a rational and meaningful way, and will form part of a continuing pattern of association; the *framing rule,* or the assumption that images faithfully replicate what they are meant to represent; the *coherence rule,* or the assumption that images will be contextualized in a narrative in an understandable fashion; and the *salience rule,* or the assumption that important or key aspects of images will maintain that status over time (p. 30).

Despite often being artificial and staged, reality television frequently gains its public credibility through its association with the news or documentary format (McNeely, 1995). Grindstaff (1995) describes programs that exploit such false credibility as "Trash TV." The genre includes police dramas and crime shows, such as *America's Most Wanted* and *Cops,* syndicated tabloid newscasts, daytime talk shows, and shows such as *A Current Affair, Hard Copy,* and *I Witness Video.*

Why is this form of entertainment so popular? Gitlin argues that reality TV restores a sense of potency to a powerless citizenry (cited in Waters, 1988). Becoming involved in current events, even if via a telephone call to the television station, helps to overcome the sense of hopeless passivity that often assaults the viewer exposed to a visual catalog of disaster, war, and violent crime during prime time news. Neal Gabler (1993), on the other hand, suggests that trash TV actually confirms Americans' view that they live in "a world gone mad, a world beyond shock, a world swirling in a moral void" (p. 3). Bill Nichols (1994) believes reality TV is a response to the (white) middle class cry of anxiety. Nichols explains,

> Beset by dreams of rising and nightmares of falling, plagued by the terror of pillage, plunder and rape, the "target" audience for reality TV (white, middle-class consumers with "disposable" income) attends to a precarious world of random violence and moment-to-moment contingency. (p. 58)

All this occurs in a "timeless, spaceless telescape of mediated reality" (Nichols, 1994, p. 59), in which the master narratives of masculinist culture are in disarray. Moreover, reality TV "continuously peeks behind the screen, flirting with the taboo and forbidden. . . . This meta-story, the ideological reduction, makes the strange banal" (p. 46).

The perversion of reality TV originates in the opportunities for spectatorship that it provides—the chance to witness the intimate confessions, failings, and transgressions of others—and in the occasions for vicarious participation in the social rituals of judgement and punishment. It should not surprise us that Gabler (1993) refers to the "democratization of perversion" in reality TV (p. 3), or that Nichols (1994) should describe it as "a perversely exhibitionistic version of the melodramatic imagination" (p. 53).

In this postmodern landscape of tele-visual simulation, we watch, see, and participate in a protracted drama in which a stream of absorbing and urgent images assails our senses. The traditional distinction between fact and fiction (or fact and fantasy) is blurred. As Nichols (1994) notes,

> Reality TV . . . plays a complex game. It keeps reality at bay. It succeeds in activating a sense of the historical referent beyond its bounds but also works, constantly, to absorb this referent within the tele-scape of its own devising. Reference to the real no longer has the ring of sobriety that separates it from fiction. . . . [T]he gap is sealed, the referent assimilated. We enter the twilight border zone. (p. 54)

In this zone, monsters are everywhere; they invade our living rooms and stare out at us from our television screens. The monster "as hypermasculine beast" (Kimmel, 1996, p. 325) is reconstructed in the ceaseless and amazing spectacle of reality TV. His deeds serve as a lesson about the thin veneer of sociality, the ease with which the individual male might slip the bonds of culture and aspire to a wild, predatory, and irrational existence stalking, cannibalizing, and eradicating Others. The victims are often women or members of other disenfranchised groups; by providing some men with a vehicle for identification, this portrayal of America as a killing field may mitigate their feelings of loss and emptiness. However, when fear threatens to overwhelm, the predatory male may be rendered different, and hence horrifying. And we may all feel safer as a consequence.

Notes

1. Film director and writer, John Waters (1996) reports that he was fascinated by car crashes as a boy. He played out his childhood fantasies of vehicular mayhem by destroying all of the toy cars he was given. His frantic mother even took him to a car junkyard to see real car wrecks. Waters reports that he was elated and exhilarated by the visit.

2. Simon Watney (1995) acknowledges that "a complex politics of representation has played prominently in the history of HIV/AIDS, as rival sets of images mobilized rival explanations of the crisis" (p. 64).

3. Cronenberg's later films rely on a what he calls a "new flesh" rhetoric, in which the body is seen as manufactured, as molded by technology. A World Wide Web page (http://www.netlink.co.uk/users/zappa/cronen.html) dedicated to David Cronenberg contains a "new flesh" directory.

4. Nicci Gerrard (1996) claims she felt repulsed by the film *Seven*. She says,

> I minded the obese marbled body slumped into a puddle of spaghetti, the bucket of vomit, the scabby living corpse putrefying, the female body genitally mutilated. For days after the film, I felt the slight sourness of panic in my stomach. (p. 88)

5. Of course, Norman Bates in *Psycho* (1960) is a classic example of the figure of the taxidermist/killer. See Niesel (1994a) for a brilliant analysis of this film and others.

6. Michael Weinberger (1995) asserts,

> Oliver Stone meticulously documents the way in which television obscures the real meaning of violence. Consider the scene in which Wayne Gale, the *American Maniacs* anchor, travels to prison to . . . interview Mickey. This scene mirrors the classic manner in which television breaks down the wall between the acceptable social element (the audience) and the unacceptable social element (the mass murderer). It has been played out many times before: one-on-one interviews which transport Charles Manson, Son-of-Sam, or John Wayne Gacy right into our living rooms.

Weinberger points out, however, that such interviews are staged in such secure settings that there is little or no risk to the celebrity interviewer; furthermore, the guards and guns can be edited out so that the viewer is unaware of their presence. This allows the viewer to submit to the illusion of some form of intimacy with the most excessive "psycho-killers" of our times.

References

Amis, M. (1996). Blown away. In K. French (Ed.), *Screen violence* (pp. 12-19). London: Bloomsburg.

Andrews, N. (1996). Muscle wars. In K. French (Ed.), *Screen violence* (pp. 144-152). London: Bloomsburg.

Badley, L. (1995). *Film, horror, and the body fantastic*. Westport, CT: Greenwood.

Barak, G. (1996). Mass-mediated regimes of truth: Race, gender and class in crime "news" thematics. In M. D. Schwartz & D. Milovanovic (Eds.), *Race, gender and class in criminology* (pp. 105-123). New York: Garland.

Benshoff, H. H. (1997). *Monsters in the closet: Homosexuality and the horror film*. Manchester, UK: Manchester University Press.

Bok, S. (1998). *Mayhem: Violence as public entertainment*. Reading, MA: Addison-Wesley.

Braidotti, R. (1994). *Nomadic subjects: Embodiment of sexual difference in contemporary feminist theory*. New York: Columbia University Press.

Burnett, R. (1995). *Cultures of vision: Images, media and the imaginary*. Bloomington, IN: Indiana University Press.

Carroll, N. (1990). *The philosophy of horror or paradoxes of the heart*. New York: Routledge.

Castells, M. (1996). *The rise of the network society.* Cambridge, MA: Blackwell.

Cerulo, K. (1998). *Deciphering violence: The cognitive structure of right and wrong.* New York: Routledge.

Chesterman, S. (1998). Ordering the world: Violence and its re/presentation in the Gulf War and beyond. *Postmodern Culture, 598,* 1-23. Retrieved March 4, 1999 from the World Wide Web: http://www.iath.virginia.edu/pmc/text-only/issue.598/8.3chesterman.txt.

Clover, C. (1993). *Women, men, and chainsaws.* Princeton, NJ: Princeton University Press.

Crane, J. L. (1994). *Terror and everyday life: Singular moments in the history of the film.* Thousand Oaks, CA: Sage.

Debord, G. (1983). *Society of the spectacle.* Detroit, MI: Black and Red.

Denzin, N. K. (1992). *Images of postmodern society: Social theory and contemporary cinema.* London: Sage.

Derry, C. (1987). More dark dreams: Some notes on the recent horror film. In G. A. Walle (Ed.), *American horrors: Essays on the modern American horror film* (pp. 162-174). Urbana, IL: University of Illinois Press.

Dewe-Matthews, T. (1996). The banning of *Boy meets girl.* In K. French (Ed.), *Screen violence* (pp. 186-195). London: Bloomsburg.

Douglas, M. (1992). *Purity and danger: An analysis of the concepts of pollution and taboo.* London: Routledge.

Dudley, W. (Ed.). (1999). *Media violence: Opposing viewpoints.* San Diego, CA: Greenhaven.

Dyer, R. (1993). *The matter of images: Essays on representations.* London: Routledge.

Ericson, R. V. (1991). Mass media, crime, law, and justice. *The British Journal of Criminology, 31*(3), 219-249.

Fine Line Features. (1996). *Crash.* Retrieved May 16, 1997 from the World Wide Web: http://netlink.co.uk./users/zappa/cronen.html.

Foucault, M. (1977). *Discipline and punish: The birth of the prison.* New York: Penguin.

French, K. (1996). Introduction. In K. French (Ed.), *Screen violence* (pp. 1-11). London: Bloomsburg.

Gabler, N. (1993, October 3). A sign of the times: When only entertainment has value. *Los Angeles Times,* p. 17.

Gerrard, N. (1996). In front of the children. In K. French (Ed.), *Screen violence* (pp. 82-90). London: Bloomsburg.

Gilman, S. (1988). *Disease and representation: Images of illness from madness to AIDS.* Ithaca, NY: Cornell University Press.

Grant, B. K. (Ed.). (1996a). *The dread of difference: Gender and horror film.* Austin, TX: University of Texas Press.

Grant, B. K. (Ed.). (1996b). *Planks of reason: Essays on the horror film.* Lanham, MD: Scarecrow.

Grindstaff, L. (1995). Trashy or transgressive? "Reality TV" and the politics of social control. *Threshold: Viewing Culture, 9*(3), 17-34.

Grixti, J. (1989). *Terrors of uncertainty: The cultural context of horror fiction.* London: Routledge.

Halberstam, J. (1991, September). Skinflick: Posthuman gender in Jonathan Demme's *The silence of the lambs. Camera Obscura, 9* (27), 37-54.

Haraway, D. (1991). *Simians, cyborgs, and women.* New York: Routledge.

Hartley, J. (1992). *The politics of pictures: The creation on the public in the age of popular media.* London: Routledge.

Hatty, S. E. (1996). *Ways of knowing: Epistemologies in a postmodern world.* Lismore, Australia: Southern Cross University.

Hatty, S. E., & Hatty, J. (1999). *The disordered body: Epidemic disease and cultural transformations.* Albany, NY: State University of New York Press.

Hawkins, J. (1996). "One of us:" Tod Browning's freaks. In R. G. Thomas (Ed.), *Freakery: Cultural spectacles of the extraordinary body* (pp. 265-276). New York: New York University Press.

Hogan, D. J. (1986). *Dark romance: Sexuality in the horror film.* Jefferson, NC: McFarland.

Horrocks, R. (1995). *Male myths and icons: Masculinity in popular culture.* London: Macmillan.

Jacobs, J. (1996). Gunfire. In K. French (Ed.), *Screen violence* (pp. 162-170). London: Bloomsburg.

James, D. (1995). *That's blaxploitation! Roots of the baadasssss'tude (Rated X by an all whyte jury).* New York: St. Martin's.

Kelly, J. (1996). Speaking up for corpses. In K. French (Ed.), *Screen violence* (pp. 196-204). London: Bloomsburg.

Kimmel, M. (1996). *Manhood in America.* New York: Free Press.

Kroker, A. (1993). *The possessed individual.* Montreal, Canada: New World Perspectives.

Levine, M. (1996). *Viewing violence: How media violence affects your child's and adolescent's development.* New York: Doubleday.

Manning, P. (1998). Media loops. In F. Y. Bailey & D. C. Hale (Eds.), *Popular culture, crime and justice* (pp. 25-39). Belmont, CA: Wadsworth.

Martinez, G., Martinez, D., & Chavez, A. (1998). *What is it—What it was! The black film explosion of the '70s in words and pictures.* New York: Hyperion.

McNeely, C. L. (1995). Perceptions of the criminal justice system: Television imagery and public knowledge in the United States. *Journal of Criminal Justice and Popular Culture, 3*(1), 1-23. Retrieved August 16, 1997 from the World Wide Web: http://www.albany.edu/tree-tops/scj/jcjpc/vol3is1/perceptions.html.

Medved, M. (1996). Hollywood's four big lies. In K. French (Ed.), *Screen violence* (pp. 20-34). London: Bloomsburg.

Newman, G. (1998). Popular culture and violence: Decoding the violence of popular movies. In F. Y. Bailey & D. C. Hale (Eds.), *Popular culture, crime and justice* (pp. 40-56). Belmont, CA: Wadsworth.

Nichols, B. (1994). *Blurred boundaries: Questions of meaning in contemporary culture.* Bloomington, IN: Indiana University Press.

Niesel, J. (1994a). The horror of everyday life: Taxidermy, aesthetics, and consumption in horror films. *Journal of Criminal Justice and Popular Culture, 2*(4), 61-80. Retrieved September, 1996 from the World Wide Web: http://www.albany.ed/scj/jcjpc/vol2is4.htm.

Niesel, J. (1994b). Review of *Natural born killers. Journal of Criminal Justice and Popular Culture, 2*(5), 113-117. Retrieved September 7, 1996 from the World Wide Web: http://www.albany.ed/scj/jcjpc/vol2is5.html.

Palmer, B. R. (1994). *Hollywood's dark cinema: The American film noir.* New York: Twayne.

Pateman, C. (1989). *The disorder of women: Democracy, feminism, and political theory.* Cambridge, MA: Polity.

Pinedo, I. C. (1997). *Recreational terror: Women and the pleasures of the horror filmviewing.* Albany, NY: State University of New York Press.

Poster, M. (1995). *The second media age.* Cambridge, MA: Polity.

Self, W. (1996). The American vice. In K. French (Ed.), *Screen violence* (pp. 71-81). London: Bloomsburg.

Shor, F. (1995). Father knows best: Patriarchal rage and the horror of personality film. *Journal of Criminal Justice and Popular Culture, 3*(3), 60-73. Retrieved May 19, 1996 from the World Wide Web: http://albany.edu/scj/jcjpc/vol3is3.html.

Skal, D. J. (1993). *The monster show: A cultural history of horror.* London: Plexus.

Skal, D. J. (1998). *Screams of reason: Mad science and modern culture.* New York: Norton.

Spring, J. (1992). *Images of American life: A history of ideological management in schools, movies, radio, and television.* Albany, NY: State University of New York Press.

Stone, O. (1994, August 16). [Online interview]. *Wired* auditorium on America Online.

Surette, R. (1992). *Media, crime, and criminal justice.* Pacific Grove, CA: Brooks/Cole.

Tarantino, Q. (1990). *Reservoir dogs* [Script]. Retrieved January 2, 1997 from the World Wide Web: http://cnuonline.cnu.edu.

Tarantino, Q. (1994). *Pulp fiction* [Script]. London: Faber & Faber.

Testa, B. (1996). Technology's body: Cronenberg, genre, and the Canadian ethos. Retrieved June 3, 1997 from the World Wide Web: http://www.netlink.co.uk/uses/zappa.html.

Tudor, A. (1989). *Monsters and mad scientists: A cultural history of the horror movie.* Oxford, UK: Basil Blackwell.

Virilio, P. (1991). *The aesthetics of disappearance.* (P. Beitchman, Trans.) New York: Semiotext.

Walker, A. (1996). Suffer the little children. In K. French (Ed.), *Screen violence* (pp. 91-104). London: Bloomsburg.

Warner, M. (1994). *Managing monsters: Six myths of our time.* New York: Vintage.

Waters, H. F. (1988, November 14). Trash TV. *Newsweek, 74.*

Waters, J. (1996). Why I love violence. In K. French (Ed.), *Screen violence* (pp. 118-131). London: Bloomsburg.

Watney, S. (1995). "Lifelike:" Imaging the bodies of people with AIDS. In A. Perchuk & H. Posner (Eds.), *The masculine masquerade: Masculinity and representation* (pp. 63-68). Cambridge, MA: MIT Press.

Weinberger, M. (1995). Natural born killers: A postmodern analysis of violence and television. Retrieved July 6, 1996 from the World Wide Web: http://www.sas.upenn.edu/~mbwenibe/centers.html.

Young, A. (1996). *Imagining crime.* London: Sage.

4

Gender Theatrics
Marking the Difference

A blank sheet of paper. On it a man draws the outline of a male figure. He fills in the outline. He has created a positive form. The space
that surrounds this positive form, this male's male, is negative space.
This is the space inhabited by women. This is the female defined.
This man takes another sheet of paper, draws the outline of a female
figure, and fills it in. This space that surrounds this positive form,
this male's female, is also negative space. This space is also inhabited
by women. This space is the female undefined. A woman takes a
blank sheet of paper and unsuccessfully attempts to draw the outline
of a female figure. . . .

   The next logical step would seem to be the female's re-figuring of
this new negative space, with appropriate variations, into a positive
form that is a "female's female." Why is this such an incredibly ardu-
ous task?

—Leah Johnson

What is this theater of men making men spanning at least three con-
tinents that is not only a representation of dazzling myths and first
times but their actualization, and not so much their actualization
but, first and foremost, a magnificent excuse for another theater, the
theater of concealment and revelation playing with the fourth wall,
the only wall that counts, the gender line fatefully implicating holi-
ness and violence?

—Michael Taussig

Two adult brothers recently collaborated on a book about their
early years. The book is written from the perspective of each brother
and acknowledges the uncertainty and selectivity of memory. Titled

Desirelines: An Unusual Family Memoir (Wherrett & Wherrett, 1997), the book is an exercise in extreme risk-taking; the contents of the book effectively tear the veil of respectability from the family's reputation. This is not without its effects. Both brothers occupy important positions in Australian public life: One is a celebrated theater director and entrepreneur; the other is a successful media figure. The brothers write openly and candidly about the often brutal and painful experiences in their family. They tell of their conformist and conventional mother, who tended the family's pharmacy business and weathered the outbursts of rage visited on the family by their father. They tell how she took solace in chain-smoking and barbiturates, and how she tried to protect her boys as best she could from their father's private and irrational behavior. They tell of discovering their father's epilepsy and drunkenness, and of concluding that family life, for him, was confusing, anxiety laden, and unfulfilling. They also tell of discovering that their father led a life of sporadic violence, punctuated by transvestism; that their father's nocturnal episodes of cross-dressing had alternated with the violence; that wearing women's clothes had somehow relieved the rising tension and militated against the use of alcohol or violence. Their mother's closet thus contained two wardrobes, and the brothers speculated that their mother had accepted their father's cross-dressing as a somewhat bizarre, if necessary, activity that gave her a respite from the violent, drunken rages.

The book tells how the elder son, Peter, began to borrow his mother's underwear as a small, frightened boy. He would don the silky garments during his father's outbursts as a way of warding off mortal fear. Later, he engaged in furtive, adolescent cross-dressing, which increased his anxiety about an identification with his violent father. The younger son, Richard, took on the role of protector once his elder brother left home. This role fell to him at a time when he was struggling with his sexuality.

Compressed in this narrative is a tale of illness, drug abuse, and the fragile and tangential character of the public face of masculinity. This highly personal narrative also illustrates the symbiotic connection between masculinity and violence; it shows how the raw and unfinished business of "becoming a man" sometimes comes at great cost, and how the demanding and insistent business of serving the ideals of masculinity can severely tax the resources of many individuals.

This chapter explores the definitions and meanings attached to concepts such as sex and gender. I review the significance of our contemporary Western constructions, especially the antithetical categories that structure the dominant dualist epistemologies and how the distinctions are maintained. I consider both traditional and revised accounts of gender, examining the role of embodiment in such accounts. I look at the link between masculinity and corporeality in Western society, exploring men's relation to and experience of their bodies, which leads to a critique of the ways in which physicality contributes to cultural constructions of masculinity. I contrast contemporary understandings of masculinity with their historical counterparts, including evolving ideas about American manhood. I also compare our Western constructions of masculinity with those embraced by traditional, pre-state societies, which allow us to contextualize current constructions in a broader historical and sociocultural frame. Let us begin by briefly examining our Western definitions of sex and gender.

Of Nature and Nurture

The existence of a conceptual distinction between sex and gender is now a commonplace assumption. The emergence of this distinction, however, has an interesting and somewhat difficult history. Before we explore this history, let us establish what is generally meant by these terms.

Sex usually refers to the biological determinants of maleness and femaleness. This includes the physiological and anatomical attributes that are derived from genetic endowments; hence it includes chromosomal patterns and the presence of hormones, such as androgens or estrogens. Labeling an individual *female* is usually premised on the possession of *XX* chromosomes and female reproductive and sexual organs. An individual will typically be labeled *male* if in possession of an *XY* chromosome pattern and appropriate genitalia. The term *sex* refers, then, to biological characteristics—chromosomes, hormones, anatomy, and physiology—and contains two categories: male and female.

Gender, in contrast, typically refers to the ascription of social characteristics to each sex. It encapsulates the dominant ideas about feminine and masculine traits and behaviors prevalent in any society at one time. Gender is thus achieved through the processes of socialization, and is comprised of psychological, social, and cultural components (Ferree, Lorber, & Hess, 1999).

Gender identity is used to describe an individual's identification with the feminine or masculine gender. It involves an individual's subjective sense of self: the core belief that the individual is a member of a specific gender category. Early sex/gender researchers, Money and

Ehrhardt (1972), described gender identity as "the sameness, unity and persistence of one's individuality as male or female (or ambivalent) in greater or lesser degrees, especially as it is experienced in self-awareness and behavior" (p. 284). Gender identity is traditionally thought to be relatively fixed by about two or three years of age.[1]

Gender roles are composed of beliefs, behaviors, norms, values, and cultural expectations appropriate to either the masculine or feminine gender. Gender roles are generally considered integral to gender identity. As Money and Ehrhardt (1972) state, "Gender identity is the private experience of gender role and gender role is the public expression of gender identity" (p. 284).

Sex roles encompass gender roles, and refer to the combination of gender roles appropriate for members of a particular sex category (see Franklin, 1988; Nadeau, 1996; Ussher, 1997). For example, Pleck and Pleck (1976) observed that the male sex role incorporates both masculine and feminine beliefs and behaviors.[2] Pleck (1981) extended his argument to formulate the concept of sex role strain; he proposed that individuals regularly violate sex roles and that the consequences of such transgression are harsher for males than females. Furthermore, according to Pleck (1981), men are socialized to exhibit dysfunctional personality traits, such as aggression and constriction of affect.

Conventions of Sex and Gender

Traditional readings of sex and gender are grounded in notions of difference. (For both explanation and critique of traditional readings, see Burke, 1996; Davis, 1995; Kimball, 1995; Schwartz & Rutter, 1998; Walsh, 1997.) The social construct of gender, like its biological counterpart, sex, articulates the multiple differences between the categories of feminine and masculine. As gender is typically about difference, it is also about boundaries. Gender, as a cultural construct, exists then to perpetuate and extend the differences implied by socially defined biological characteristics.

Cultural constructions of difference, located in biology and behavior, are reflected in the policies and determinations of social institutions (Rado, 1997). A recent decision by the Court of Justice of the European Communities in the case of *P v. S* (1996) upheld the right of a transsexual to complain of sex discrimination if she or he receives biased treatment. However, the English courts are still required to distinguish between the social category of gender and the biological category of sex, because the transsexual's legal sex is incongruent with her/his acquired gender (Loux, 1997). Consequently, in the case of transsexualism, or *gender identity dysphoria* as it is sometimes known, difference is understood to be inscribed on the body at birth and is therefore irrevocable.[3] This immutable difference cannot be erased, according to prevailing English law, by the reissuing of a birth certificate ascribing the "opposite" sex to the applicant. This rigidity surrounding the relation between gender, sex, and embodiment is a peculiarly Western preoccupation. Many other cultures tolerate more elastic arrangements (see Lorber, 1994).

Feminist theorists of difference, who often derive their inspiration from Freud and various post-Freudian scholars, have provided rich accounts of the origins and meanings of this difference (see Chodorow, 1978; Eichenbaum & Orbach, 1983). These theorists focus on the development of emotional and cognitive disparities between men and women (see Gilligan, 1982). According to Hare-Mustin and Marecek (1988), there are two perspectives on the construction of gender as difference: One is concerned with the exaggeration of differences; the other is concerned with the minimization of differences. The former perspective is described in terms of *alpha bias.* Views of gender differences as dichotomous, enduring, and inevitable typify this perspective. This view is reflected in Western philosophical thought, from Descartes and Bacon through to Locke and Rousseau. Hare-Mustin and Marecek claim that Freudian and feminist psychodynamic approaches also reflect this alpha bias. *Beta bias,* on the other hand, is the tendency to de-emphasize differences, a perspective reflected in theories and social policies that focus on egalitarianism and equality of opportunity.

For many feminist scholars, however, the debates surrounding gender hinge not on mere differences, but on hierarchies of dominance and submission. Catherine MacKinnon (1987) speaks of the power and violence of difference in her now famous observation that

> constructing gender as difference, termed simply the gender difference, obscures and legitimizes the way gender is imposed by force. It hides that force behind a static description of gender as a biological or social or mythic or semantic partition, engraved or inscribed or inculcated by god, nature, society (agents unspecified), the unconscious, or the cosmos. The idea of gender difference helps keep the reality of male dominance in place. (p. 3)

Discovering the Sex/Gender System

Despite its controversial aspects, the concept of gender as difference or as boundary has remained popular, and the concept of a sex/gender system continues to have currency in many fields of scholarship.

The sex/gender system is the product of research and theorizing on transsexualism (see Robert Stoller, 1968). However, it was taken up by feminist sociologist Ann Oakley in her book *Sex, Gender and Society* (1972). Three years later, social anthropologist Gayle Rubin (1975) argued that both sex and gender are socially constructed:

> Sex is sex, but what counts as sex is equally culturally determined and obtained. Every society also has a sex/gender system—a set of arrangements by which the biological raw material of human sex and procreation is shaped by human social intervention and satisfied in a conventional manner, no matter how bizarre some of the conventions might be. (p. 165)

> At the most general level, the social organization of sex rests upon gender, obligatory heterosexuality, and the constraint of female sexuality. Gender is a socially imposed division of the sexes. It is a product of the social relations of sexuality. (p. 179)

The positing of this sex/gender distinction permitted discussion of the social determination of gender, and avoided the pitfalls of biological reductionism. Subjectivity, then, could be interpreted within the framework of gender; socialization into masculine or feminine identities was seen as central to the production of the gendered subject.

According to this view, social inequities or harms directed at one gender by the other could be remedied through resocialization. Such solutions have been proffered in many areas; for example, it has often been suggested that the way to alter problematic behavior exhibited by men (e.g., violence, lack of nurturance, or other expressive behaviors) is to change socialization practices. There have been calls, therefore, to involve men in childrearing, or to raise boys in a way that does not instill extreme masculine values or reward exaggerated masculine behaviors.

According to Gatens (1983), these approaches are premised on the idea of the neutral body, of the arbitrary coupling of gender and sex:

> What I wish to take to task in implicit or explicit investigations of
> gender theory is the unreasoned, unargued assumption that both the
> body and the psyche are post-natally passive "tabula rasa." That is,
> for theorists of gender, the mind of either sex, is a neutral, passive
> entity, a blank slate, on which is inscribed various social "lessons."
>   The body, on their account, is the passive mediator of these in-
> scriptions. (p. 144)

The proponents of resocializing (or de-gendering), according to
Gatens, base their argument on a rationalist view of consciousness and
a belief that it is possible to alter individual experience through substituting one set of cultural practices for another. For these proponents,
the sex/gender distinction mirrors the body/mind distinction; socialization theorists are thus positioned within the parameters of the
dualistic notions of the body.

In contradistinction to this is the call to focus on the sexed subject, not just the "physical body, the anatomical body, the neutral,
dead body, but the body as lived, the animate body—the *situated*
body" (Gatens, 1983, p. 150). I investigate this assertion more fully in
this chapter. First, however, I briefly explore the implications of different theoretical approaches to gender.

Gender: Traditional and Revisionist Accounts

Conventional accounts of gender and its development draw on
the concept of core gender identity—the assumption that subjectivity
is shaped by gender (see Beall & Sternberg, 1993; Stoller, 1968).
What does this mean for masculinity? Psychoanalytic theory argues
that masculinity is a specific organization of psychic structures, con-
sisting of multiple, ambiguous desires, emotions, and fantasies, which
arise out of the dynamics of particular family relationships. Suffice it
to say at this stage that Freudian psychoanalysis represents one of the
first attempts to theorize the acquisition of masculine identity. Freud's
discursive statements on the Oedipus Complex and his *Three Essays
on the Theory of Sexuality* (1953) set the groundwork for an architec-
tural approach to gender. Socialization theory argues that masculinity
is composed of a cluster of socially accepted behaviors learned
through observation and imitation of significant role models such as
parents. Role theory proposes that masculinity can be regarded as a set
of social scripts, the substance of which is acquired in early childhood.

Revisionist accounts of gender reject the idea that masculinity is embedded in a fixed and stable gender identity. Consistent with postmodern readings of subjectivity in which the self is viewed as fluid and changeable, masculinity, in revisionist interpretations, is no longer understood as the expression of an inner essence. As Michael Kimmel (1994) notes, "I view masculinity as a constantly changing collection of meanings that we construct through our relationships with ourselves, with each other, and with our world" (p. 120). Homi Bhabha (1995) maintains that "masculinity, then, is the 'taking up' of an enunciative position, the making up of a psychic complex, the assumption of a social gender, the supplementation of a historic sexuality, the apparatus of a cultural difference" (p. 58). Asserting the ambivalent and uncertain nature of masculinity, psychotherapist Roger Horrocks (1994) states, "It makes sense to see masculinity as heterogeneous, contextually sensitive, interrelational" (p. 5). This stance is in contrast to traditional perspectives, which view masculinity as a deep-seated, resilient, and persistent aspect of individual character or personality.

Prominent among the revisionist theorists is the work of Bob Connell. In a radical departure from the traditional perspectives on gender, Connell proposes (1987) that we conceptualize gender as "practice organized in terms of, or in relation to, the reproductive division of people into male and female" (p. 140). Furthermore, gender practice can be organized in terms of numerous social categories; hence gender, according to Connell (1987), is "a linking concept," connecting divergent fields of social practice to "the nodal practices of engendering, childbirth and parenting" (p. 140). Gender is, then, a process and not a condition of the individual (see Lorber, 1994). Rather than reify gender, Connell (1987) invites us to think of gender as a verb—a dynamic process situated within sociality.

Following Jill Julius Matthews (1984), Connell also proposes the existence of a *gender order,* a pattern of gendered power relations that emerges out of the exigencies of history. A *gender regime* is the manifestation of this structured gender order within a particular institution. The gender order and the gender regime rest on the division of labor, the hierarchies of power, and the social constitution of desire and sexuality (cathexis). Connell recognizes the significance of force and violence in all these domains.

In one of the most influential statements in contemporary social theory, Connell posits the existence of masculinity and femininity as multivalent concepts. Rather than rely on the unitary and homogeneous constructions of gender incorporated in much previous theory, Connell explores the idea of multiple masculinities coexistent within the gender order. Connell (1987) declares,

> There is an ordering of versions of femininity and masculinity at the level of the whole society. . . .
>   This structural fact provides the main basis for relationships among men that define a hegemonic form of masculinity in the society as a whole. "Hegemonic masculinity" is always constructed in relation to various subordinated masculinities as well as in relation to women.
>   There is no femininity that is hegemonic in the sense that the dominant form of masculinity is hegemonic among men. (p. 183)

However, according to Connell (1987), there is a version of femininity that is given prominence, that is emphasized.

Hegemonic masculinity is the publicly avowed, preferred model of manliness. It depends on the circulation of mass media ideologies and images for its survival and prosperity. Many of the images of hegemonic masculinity are aspirational, depicting fantasy or fictional characters whose attainments represent the extremes of socially approved masculine achievements. Such public forms of masculinity and their private counterparts sediment differential power relations between men and women. Hegemonic masculinity is, then, the cultural manifestation of men's ascendancy over women. Although forms of hegemonic masculinity are established and maintained via mass media and institutional doctrines and practices, they are not inconsistent with the use of force or violence. However, as Connell (1987) points out, women may also feel oppressed by nonhegemonic forms of masculinity; subordinated masculinities, such as those embraced by gay men for example, may not empower women, and indeed may contain tendencies toward gender hostility or even misogyny.

Connell's revisionist work on gender has found its way into many spheres of social science scholarship. Messerschmidt's *Masculinities and Crime* (1993) adopts Connell's notion of hegemonic masculinity, and argues that crimes committed by men can be understood as attempts to accomplish masculinity when other means of demonstrating manliness are curtailed or unavailable. Messerschmidt claims that marginalized and excluded groups of males, such as African American or Hispanic American youths, may display an oppositional masculinity born of resistance. Middle-class, white males, by contrast, may embrace an accommodating masculinity, embodying hegemonic concerns with career and social achievement. Messerschmidt's thesis, therefore, emphasizes the relational and hierarchical character of masculinities (see also Donaldson, 1993).

Another revisionist gender theorist is Judith Butler. In her book *Gender Trouble* (1990), Butler outlines a performative notion of gender. In this interpretation, gender is an array of social practices that adhere to individuals as they internalize social structures. In her later work, Butler (1995) maintains that gender "is produced as a ritualized repetition of conventions, and that this ritual is socially compelled in part by the force of a compulsory heterosexuality" (p. 31). The psychic illusion of a core gender identity is a catalyst to the continual performance of gender. Furthermore, femininity, according to Butler (1995), is cast as the spectacular gender; it can be regarded as an ideal that is only ever imitated and never fully inhabited.[4]

Symbolic social structures, such as law, reinforce the idealized gender categories and cast out identities that disturb the socially proper gender divisions. These ejected identities become "zones of uninhabitability" (Butler, 1993, p. 243). Butler notes, however, that "repetitions of hegemonic forms of power" can also be opportunities to expose or disrupt the naturalizing functions of gender discourse. Butler thus recognizes the resistant and disruptive potential of ostensibly conventional practices, such as those installed within juridical discourse, for example.

As we shall see, this interpretation of gender has been very influential. Below, I return to the concept of the sexed body and its relation to masculinity.

Masculinity and Corporeality

Within the epistemological heritage of Western society, the body has traditionally been conceptualized as the material container for either the soul or the intellect. As we saw in Chapter 1, Descartes's writings were premised on the notion that the body could be equated with a machine; according to Descartes, the body was simply *res extensa,* matter animated by mechanical forces. Descartes attempted to distance bodily experiences, such as disease and pain, from the subject by substituting a third-person for a first-person perspective. Moreover, he severed the attributes associated with subjectivity from the body. Identified primarily with physical sensation and divorced from higher cognition, the body occupied the position of Other. The bifurcation between the body and mind or soul relegated the body to the status of a degraded entity. Descartes wrote, "I am a thinking body. I *possess* a body with which I am intimately conjoined"; however, he continued, "this 'me,' . . . the soul by which I am, is entirely distinct from the body" (quoted in Leder, 1990, p. 126). The body, according to Descartes, was a deceptive and limiting presence, with distinct boundaries, that enclosed the self. Cartesian ontology rested on the distinction between *res extensa* and *res cognitans,* privileging of the latter over the former. Cartesian method provided the key to transcending the body; scientific knowledge was gained through the process of denying and controlling the body. Leder (1990) notes that "a certain telos toward disembodiment is an abiding strain of Western intellectual history" (p. 3).

Jane Gallop (1988) asserts that the mind/body split integral to the Cartesian model is an image of extraordinary violence. Furthermore, she believes that the Western philosophical tradition has failed miserably to "think through the body": "Rather than treat the body as a site of knowledge, a medium for thought, the more classic philosophical project has tried to render it transparent and get beyond it, to dominate it by reducing it to the mind's idealizing categories," she writes (pp. 3-4).

In contradistinction to this tradition, we now acknowledge that subjectivity and corporeality are intimately entwined, and that the body mediates the experience of the external world. Consequently, the senses interpret and construct; a corporeal self responds to stimuli that impinge from beyond the borders of existence. Relationships are grounded in a reciprocity of sensory exchanges; touch, sight, aroma, and speech all rely on the vicissitudes of embodiment. The body contributes to the formation of subjectivity; indeed, the involvement of the body is central to the experience of self.[5] (See Armstrong, 1996; Csordas, 1994; Foster, 1996; Halberstam & Livingston, 1995; Kay & Rubin, 1994; Lingis, 1994; Young, 1997).

What of men's bodies? Below I examine how masculinity and physicality are intertwined. First, I consider men's relationship with their bodies, and then review the ways in which men conceptualize embodiment.

Male Bodies: Hide and Show

Men often view their bodies as instruments: flesh in the service of an objective or a desire (Seidler, 1997). Men are frequently depicted in the public arena as "talking heads" divorced from their physicality. In these representations, corporeality is de-emphasized in the pursuit of political or social credibility. It is almost as if the public acknowledgment of embodiment is, for men, a liability.

Ironically, the male body is not only an instrument, but also a weapon (Messner, 1997). Sociologist Bob Connell (1983) remarked, "What it means to be masculine is, quite literally, to embody force" (p. 27). Margaret Atwood (1996) reiterates this idea: "Men's bodies are the most dangerous things on earth" (p. 3), she writes, referring to the fact that men kill other men in both war and peacetime, and also that men sexually assault and kill women and children. "Why do men want to kill the bodies of other men?" she asks, while observing that, today, men are "most afraid of . . . the body of another man" (p. 3). Violence, as we shall see again later in this chapter, is integral to masculinity.

Consistent with the centrality of force to masculinity, men are taught to occupy space in ways that connote strength, potency, and assertiveness. A corollary of these body-reflexive practices (Connell, 1995) is the translation of the male body into a physical project, subject to the will and motivation of its "owner" (see Armstrong, 1996). This view of the body leads to an achievement-oriented approach to masculinity—one reflected in sport and pornography. As Susan Bordo (1996) notes, "The ideal is to have a body that is hard as a rock, without looseness or flaccidity anywhere. . . . [M]uscles today are the mark of mind over matter" (p. 290). This achievement-oriented masculinity produces a solid, impervious, and self-sufficient body. It is a body both desirable and threatening. Yet, as we shall see below, it is ultimately a fragile creation, defined by its own failures (Connell, 1995). The perfectible body, the emblem of masculinist cultures from classical Greece onward, may prove elusive (Dutton, 1995). Discourses of the self-built and carefully engineered body may clash head-on with the lived experiences of unreliable and somewhat strange physicality.

Living in the Male Body

Men's experience of the body is often epitomized by feelings of alienation and absence. Indeed, men will frequently speak of the foreign character of their own bodies, as if they are referring to a physical entity that is not integral to their identity as male subjects. Gallop (1988) notes that "men have their masculine identity to gain by being estranged from their bodies" (p. 7).

This experience of alienation from the body may surface, paradoxically, in the arena of sexuality. Referring to St. Augustine's lament that "sometimes the impulse [of desire] is an unwanted intruder, sometimes it abandons the eager lover" (1972, p. 577), Leder (1990) claims that sexuality "exhibits a visceral autonomy" (p. 137). Furthermore, he declares that "just as the body is remembered when pain or sickness interferes with our intentions, so too when powerful passions rebel. At such times the body dys-appears, surfacing as an alien or threatening thing" (p. 137). On the basis of this, Leder claims that the Cartesian paradigm has a foundation in experience. In contrast to the assumption that the dualist view of the world reflects a denial of lived experience and the valorization of incorporeal reason, Leder asserts that the experience of the body supports and validates Cartesian dualism. This peculiarly masculine view of the body—in which the body is alternatively viewed as absent or alien—reverberates through much recent writing and scholarship on masculinity. John Updike (1996), for example, describes the moment of sexual excitement as follows:

> Men's bodies, at this juncture, feel only partly theirs; a demon of sorts has been attached to their lower torsos, whose performance is erratic and whose errands seem, at times, ridiculous. It is like having a (much) smaller brother toward whom you feel both fond and impatient; if he is you, it is you in curiously simplified and ignoble form. . . .
>
> To inhabit a male body, then, is to feel somewhat detached from it. It is not an enemy, but not entirely a friend. (p. 10)

Margaret Atwood (1996) playfully comments,

> The thing is: men's bodies aren't dependable. Now it does, now it doesn't, and so much for the triumph of the will. A man is the puppet of his body, or vice versa. He and it make tomfools of each other: it lets him down. Or up, at the wrong moment. (p. 4)

This detachment and alienation from (aspects) of the male body can, however, have other consequences. Men often view their bodies as low maintenance propositions (see Updike, 1996), and so neglect their health until the advent of a physical crisis. This crisis can both reflect and magnify these feelings of detachment and disconnection. Speaking of his increasing alienation from his physicality, and eventual decline into illness, the academic David Jackson (1990) says,

A widening split grew between my mind and my body. I felt increasingly out of sync with my body, using it to carry around my brain but being estranged from its specific needs and rhythms. . . . [E]ventually I collapsed physically in February 1986 [and] it was with a sense that my body had decided to claim its revenge on an indifferent, arrogant intellect. (p. 59)

Under the heading "Falling apart," Jackson describes the rebellion of his body:

I was reconnected to the life and history of my body at the moment when I collapsed in a total heart-block while teaching. It was the point at which my body dug its heels in and refused to go on obeying the imperious demands of my head. . . .

It was the first time in my life that my body, which I had been holding so firm and tight for so long, had completely let me down. (p. 59)

In hospital, the absent body began to manifest itself:

I became intensely aware of my body's moods, its daily movements, its sudden swings, my distinctive heartbeat like a personal thumbprint, its aches and pains in a way that previously living through rational intellect had distanced me from. (p. 61)

This relation to the body, characterized by denial and rejection, contains within its outlines another process: the negotiation of boundaries. The failure to detect the presence of the body and the attempt to exile the experiences of the body reflect a concern with demarcating the self from others. Leder (1990) discusses the necessity of preserving boundaries:

My body is . . . that whereby I am localized and bounded, marked off as separate from other parts of the world. To perceive, I must inhabit a particular perspective and maintain some separation from the thing perceived. To live I must preserve a boundary across which I metabolically take in or give out. (p. 201)

And how might one be "marked off as separate from other parts of the world" and "the thing perceived"? Our collapsed writer, David Jackson, provides us with an answer:

On one level, heterosexual relations have historically shaped me to embody superiority over women in my bodily relations. Practically, this means holding my body in a firmly decisive way that marks me off from an imaginary woman. Often this means that thrusting, driving and pushing . . . have been naturalized in my heterosexual body. (p. 57)

The imperative to delineate a boundary that excludes the "imaginary woman" through the "thrusting, driving and pushing" of heterosexual activity betrays the existence of powerful emotions. That survival depends on preserving the boundary may indicate the pervasive terror of being absorbed or devoured. This terror may arise whenever the intellect (reason) succumbs to the body (desire). Jackson speaks of the fear of annihilation underscoring his collapse (Jackson, 1990, p. 59):

I suddenly became dizzy and light-headed. I felt as if I was being sucked into the darkening, spinning centre of a whirlpool. Before, when I had experienced dizzy spells, I had felt as if I had lurched towards the centre of the whirlpool and then veered back to the calmer fringes of the slack, outer circle. But now I couldn't stop myself being swallowed, deeper and deeper. There was just a terrifying, revolving swirl encircling me, dragging me in. I could feel my knees buckling. I sensed that I was caving in and falling.

And yet this terror at the disappearance of identity, the eradication of the self, is matched by the wish to transcend the boundaries. Mergence may become a compelling fantasy. Thus, Jackson informs us,

I dream of a lost body. I dream of a body I desire. I envy bodies that can drift and swirl like uncoiling strands of water-weed. I dream, in slow motion, of having a seal's body. I sense the way a seal can become a part of its liquid element, slipping drowsily through green fathoms. I can imagine the lightness of a seal's swaying rolls. I'm full of frustrated desire for the way it delights in the casual play of its own sleek movement. (p. 47)

Similarly, talking of the development of subjectivity, Leder (1990) says that

the lived body, as we have seen, is far more than a perceiver/perceived. Beneath the sensorimotor surface lies the anonymous strata of the visceral, a prenatal history, the body asleep. . . .

In the depths of my past (as an embryo) I encounter the same viscerability that resides in the depths of my inner body and the depths of sleep. The conscious, active "I" is in every direction outrun. (pp. 60-61)

For David Jackson, the frustrated desire of which he writes is but a tantalizing dream, a psychic impossibility. To dissolve the boundaries and become one with the "imaginary woman" or the "liquid element" would instill terror and threaten survival. In masculine experience, the body literally marks off one individual from another, establishing physical boundaries that have their parallel in the demarcation of psychic territory.

Gendered Embodiment

While men may be alienated from the lived body, women may be estranged from it through a process of splitting, which ensures that the body as experienced is severed from the social meaning attributed to that body. This splitting is achieved through the objectifying gaze of the Other; the rupture between the lived body and the body as object occurs at the point of incorporation by the Other's gaze. The internalization of the body as object renders women's perception of the body problematic; the body is transformed into a foreign entity, one *inside* social relations but *outside* the self.

Consistent with the alienating project of the Other, women's bodies are often viewed as assembled bits that are inherently flawed; hence discourses of the female body frequently portray women's reproductive capacities in terms of biological otherness (see Diprose, 1994). The "difference as pathology" perspective permeates public discourse in several fields, especially medicine and law. Within this perspective, women's reproductive functions transform the body into an abnormal organism; femaleness, as diseased state, is defined and delimited by maleness, as healthy norm. The construction of the female body as a morass of dislocated and malfunctioning parts, in which the bodily depths are in chaotic flux, is matched by a focus on the importance of the surface of the female body. This cultural construction of the female body translates into the vocabulary of deficiency and desire: an acknowledgment of lack, followed by attempts at corrective action.

Discourses about the need to control the unwieldy female body through regimes of diet and exercise echo through the weight reduction, beautification, and health industries.[6] This push to remake the female form reinforces the dominant definition of the female body as diseased; the voluptuous boundaries of women's bodies are pronounced abnormal and unsightly. Body reduction (and the attendant shrinking of female sexuality) become a normalized practice (see Davis,

1995; Shaffer, 1997). The more compact the female body, the more taut its surface, the more efficient it is as a container of female desire. Within this aesthetic, female sexuality is viewed as less likely to encroach on other (male) bodies or to overwhelm the body in which it resides. Social order, with its corollary of female restraint, is thus maintained.

The objectifying and alienating gaze of the Other structures women's perceptions of the body and produces behavior supportive of this project. Bordo (1993) demonstrates how anorexic women have incorporated the dualist notion of the body as a site of confinement, limitation, and danger; subduing and controlling the body become the behavioral objectives within this construction. According to Bordo, this process culminates in the extinction of the experience of desire, which for anorexic women is represented as the cessation of hunger. The bodily depths are viewed as outside the self; for example, Bordo (1993) cites a woman who says she ate because "my stomach wanted it" (p. 63). Furthermore, hunger, like disease, is conceptualized as an alien force, rather than the expression of self-regulating and healthy mechanisms. This attempt to subdue and control the errant body is intimately connected to female sexuality. Becoming "fat" (that is, more abundant) is tantamount to succumbing to the tide of lascivious desire. This may also be associated with ideas of internal decay. Bordo (1993) cites another woman who claimed that after eating sugar she felt "polluted" and rotten inside.

However, as we see, these images of defilement are not limited to the present time or Western society. The concept of women's bodies as repositories of lust (and contagious disease) is widespread. The response of the female anorexic (or the female bodybuilder) to these images—and the consequent attempt to eradicate or harden the fleshy female morass—is predictable (see Bordo, 1996).

Muscular Masculinity:
Men and Sport

Sport has, for a long time, occupied an important niche in American society (Messner, 1992; Tudor, 1997). According to Gorn and Goldstein (1993), the origin of American sporting culture can be found in pre-industrial England. In colonial America, sport took various forms in different regions: In urban centers like New York, blood sports were particularly popular; in the southern colonies, it was horse racing. No matter what form sport took, it provided a symbolic context for the conflict and competition of modern capitalism (Gorn

& Goldstein, 1993), and debates about identity (Bale & Philo, 1998). However, sport also provided the ideal setting for the articulation of aspects of modern masculinity.

The emergence of organized sports served to deflect fears of feminization among middle-class men, and generated new arenas for asserting male superiority (Messner, 1990). Indeed, as Connell (1995) argues, "In historically recent times, sport has come to be the leading definer of masculinity in mass culture. Sport provides a continuous display of men's bodies in motion" (p. 54); hence the embodiment of masculinity in organized sports is critically important. As Connell writes, "True masculinity is almost always thought to proceed from men's bodies—to be inherent in a male body or to express something about a male body" (p. 45).

In the individualistic and narcissistic subculture of bodybuilding we find the clear translation of masculinity into both behavior and appearance (Heywood, 1998; Moore, 1997; Simpson, 1994). Klein (1993) refers to the homophobia, fascism, and hypermasculine tendencies in this subculture, with its "comic-book" masculinity. Fussell (1996) describes our era's "bodybuilder americanus" as a "caricatural distortion" (p. 43), an exaggerated interpretation of masculinity in which a muscular body is a vital prop in the contemporary masquerade of manliness. "It does look as if everyone has swallowed an air hose," observes a bemused Fussell (p. 43).

Organized sports generally involve spectacular contests, in which fit and muscular bodies are pitted against each other. Such contact between bodies is inherently physical; however, it is also often violent. Michael Messner (1997) speaks of the body as weapon: the hardening of the body into a potential instrument of harm. Violence may occur between the players on the field, or between spectators, as is the case in British football hooliganism, which has a longstanding, if notorious, tradition. War metaphors sometimes invade football talk, as if organized sport and organized violence are interrelated. As McBride (1995) exclaims, "Football is not just a war but rather a game of sexual encoding that employs both castration and phallic rape imagery to describe the domination of the enemy" (p. 92). Not surprisingly, attendance at professional football games has been linked to violent assaults on women (White, Katz, & Scarborough, 1992).

Sport is, then, embedded in the modern gender order (see Parker, 1996). Sport has been integral to the social processes of making men—of instilling the avowed qualities of manliness in young men and of instructing all men, regardless of age, in the radical opposition between men and women in society. The opponent (or enemy) becomes gendered—that is, feminized—within the contours of modern sporting discourse. This process of inculcating masculinity through sport began in earnest, in Britain and elsewhere, during the last century. Associated with ideologies of empire and nationalism, and with the creation of militaristic styles of masculinity (Mangan, 1996), sports brought forth an emphasis on the quest for moral manliness (Chandler & Nauright, 1996).

Today, organized sport remains preoccupied by gender-related concerns (Hall, 1996; McKay & Messner, 1997). Issues of power, violence, and sexuality are at the core of debates about sporting endeavors (Messner, 1994). Laurel Davis (1997), for example, describes how the publication of the *Sports Illustrated* swimsuit issue reproduces hegemonic masculinity and marginalizes the perspectives of women, gay men, and people of color. Arguably, such divisive and biased publications are reminiscent of the propaganda of combat. Perhaps we could regard the swimsuit issue, with its scantily clad, idealized female bodies, as a war manual that prepares the wary to recognize the enemy—and, of course, also depicts the enemy in a nonthreatening form fit for visual consumption. The juxtaposition between the masculinity of the moving body of the sportsman and the femininity of the fixed body of the sports model reaches its zenith here. Furthermore, the body of the sportsman gains in power by being looked at, while the body of the sports model, as sexualized, photographic image, is stripped of power.

Military Violence:
Men Behaving Badly

The historiography of war has increasingly concerned itself with the issue of masculinity. It is now proposed that warfare and the militaristic masculinity integral to combat are an important means by which young men are socialized into the essential ingredients of contemporary manliness. This gendered education is instilled in a number of ways. First, mythologies of war and past battles fought circulate throughout society sanctifying the killing and destruction of warfare. Examples of such mythmaking abound, but one instance will suffice here. Recently, an Australian travel agency issued a call to join the 1998 *Battlefield Tour of Gallipoli and the Western Front*. In jingoistic language, the potential war history tourist was invited to walk the famous World War I battlefields of Turkey and France and be instructed by the tour guides on the maneuvers and effects of war.

Another strategy employed to engender the military lessons of manhood involves the religious consecration of war by mainstream churches. This move helps to convince the population that war is both purposeful and meaningful, and also effectively sacralizes war. A third strategy involves the deployment of military rituals involving uniforms, flags, and music. Such visual manifestations of militarism are displayed and promoted as a means to glorify war (see Ehrenreich, 1997).

Despite this gendered education, we now know that the psychological costs of the formal induction into an organized culture of violence are extremely high (Grossman, 1996). We also know that many men are repulsed by killing, and are unable or unwilling to engage in lethal combat (Ehrenreich, 1997). Reviewing the meaning and significance of the shell shock suffered by soldiers in World War I, Elaine Showalter (1987) concluded that this affliction could be regarded as a type of male hysteria. She argued that ordinary soldiers attempted to formulate masculine identities that reconciled the contradictions between the hypermasculine battle rhetoric of governments and the humbling and enervating effects of combat. This attempt to reconcile the inconsistencies was based on a recognition of the yawning divide between the ideologies of masculinity propagated by the state and the lived experiences of individual men. Consequently, the efflorescence of hysterical symptoms manifested by individual men during wartime can be read, according to Showalter, as a temporary exit from the public demands of the masculinist social order (see Pugliese, 1995).

Of course, the trials and tribulations of war do not begin and end with combat. The soldier's return to the employment and familial responsibilities of civilian life may provide men with opportunities to compose new masculine identities and to shed the frailties and failures brought on by war. This process, however, is not always successful. Men are often left feeling exposed and vulnerable (see Dawson, 1994). Indeed, the repatriation experience is often steeped in the tensions between memory and anticipation (Garton, 1995).

Needless to say, the business of war still prospers during peacetime. The practices and behaviors integral to military training academies indicate that the relentless march of gendered socialization so central to warfare continues unabated in the absence of military threat or engagement (see Stiehm, 1996). Recent revelations of military misconduct indicate that this is so. To make sense of these occurrences, we need to place them in the larger context of the role and function of military institutions.

Modern military institutions are strongly bounded in a multiplicity of ways, as is represented in their spatial organization and in their codes of secrecy. The psychological estrangement from everyday life, inculcated through the disciplined training of military personnel, furthers this process of demarcation. The boundedness of military institutions is concordant with the articulation of masculine identities and the intense development of masculinist behaviors in these settings. The archaic figure of the warrior, with its deep connection to masculinities, reappears here in the guise of the modern military man.

The traditional link between masculinity and the legitimized violence of warfare has been undermined to some extent by the introduction of greater numbers of women into military service. This process of gender integration, however, has produced high levels of anxiety; it appears to threaten the boundedness of the military institution and the separation of men and women, which is viewed as critically important. According to this fearful perspective, the presence of women dilutes the masculine character of the institution, erodes the solidarity of the body of fighting men, and introduces confusion and conflict to the system of loyalties. There are also fears that the admission of women to the military machine will destabilize or even pollute it. Morgan (1994) convincingly argues that at every turn there is anxiety that the symbolic order will implode if full gender integration occurs. This apprehension is sparked by "the apparent loosening of boundaries between women and men, and the weakening of the links between nation, the military, and gendered identities" (p. 171).

Nowhere is this perspective more evident than in the recent spate of sexual scandals that have rocked American military institutions (see Francke, 1997; Harrell & Miller, 1997; Herbert, 1998). The Tailhook incident of 1991 stands as a defining moment in the sexualized warfare that continues to plague these institutions. In this incident, a large number of female naval aviators were harassed and sexually assaulted by colleagues during a convention in Las Vegas (see Zimmerman, 1995). More recently, the sex scandal at the Aberdeen Proving Ground in Maryland erupted after a complaint of rape by a female recruit against Staff Sergeant Delmar Simpson. Simpson was accused of sexual misconduct by a further 26 female soldiers. Simpson's superior officer, Captain Derrick Robertson, was charged with sexual assault offences for his part in what became known as the Aberdeen rape ring. Simpson was sentenced to 25 years in prison for the rape of six female recruits. Others were court-martialed or faced disciplinary action. In an even more bizarre series of accusations and disclosures, the Sergeant Major of the U.S. Army, Gene McKinney, was charged with a series of sexual assaults. McKinney was convicted in 1998 of obstructing justice, but was cleared of the 18 sexual assault charges brought by six women. He was demoted one rank and given a formal reprimand. More recently, Major General David Hale was formally accused of conducting improper relationships with the wives of four of his subordinates. He was permitted to retire while under investigation.

Of course, some commentators perceive the current situation in different terms, asserting that efforts at gender integration are essentially attempts to demasculinize the military. We might speculate, however, on the reverse impact of this process—that gender integration might be part of a project to raise the status of women by masculinizing some of their number. We are perhaps reminded, here, of the 1997 film *G. I. Jane*. In this film, a female recruit in the army's elite commando squad screams at her opponent, during a violent brawl, "Suck my dick!" This denunciatory invitation and the female recruit's obvious physical prowess mark a turning point in the movie. The recruit, played by Demi Moore, starts to become "one of the boys" after this event.

Access by women to the hallowed role of warrior arguably increases women's status; at the same time, it disturbs and unsettles men's confidence in their superior status. The disappearance of *difference,* implied by gender integration strategies, may provoke a defensive and hostile attack. Institutionalized violence might then be regarded as a masculinist tactic invoked to shore up a failing sense of manliness.

Historicizing Masculinity

The critical examination of masculinity in the contemporary context is an ongoing and exhaustive project. The theoretical and experiential interrogations of gender and sexuality in today's society have led to a sustained interest in prior constructions and definitions of masculinity (see, for example, Carnes & Griffen, 1990; Mangan & Walvin, 1987; Roper & Tosh, 1991; Rotundo, 1993). This interest derives from a recognition of the malleable nature of the cultural imagery that captures ideas about bodies, sexuality and gender.

The project of historicizing masculinity—of acknowledging the myriad ways in which the social parameters of maleness are constructed—involves an analysis of what Clare Lees (1994a) calls the four big *P*s: power, potency, patriarchy, and politics (see also Lees, 1994b). Definitions of masculinity, situated in these domains, shift over time; these definitions respond to changing relations between men and women, as well as to alterations in social and scientific knowledge about the human body, sexuality, and reproduction. Masculinity is also multivocal or plural in any society at any given moment. Lived expressions of maleness assume a variety of forms; constructions of masculinity are neither monolithic nor all-encompassing. There is also a range of means or processes whereby masculinity is established or achieved. Masculinity is, then, composed of a series of possibilities, each awaiting exploration. The act of exploration and enactment reflects the unstable, changeable nature of masculinity, which has been described as "a culturally specific process of becoming" (Cohen, 1997).

Below, I briefly explore the implications during selected cultural moments of the fragility of gendered identity and the interdependence of masculinity and femininity. Historicizing masculine identity helps to make sense of the conundrums and paradoxes that surround current debates about gender in society. I should note here that the analysis of the historical formation of masculinity owes a profound debt to feminist scholarship.

Medieval Masculinities

Masculinities, in the context of the Middle Ages, appear to take a diversity of forms, which are described, directly and indirectly, in the texts that have come down to us from the 12th to the 14th centuries. Our knowledge of medieval constructs of gender is, thus, limited by the body of written materials available to us. Nevertheless, these texts provide us with a detailed, if fragmented, perspective on medieval notions of sex and gender.

The poetic and didactic texts of the Middle Ages tell us that formations of masculinity were distributed along a continuum. At one end of the spectrum lay heroic masculinity, an exaggerated and idealized construction that served as a benchmark in medieval society. Heroic masculinity centered on dominance and defeat; the attributes of heroism were codified within prescriptions about action and movement. Moreover, heroic masculinity was essentially spectacular and performative, and was largely antithetical to the institution of marriage or the sphere of domesticity. At the other end of the spectrum were the sanctifying practices of religious devotion. In this interpretation of masculinity, subordination to spiritual authority and ecclesiastical rules went hand in hand with bodily regulation and denial. Disavowal of female company was also relevant here, although it carried connotations of spiritual purity rather than allusions to mobility and conquest.

Despite these differences, all forms of medieval masculinity were embedded in a matrix of social, political, and anatomical relations. Nothing was fixed or static. As Will Sayers (quoted in Cohen et al., 1995) notes,

> Effective masculinity was constantly on trial and . . . the individual efforts of the would-be hero were continuously accompanied by glances temporally and spatially forward and back, above and below, right and left.

The fluid and mutable character of masculinity in the Middle Ages was evident in the preponderance of myths of masculine parthenogenesis, of the ability of the male to conceive and give birth (see Zapperi, 1991). According to Jeffrey Cohen (1994), this parthenogenesis was tantamount to the uncoupling of gender from corporeality, and indicated that notions of sexual dimorphism were overlaid with richly embroidered fantasies about procreativity.

Indeed, it would appear that medieval society subscribed to concepts of sex and gender that were remarkably remote from our own (see, for example, Fradenburg & Freccero, 1995; Lomperis & Stanbury, 1993). Carol Clover (1993) recently claimed that Old Norse texts assumed the existence of only one gender, and this was the gender of power and domination. Drawing on Laqueur's (1990) theory of a one-sex model in pre-Renaissance Europe,[7] Clover (1993) attempts to show that concepts of gender were embedded within ideas of "winnable and losable attributes" (p. 379). Thus, although males enjoyed a preexisting social advantage, according to Clover, women who exhibited the valorized characteristics associated with power and authority (for example, settling feuds, controlling land, and defending themselves) were often considered masculine. By contrast, men who refused the opportunities afforded by masculine exploits were not considered masculine. Clover (1993) asserts that the gendered cultural system outlined in Old Norse texts described a society "in which being born male precisely did *not* confer automatic superiority" (p. 380). The benefits and prestige attached to masculinity had, then, to be earned by men and women through appropriate public displays, and these public activities had to involve other men (see also Dockray-Miller, 1998).

Some scholars have challenged the basic theories on which Clover builds, pointing to the way Laqueur's work neglects alternative, but influential, constructions of sexuality and gender that prevailed in the medieval era. These authors maintain that Laqueur focused on particular aspects of the Galenic model, but neglected the contribution of the humors in constructions of gender identity (see Paster, 1993). Heat, for example, was thought to be a marker of physiological maleness; it was essential for semen production and ejaculation. Carol Everest (1994) notes that "the manliest of men [had] abundant innate heat" (p. 9). Furthermore, the concentration on the genital differentiation implied in the narrow interpretation of the Galenic model by authors such as Laqueur (1990) marginalized the significance of the female body in the high Middle Ages (see Bynum, 1984, 1991). Such approaches also obscure the significance of femaleness and feminine imagery to monastic devotional discourse in the 12th and 13th centuries (Holsinger, 1994).

Consequently, it is perhaps useful to regard the sex/gender system of the Middle Ages as a "cluster of gender-related notions, sometimes competing, sometimes mutually reinforcing, sometimes constraining, sometimes consistent, sometimes ad hoc" (Cadden, 1993, p. 9). Rather than giving prominence to sexual differences (or genital variations), medieval thinkers, drawing on the Hippocratic, the Aristotelian, the Galenic, and the Soranic paradigms, often emphasized other distinctions. Cadden (1993) quotes one authority, for example, who proclaims that "the male differs from the female in three [ways], namely, complexion, disposition, and shape. And among these the complexion is the most fundamental" (p. 170). Recognizing the different ways in which medieval writers conceived of gender does not deny the significance of the relational character of gender constructions; it does, however, highlight the dangers of adopting a presentist approach, which suggests that our modern preoccupation with biological (and especially genital) differences was as important in the medieval era as it is in our own.

Enlightenment Masculinities

Heroism, imbricated deeply within medieval constructions of masculinity, was carried forward into modern understandings. The political theorist Thomas Hobbes, whose life spanned the late 16th and the early 17th centuries, articulated the basic contours of modern heroic masculinity. Hobbes's account of human experience, embedded in nature, and his theory of the conditions needed to produce stable and legitimate civil authority are well known. What is less visible is Hobbes's conception of the masculine subject, although Hobbes's description of the human condition contains many gendered statements that provide us with an insight into how he conceived of masculine and feminine.

Hobbes was preoccupied with the dangers posed by "the passions" and the need to direct and guide their expression in society. As Christine Di Stefano (1991) states, "Man is portrayed by Hobbes as a kind of desiring machine" (p. 78). Desire, however, was configured as a private and individual experience, requiring the constraint of rules or norms in civil society to generate social equilibrium. Hobbes's conception of a civil society was based on a definition of human subjectivity in which individual identity is strictly differentiated and functions according to exclusionary principles. Hobbes's conception of a civil society was based on this conception of human subjectivity, and Hobbes's civil order, "with its contractually designated and minimally conceived obligations designed to counter the dangerous social perplexities of proximity and ambivalence, assumed distinctly modern masculine characteristics" (Di Stefano, 1991, p. 89).

Extricating himself from the state of nature, emergent modern man was instructed by Hobbes to embrace a radical atomism, an individualism of heroic proportions. The full horror of the state of nature was on display so that the orderliness and predictability of civil society could become both a refuge and a salvation from the dark natural forces of decay and destruction. The medieval, premodern brand of heroism, bent on the slaying of enemies and triumphant encounters with perilous and malevolent powers, was banished in this account. In its place was a peaceful, nonviolent civil order, buttressed by obedience to a political credo of rights shared amongst men and instituted by a powerful sovereign.

In the political pronouncements of John Stuart Mill we begin to see the introduction of internal, rather than external, controls on the individual. Mill divided society into active and passive types, with the intellect being the distinguishing criteria. The active character type shaped and furthered the human condition, struggling against the downward pull of nature. As Di Stefano (1991) so eloquently expresses it, for Mill, life was "a constant struggle against the quicksand of regression as the insistent forces of decay beckon from the sinister periphery of civilization" (p. 152). For Mill, nature was a hostile and

threatening presence that must be controlled and tamed. In an extraordinarily transparent statement, Mill declared,

> Nature impales men, breaks them as if on the wheel, casts them to be
> devoured by wild beasts, . . . poisons them by the quick or slow
> venom of her exhalations, and has hundreds of other hideous deaths
> in reserve. (quoted in Di Stefano, 1991, p. 153)

It is against this background of odious violence and destruction
that Mill offered his account of human civilization. According to Mill,
each individual must confront the destabilizing and dangerous aspects
of nature that reside in the human character. Self-control and self-
discipline were the weapons vital to this struggle; only they could preserve the individual from the threatened encroachment of vindictive,
feminized nature. Reason—and Mill's distinctive methodological individualism (Di Stefano, 1991, p. 163)—was critical to man's perpetual
endeavors to establish and maintain culture. This ascendancy of civilization over nature also depended on sovereignty over self, of mind
over body. Di Stefano (1991) is undoubtedly correct in stating that
Mill propounded a highly masculine view of the subject—a subject exposed to "horrific vulnerability" (p. 167), separated radically from the
natural world, and dependent for survival on strict differentiation
from others. Di Stefano (1991) labels this the "rule-legislating, self-
disciplined, and civilized self" (p. 17). This self heralds the introduction of a modern disciplinary masculinity.

New World Masculinities

The conquest and settlement of America in the 16th century was
infused with complex and exaggerated constructions of masculinity.
These constructions buttressed the actions of those who arrived, providing both a rationale for current behavior and a template for future
behavior. As in other conquered lands, the settlers quickly laid claim
to natural and social assets, and developed a strong and sustained
resistance to the forfeiture of these benefits and advantages (see
Madsen, 1994). These actions translated into an ideology of triumphant masculinity and a politics of extermination and exclusion.
Freed to a large extent from British and European conventions, American men ventured forth to create new styles of masculinity. Below,
I examine a few of the cultural watersheds that marked the shifts in
this stylistic landscape.

Prior to the Civil War, the arrival of immigrants sparked demon-
strations and riots, as American-born men feared work-related dis-

placement. Working-class white men designated African American slaves the despised Other; racial differences, expressed in the form of virulent racism, provided a means for working-class white men to overcome anxieties about immigration and employment. However, in the 1830s, the working-class male was delivered a political savior in the figure of Andrew Jackson. Jackson, a military hero, assumed a hypermasculine stance during his presidential campaign; he championed the cause of the working man, whether rural or urban, and raged against the influence of the financial institutions and the Indians. The former were viewed as vestigial reminders of the overly refined and effete character of European society. The bank was described as a devouring feminine force that would produce dependency among decent working men. As such, it was reviled (Kimmel, 1996). The Indians were viewed as brutal savages requiring colonization. The language of paternalism and protectiveness provided a moral license for the dark history of terror perpetrated against the Indian nations.

The 19th century also saw the cultural production of the cowboy. Late in the century, the previously rough and dirty herder was transformed into the brave and courageous "man of the frontier," willing to enter unknown and dangerous territory and prepare it for habitation. As he pushed forward into alien and hostile spaces, the cowboy rejected the comforts of romantic or sexual relationships. He circulated, according to the cultural documents, in an ever-onward movement and in a world of males. He was self-reliant, emotionally contained, and supportive of other men. He was celebrated in the open-air theater of the rodeo, a convention established at the end of the 19th century, and in the literary genre of the Western, initiated by the publication of Wister's novel *The Virginian* in 1902 (Kimmel, 1996). As we shall see in the next chapter, the figure of the cowboy and the mythic places he inhabits still thrives in America today.

The twin pressures of racism and xenophobia continued to color social experience in the early part of the 20th century. Bederman (1995) traces how the cultural ideals of Victorian manhood were reformulated into an aggressive and sexualized masculinity that celebrated both the virility of so-called "primitive" men and the refined character of "civilized" men. He shows how race, nationalism, and notions of evolution were threaded together to form the platform that supported a reinvigorated masculinity.

In the early decades of the 20th century, World War I provided many men with a socially approved masculine role (see Bourke, 1996). Although considerable numbers of men suffered from the traumas of war, there was general optimism about the prospects for the economy. The Great Depression of the late 1920s and early 1930s ushered in a phase of personal and collective desperation, as a quarter of all American men found themselves unemployed. During the 1920s, fraternal orders began to attract more members and more social criticism. More insidiously, the Ku Klux Klan flourished with an upsurge in racially motivated violence.

At the same time, the popularization of psychology for mass consumption led to the publication of many books dealing with family life and child rearing. This gave men a new arena in which to enact masculine behaviors and recuperate some positive feelings of self-worth. However, there was elevated anxiety about gender differences and, particularly, male homosexuality. Kimmel (1996) notes that "tabloid newspapers terrified and titillated their readers with stories of degenerate child molesters who committed acts of unspeakable depravity" (p. 205). As we have seen, this is not an unfamiliar theme in American society.

Not surprisingly, the scientific discipline of psychology moved into the hiatus created by the creeping doubts about gender-based distinctions. In 1936, the psychologists Terman and Miles developed a psychometric scale measuring masculine and feminine attributes. With the advent of this test, gender differences could be inscribed on the general population, and variance from the norm could be ascertained for both individuals and groups. Socially constructed gender differences were thus scientized and legitimized.

Emerging from this popular concern about "gender blending" were two remarkable heroes: the appropriately named aficionado of body building, Charles Atlas, and the masculine fantasy hero, Superman, whose metropolitan alter ego, Clark Kent, seemed to represent the condition of everyman. The metropolis also threw up Americanized versions of another heroic tradition: The hard-boiled detective strode out of the pages of stories and books by the likes of Hammett, Chandler, and Spillane. Like the cowboy, the detective occupied a universe largely devoid of sweethearts or wives, but replete with temptresses and *femmes fatales*. This stylistic interpretation of American manhood was literalized in Ernest Hemingway's short story collection *Men Without Women* (1927). Here, Hemingway "searche[d] among the shards of European culture for a lost American manhood" (Kimmel, 1996, p. 214). Masculine scenarios, it would seem, were difficult to fix in place. Slippage and even disappearance were distinct possibilities. Only the continual cultural renewal of opportunities to *demonstrate* masculinity would forestall a serious crisis at the individual and social level.

World War II provided another generation of American men with the opportunity to engage in militaristic styles of masculinity. However, as with World War I, cracks and fissures soon opened up, and the public became aware of the existence of the psychologically damaged returning soldier. Women were encouraged to indulge and nurture these men, and to yield to men's domestic and familial authority.

Following World War II, the arena of the family came increasingly to symbolize a relational space in which men could assume new forms of masculinity. The significance of fatherhood to concepts of manliness rose sharply, and fathers were viewed as essential to their sons' development. Furthermore, the involvement of fathers in their sons' upbringing was seen as a strong deterrent to juvenile delinquency. Good fathers were seen as central to the perpetuation of the social order, and father absence was believed to have negative consequences for both young men and society in general. In fact, good fathers were viewed as the antidote to the manipulative influence of some mothers, whose overinvolvement with sons was understood to be a causative factor in some social ills and many psychological disorders.

During the 1950s, doubts about the cogency of men's authority at work were exacerbated; the allegorical drama *The Incredible Shrinking Man* (1953) appeared the year after *The Invisible Man* (1952). McCarthyism generated a tide of fear and accusation about political beliefs and sexual preferences (Kovel, 1997). There were stirrings in the African American community; the refuge of racist beliefs was disappearing. In the face of these apparent dead ends, the entertainment industry buoyed American men with the positive portrayal of fathers on television, and the strengthening of masculine frontier fantasies. The actor John Wayne and the hypermasculine characters that he played assumed an important role in the project of rescuing fragile American manhood (see Davis, 1998; Wills, 1997).

Another source of consolation for some men was the production of the magazine *Playboy*. Appearing on newsstands in 1953, this publication took up the debate about the feminization of American men. Alongside the confrontational writings of Norman Mailer, *Playboy* provided a metaphoric place of escape for apparently besieged men. As women entered more and more previously masculine preserves, Mailer's didactic writing and the texts and images of *Playboy* were a solace and a comfort.

The 1960s and 1970s stripped away many of men's asylums. The civil rights movement and, later, the women's movement undermined the ideology of the self-made white man who wielded authority and accrued advantages. The entitlements of the dominant male groups were now seriously in question. As Kimmel (1996) states, "The constant search for some masculine *terra firma* upon which to ground a stable identity had never provided a firm footing. . . . [B]y the 1960s gradual erosion and uneasy footing had become a landslide" (p. 262). Work was no longer a satisfying ground for proving masculinity. And arguably the most unsettling event for men's definitions of self was the Vietnam War.

The war in Vietnam produced a deeply felt cultural vulnerability (see Martin, 1993). Gerster (1995) declares, "Vietnam remains the crucial destination in the cultural itinerary of an entire generation. Hanoi, Da Nang, Hue, Nui Dat, Saigon—these are the talismanic place names of the 1960s, carved on the collective memory" (p. 223), and yet the Vietnam War was a military encounter that went horribly wrong. The cultural models of masculinity available to men during and after World War II—soldier, breadwinner, and family man—were twisted beyond recognition for the young men who fought in Vietnam (Karner, 1996). Warfare in Vietnam was fraught with contradictions, as the exoticism of Asia and Vietnam itself (see Said, 1991) was reconfigured as an illicit space of pain and death. Masculinist fantasies of the sexually alluring Orient awaiting colonization coalesced with fantasies of evisceration, of emptying out the putrid contents of this place of death. Not surprisingly, a great deal of the cultural imagery that emerged from the Vietnam War emphasized the implied and actual threat of castration. Such threats were thought to emanate as much from the assorted prostitutes and bar girls who entertained the troops as from the bullets and bombs of the enemy. For example, Gerster reports on the belief that Vietnamese women deliberately contracted venereal diseases in order to infect foreign troops, or even inserted razor blades into their vaginas to harm the U.S. and Australian soldiers (p. 231; see also Theweleit, 1987, for an analysis of the gendering of violence in war).

Thwarted by their desire to emulate their fathers, many returning soldiers experienced a profound loss of self. Vietnam survivor narratives often turn on a desperate search for the prior, unified self; however, many narratives also refer to the deep inner divisions and rifts that refuse to be healed (Loeb, 1996). I review, in the next chapter, how some of these Vietnam-related anxieties and experiences have been captured on film (see Katzman, 1993; Selig, 1993).

This cultural crisis of confidence in masculinity translated into open questioning of the social definitions of manliness. Men's liberation, which began as a movement in the mid-1970s, threw the spotlight directly on such issues as the male sex role and such problems as sex-typing. Androgyny became popular, both as a topic of discussion and as a practice, even as there was also a boom, from the 1960s onwards, in pornographic magazines and other materials directed at a male audience.

A pronounced emphasis on exaggerated masculine values and behaviors materialized in the 1980s. A fresh aggressivity informed American politics under Ronald Reagan. Reagan and his successor, George Bush, lived out the cowboy character with a vigorous combativeness not witnessed for some time. American foreign policy became inflected with masculinist rhetoric, as America stood up to the "evil empire" and fought the "war on drugs." Of course, the 1980s also witnessed the appearance of the "wimp": the warm, supportive, and compassionate player in the gender game. A variant, the SNAG (the sensitive, new age guy), was alternately embraced and reviled. American men seemed as confused as ever, caught between polarized styles of masculinity, all of which were subject to caricature. However, the phenomenon of the "angry white male," beleaguered and cornered by affirmative action programs and the discourse of rights and entitlements, seemed real enough. Equally real was the burgeoning of new male fraternities—the political groups that advocated for men in society. I examine the politics of masculinity in the next chapter; below, I consider the definitions and constructions of masculinity in cross-cultural contexts.

Masculinities in Traditional Societies

Concepts of gender in traditional, precontact societies revolve around the relationships between spiritual creation and human reproduction, the constructions of anatomy and character, and the maintenance of religious well-being and social equilibrium. Below, I briefly explore some of these dimensions of gender, concentrating, in the main, on societies in the western Pacific region, principally Papua New Guinea and the islands that constitute Melanesia. As we are interested in traditional constructs, and not those introduced by Western missionaries and other cultural groups, I focus on early anthropological studies. In recognition of the significant social change now visited on the societies under review, I use the past tense to describe these societies; this is not intended to imply the extinguishment of all the ideas and practices described, but is intended to alert the reader to the volatility of the "ethnographic present" (Ernst, 1991).

Let me begin by providing some background to the issues at hand. In the Highlands of Papua New Guinea, there has traditionally been a strict opposition between the lifestyle and implicit value of each gender, with male antagonism and hostility being directed specifically at women. For example, the Mount Hageners of the Western Highlands of Papua New Guinea exhibited very rigid and categorical thinking in connection with gender ascription (Strathern, 1978). The strict opposition of all things male and female (although actual words for such categories did not exist) was accomplished through the establishment of a dichotomy between male and female spheres of labor, social influence, and religious importance. Such a polarization, Marilyn Strathern (1978) believes, was a masculine creation, although the women formally acknowledged its existence. The demarcation between the sexes was consistently fierce, encompassing behavior, interests, appearance, and access to religious worship. Women were perceived as being less capable and associated with failure and all things insignificant and unimportant. Women could achieve a spurious social prestige by behaving more like men, but they were unable to acquire legitimate masculine power. Similarly, a man of little achievement may become "like a woman."

Fecund Males: Masculine Parthenogenesis
and Its Variants

Unlike our own society, in which males' participation in procreation beyond insemination is not generally acknowledged, ideologies about human reproduction in other societies markedly shift the balance between males and females. Sometimes this involves heightened participation by males in procreation, and sometimes it involves the denial of the female contribution to the processes of reproduction as we understand them.

Among the Iqwaye of Papua New Guinea, the original, mythopoeic creation of the first man was thought to be a self-creation (autogenesis). The first man created other men by forming lumps of clay, which he then inseminated. The first woman was created, through metamorphosis, out of one of the first men. Omalyce, the cosmic male initiator, was conceptualized as containing the seeds of femaleness within his body. The primordial act of creation, however, was an essentially male affair; there was no acknowledged female sex. These cosmological beliefs translated into specific configurations of the sexed body in Iqwaye society; as Mimica (1992) states,

Maleness and Femaleness, i.e., man's and woman's bodies [were]
two species of embodiment of this single bodily genus—the phallus.
. . . Man's body [was] bisexual, but in terms of the Iqwaye cultural
notions it really [meant] that it [was] bi-phallic, for phallus . . . [was]
generic sex. Woman's body [was] mono-phallic, i.e., monosexual.

Consequently, in women, the vagina was the analogue of the penis
and the mouth, with the two being the inverse of each other. But the
vagina was thought to lack a penile component; instead, the entire
female body was conceived of as phallic and as devoid of the capacity
for self-closure.

In Chagga society, there was an accepted symbolic opposition
between "open" women, with vaginas that could menstruate and give
birth, and "closed" men, with orifices that retained feces and blood.
The opposition between open women and closed men was premised
on important conceptual parallels between female procreative functioning and male digestive functioning. For example, in Chagga cosmology, the original anal plug, the *ngoso*, representative of primordial
masculinity, was thought to be obtained by theft from the women.
Furthermore, in everyday life, pregnancy was conceptualized as the
female *ngoso*, with the woman being closed at the height of fertility.

Despite a familiarity with the relationship between ovulation, sexual intercourse, and pregnancy, the men in Chagga society persisted in
the belief that they, too, could become pregnant with fecal children
during their procreative years. Men, at the conclusion of this procreative period, acknowledged the "resumption" of defecation. Men also
believed they contributed significantly to the creation of the fetus.
Semen was equated with the nourishing mother's milk; semen was the
milk a man fed the vaginal mouth to make a child. Consequently, male
semen created the child, and female milk nourished it after birth.

The Onabasulu of Papua New Guinea emphasized the male contribution to the ongoing development of young men. The "insemination" of young males during initiation rites was viewed as critical to
their growth. This insemination derived from the cosmological beliefs
of the Onabasulu, and was achieved by the application of adult semen
to the skin of the young men. The cultural imperative of inseminat-
ing young males was a staple feature of many societies in the Great
Papuan Plateau and the adjoining Strickland River. The Kaluli, for
example, employed anal intercourse, and the Etoro used fellatio
(Ernst, 1991).

Procreative functions were the focus of attention in other societies. The Hua of the Highlands of Papua New Guinea attempted to

imitate menstruation, although men publicly espoused the view that female menstruation was a disgusting process (Meigs, 1976). In addition, the males claimed that they, too, could become pregnant. Indeed, for the Hua such a belief was so compelling that some informants maintained that they had witnessed the removal of the fetus from the male body; interestingly, such a "birth" was said to be accomplished by inserting a bamboo tube into the man's abdomen and withdrawing the fetus in the subsequent blood flow.

Male pregnancies were simply termed *Kupa* or "stomach." Impregnation occurred through oral incorporation—that is, the ingestion of food—and was not a rare condition. There was also some suggestion that anal intercourse would lead to pregnancy (Meigs, 1976). Both sexes, therefore, possessed the potential to become pregnant, as conception could occur in the womb, in abdominal tissue, or in the intestine; the only significant difference between the genders was that women possessed a birth canal, and so could deliver the fetus through the vagina.

In the absence of the opportunity to observe birth in any animal other than the domestic pig, the Hua males formulated an idiosyncratic model of internal anatomical structure. In animals such as the dog, pig, mouse, or human, birth was assumed to take place via an organ composed of both the urethra and the vagina; the intestine led either into the rectum or the womb. Young girls were thought to possess a closed birth passage, as were menopausal women, although some informants believed the latter possessed no such organ (Meigs, 1976).

Meigs (1976) commented on the Hua construction of male pregnancies as follows:

> It should be emphasized that Kupa is a feared and abhorred condition. Yet one cannot resist suggesting that it is also desired. All the physiological facts deny the premise that males can become pregnant. However, I would submit that the reason males believe they can become pregnant, and believe in the fake fetuses provided by the medicine men, is that they are highly motivated by psychological reasons to do so. They appear to possess a will to believe that they are fertile. (p. 397)

As we have already noted, the males of Hua society also explicitly imitated menstruation. This took two forms: first, the letting of blood in order to release fluid and prevent clotting, especially in men suffering from *Kupa*; and, second, the ingestion of plants that possess a red juice, as these plants apparently possess the power to disperse clots of blood and purge them from the intestine.

In addition, the Hua males engaged in other forms of female-imitative behavior. They attempted to incorporate female qualities by ingesting foods that supposedly possess these qualities: rapid growth, a soft, moist interior, and fecundity (Meigs, 1976). Men, in secret, also ate possum, a "female" food capable of causing a male pregnancy, and blood, which they conceptualized as female.

Other New Guinea societies in which males traditionally claimed the need to menstruate included the Gahuka-Gama and the Gururumba. The former possessed an initiation ceremony in which the young neophytes were forcibly bled from the nose and instructed in the art of voluntary vomiting. These activities were practiced during their period of induction into the men's group, and repeated at later intervals. The nose bleeding was explicitly labeled male menstruation; of female menstruation, they possessed a great fear (Read, 1952).

In most Melanesian societies with initiation ceremonies, the rites reflected "male anxiety concerning, and most probably envy of, menstruation and childbirth. . . . Male ritual and female physiology, though opposed to one another as mystical forces which must be kept apart, [were] nevertheless sometimes equated" (Allen, 1967, p. 17). Indeed, the men of Wogeo referred to their penile incision blood as their menstruation (see Hogbin, 1970), as did the Arapesh (Mead, 1935). The Chimbu practiced nose bleeding instead of penile sub-incision; nevertheless, the equation between initiation and menstruation was still explicit (Nilles, 1943). The sacred flutes used in initiation ceremonies were called *koa*, a word used when a boy had been initiated and a girl had experienced her first menses. *Koa* was also used to refer to both menstrual blood and female sexual organs.

The Gahuka-Gama of the New Guinea Highlands practiced strict initiation rites from which females were excluded; these rites epitomized the denial of the female contribution toward procreation. The males of Mount Hagen in New Guinea practiced a more general denigration. Marilyn Strathern (1972) noted that the "men say that women of exceptional ability obviously started off life in their mother's womb as male, only happening to be born female" (p. 161). The Mount Hagen men possessed no initiation rites by the 1970s, but employed two vehicles—one concerned with ideology and one concerned with religion—to express their attitudes toward women. First, in order to deal with the physiological paradox of women's apparent power in childbirth, men admitted of women's prestige "only in relative and not absolute terms" (Strathern, 1978, p. 185). Men believed that they continued to contribute to the development of the fetus after conception; it was the male responsibility to mould the growing child with constant donations of sperm until at least the fifth or sixth month, or the child would be classified as incomplete. Such conceptions, of course, indirectly acknowledged the reproductive power of women; however, this source of influence was diminished by the general denigration of all things female, and by the appropriation of female power in the religious cult known as the *Amb Kor.*

In the context of the Mount Hagen Female Spirit cult, or the *Amb Kor,* mortal women were assigned an essentially negative value. The Female Spirit, associated with white, the color representing male fertility, was portrayed in myth as distinctly asexual (Strathern, 1979). Her vagina was closed, and the menstrual fluid of mortal women was supposedly as dangerous to her as it was to the men. The Female Spirit appeared, then, to represent a variety of pseudomaleness, cleansed of the carnal sexuality of women, yet possessing women's reproductive power. The ritual involved in this cult served quite explicitly to invoke female fertility. The men collected and buried the wombs and stomachs of female pigs in holes or earthen ovens; they built three secret cult houses, the last, the "inner sanctum" (Strathern, 1972, p. 42) was secluded behind a high fence; and after performing several sacred acts, the ritual culminated in the dance of the men. On one level, the men represented the Spirit herself: Andrew Strathern (1979) maintained that the dancers became "of female gender in 'helping' the spirit to show herself at their dance" (p. 48). On another level, however, the ritual demonstrated both the symbolic confinement of the Female Spirit and the control of the men over the cult. Interestingly, men conceived of this male-identified goddess as a beautiful young woman, a spiritual bride, adorned in the decorative attire of olden times. This nostalgic vision of the goddess, a view possessed exclusively by the men, was represented by primordial stones that had apparently emerged from the earth at the dawn of time. Commenting on the significance of this cult, Marilyn Strathern (1978) noted, "Men do seem to contrive always to make it seem that power is on their side. If women bear children, men in their cults control the essential source of fertility" (p. 175).

Accompanying such a negative categorization of the female gender was the existence of a women's pollution cult. Women and men lived separately, an arrangement that tended to emphasize the demarcation between the sexes. Furthermore, female sexual and reproductive processes were thought to be especially dangerous to men, and sexual intercourse could only occur under certain conditions. Indeed,

Sillitoe (1998) claims that New Guinea Highlanders suffered from *horror mulieris,* a fear that women could pollute and kill men as a result of the power vested in their reproductive organs. In the pollution cult, the female was thought to transfer her pollutant qualities to her male lovers and her offspring. At menopause, the female was eligible to join the category of untainted males, composed of both virginal and sexually experienced men. Members of the pure category were considered to be "like men," while members of the polluted category were said to be "like women," regardless of their gender. Such fluidity of gender classification permitted the male a significant degree of participation in the social life of women, an analog, perhaps, to their spiritual participation in the reproductive life of women.

The Hua of the New Guinea Highlands also possessed highly developed ideas about pollution. Threats of pollution emanated from bodily emissions, carriers or containers of these emissions, and certain symbols (Meigs, 1978, 1984). However, pollution did not eventuate from objects or substances that produced disordered, anomalous, ambiguous, or marginal phenomena (see Douglas, 1966). Rather, pollution attached to acts of body invasion—of the entry of the object or substance in question into the body. This undesired breakdown in bodily boundaries could take place through a number of pathways: the breaching of the membrane of the skin, for example, or the involuntary tasting or touching of a potentially polluting object or substance. For the Hua, unwanted impositions on the body could occur via all five senses; for example, if a man or a boy inadvertently caught the smell of a menstruating woman, his strength could be severely curtailed (Meigs, 1978). The perception was that these unsolicited entries into the body or the body's sphere of awareness were associated with decomposition or decay, and could increase the quantum of pollution.[8] As in contemporary American society, feelings of disgust were integral to Hua conceptions of pollution. The individual, affected by the encroachment of polluting objects or substances, reacted with pronounced feelings of revulsion (see Miller, 1998).

These ideas about pollution parallel the specific constructions of the sexed body in modern Western society. Women's bodies, in the West, are often viewed as porous and subject to leakage, and are hence inherently impure. These notions resonate with Western ideologies about the closed, controlled, and well-mannered body of the modern private citizen (see Elias, 1994), the so-called "positive body" (Barker, 1984) or "classical body" (Bakhtin, 1984) that emerged during the 17th century. This privatized and contained body, modeled on a masculine ideal, can be contrasted against the "grotesque body" (Bakhtin,

1984), which is characterized by its openness and its orifices, which lack closure. Women's bodies, with their cyclical nature and reproductive potential, are often culturally coded as grotesque (Russo, 1995). Women's bodies threaten to "'spill over' into social space, breaching its order—in particular, the basic distinction between inside and outside, person and world" (Comaroff & Comaroff, 1992, p. 74). The unbounded character of women's bodies—as sexed objects in contemporary Western society—incites fear in the masculine imagination. Janet Wolff (1990) claims this fear is associated with the cultural trope of the "monstrous-feminine," in which the terror of reincorporation into the maternal body features prominently (see also Creed, 1993).

Of Threat and Danger

There are at least two remarkable aspects to the construction and articulation of gender in particular cross-cultural contexts. The first is that femaleness was often understood to be self-sufficient and maleness to be contingent.[9] This differential and asymmetrical relationship between femaleness and maleness was manifest in all spheres of sociality (see Strathern, 1996). Writing of the Foi of Papua New Guinea, Weiner (1987) asserted,

> Men lack the power of menstruation and hence of childbirth. The continual regeneration of female procreative substance and of birth itself is an aspect of the innate flow of vital energies that comprises the Foi realm of "nature." In order to control and channel this innate female power, men control wealth items in the form of bridewealth, which transforms female birth into the artifice of male patrilineal continuity and social cohesion. (p. 263)

The second remarkable aspect of gender construction in cross-cultural contexts is the frequent constitution of women as the dangerous sex (see Hatty, 1991; Hays, 1966).[10] In modern industrialized societies, however, it is generally men who are designated as dangerous (i.e., who possess the greatest capacity to cause harm to others). Sherry Ortner (1978) was puzzled by this apparent reconfiguration of intersexual threat in contemporary Western societies. Ortner noted that it presented a reversal of the often found relationship between gender and danger; feminized threat was frequently visible in ritual practices and religious ideologies in traditional societies, but was largely expunged (or obscured) in the West. But Barbara Smuts (1992) views these discourses about gendered danger as continuous rather than opposed, maintaining that pre-state ideologies about gender are perpetuated in today's society. She alleges that ideologies about "safe" (i.e., untainted) and "dangerous" (i.e., polluted and polluting) women are now split along class lines. Smuts (1992) claims that the "pure" label is reserved for middle and upper-class women, and the "dirty" label is allocated to poor, working-class women. "By depicting [working-class] women as whores," states Smuts, "high-status men can attribute their sexual exploits to the women's voracious sexuality, drawing attention away from the coercive tactics they employ to gain access to these women" (p. 26).

This ideology of gendered threat relies heavily on the utilization of violence by men—in intimate relationships, in public places, and on a national and international scale. Violence, as the prerogative of the dominant gender, is invoked to sustain this position of social superiority. We have already examined how this masculinist imperative shapes individual and group behaviors. Violence is also invoked in transactions between men. Displays of hegemonic masculinity involving violence assert the primacy of this version of manliness and marginalize alternative versions. However, Connell (1995) asserts that "violence is a part of a system of domination, but is at the same time a measure of its imperfection. . . . [Furthermore] the scale of contemporary violence points to crisis tendencies . . . in the modern gender order" (p. 84). It is to these crises and their explanations that I turn in the next chapter, where I consider the ways in which masculinity is represented in the visual apparatus of contemporary Western society, especially in cinema.

Notes

1. The processes whereby gender is constructed are revealed in instances in which an individual's biological sex is ambiguous, as in so-called intersexed infants. Kessler (1990) has shown that biological factors are paramount in determining an infant's gender. Consequently, the possession of appropriate genitalia is fundamental to the allocation of an individual to one gender or the other. However, the male gender operates as the standard, and the female gender occupies the status of a default gender. When an infant is born with inadequate genitalia (in terms of size or form)—such as with a small or misshapen penis—corrective surgery is often recommended. Furthermore, the parents are often advised by medical authorities to rear their child as a female (albeit the barren variety). Thereby, ambiguously sexed infants are normalized, and society's two-gender system is affirmed (see Fausto-Sterling, 1995).

2. Of course, as we shall see, discourses relating to gender and sexuality shift over time, and so the Plecks' observations are relevant for a specific time period.

3. For a discussion of this issue, see the following texts: Beemyn and Eliason (1996), Bullough, Bullough, and Elias (1997), Califia (1997), Devor (1997), Ekins (1997), and Halberstam (1998).

4. Perhaps this is what entertainer Barry Humphries (also known as Dame Edna Everage) meant when he said, "Australian women are the best female impersonators in the world."

5. One of the most influential scholars of the body has been Foucault. He has demonstrated that the body cannot be regarded as a given, but is the product of cultural processes that discipline, train, mark, and shape the body. The body is produced through the intervention of historically specific institutional processes and practices. Self-regulation, supervision, and discipline are the vehicles whereby the effects of power are deposited. The body is also susceptible to the actions of the Other; it may be scrutinized, categorized, judged, and perhaps tortured. The body is thus constituted in a sociopolitical field. Yet resistances occur to the imposition of these disciplinary regimes; the body can never be transformed into a docile entity. In its capacity for resistance, the body displays a subversive power to redefine and codify itself anew.

Another scholar who has made a major contribution to writings about the body is Elizabeth Grosz (in particular, see Grosz, 1994; Grosz & Probyn, 1995). She contends that the modern body presupposes a hidden or private depth, obscured beneath the surface. Thus, the modern body is read according to external signs or symptoms and in terms of its concealed regions. However, bodies are also inscribed. The surface of the body may be elaborated voluntarily or involuntarily, with or without violence. Social institutions may inscribe the body by force—confining, constraining, watching, and categorizing, in the prison, psychiatric facility, or hospital—and reorganize the body into a "text" that resonates with sociocultural narratives. The body may be incorporated into the Other's project; only the corporeal surface may remain to be inscribed, inspected and supervised.

Grosz (1994) notes that bodies

> cannot be adequately understood as ahistorical, precultural, or natural objects in any simple way; they are not only inscribed, marked, engraved, by social pressures external to them but are the products, the direct effects, of the very social constitution of nature itself. (p. x)

6. Best (1991) demonstrates how the undergarment company Berlei generated complementary images of women's bodies in advertisements during the 1920s. One image suggested that women's bodies were composed of excess flesh, and hence were blighted. Another image suggested that such flaws in the contours of the body could be rectified by the wearing of a corset. Like dieting, this was a strategy of containment and control. Interestingly, it coincided with a rising tide of concern about femininity in women.

7. This model viewed the male body as the basis for all anatomical theory. The one-sex model, based on this male standard, reflected the fact that males were considered "the measure of all things" (Laqueur, 1990, p. 62). Femaleness did not exist "as an ontologically distinct category" (Laqueur, 1990, p. 62). The model held that male and female bodies were simply mirror images of each other. Even with blood, semen, milk, and other bodily fluids, precise parallels were drawn as to their functions in male and female bodies. The propensity to view the female body as simply a variation of the male body extended into the realms of medical vocabulary. Laqueur pointed out that, in fact, there was no precise medical nomenclature for female genitals or the reproductive system generally until after the Renaissance. However, the one-sex model did envisage that both men and women could gain pleasure from sexual relations, and postulated that there was a causal association between orgasm and conception.

8. The exception to this conceptual schema is the category of substances known as poisons. Although certainly dangerous to health and well-being, they do not necessarily produce decay (except insofar as they lead to death). In contrast, several classes of disease are viewed as "polluting" in contemporary society, even though they are not contagious (see Hatty & Hatty, 1999).

9. This is not to suggest that gender duality, based on a two-sexed (male/female) model is evident in all cross-cultural contexts. Fitz John Porter Poole (1996) has conducted fieldwork with the Bimin-Kuskusmin of the West Sepik area of Papua New Guinea. He notes the existence of prominent cultural imagery about androgyny among these people.

10. Conceptions of women gleaned from ethnographic sources frequently contained similar core values: for example, that the women originally enjoyed a powerful position in society (Hiatt, 1978). In a fascinating article, Chris Knight (1988) argues that the source of this original female power lay in menstrual synchrony. When this broke down, according to Knight, the mythic symbolism and significance of the synchrony was assumed by the men; hence the initiation ceremonies, many of which purported to imitate menstruation, were derivative of prior female experience.

Another staple theme was that women possessed an insatiable sexuality that was extremely dangerous (in both a ritual and a physical sense) for the men. Berndt recorded the following myth from the Mara of southeast Arnhem Land the following myth, which illustrates the above themes:

> A long time ago an old woman called Mumuna lived alone with her two daughters. By making a smoky fire, she attracted men to her camp, then welcomed them with food and invited them to spend the night with the daughters. Later, while they slept deeply from sexual exhaustion, she dropped boulders on them. The next morning she cooked and ate them, then regurgitated them onto an ant-bed. Their bones can be seen today in the form of stones.
>
> The attitude of the daughters was equivocal. On the one hand they relished the sexual role that their mother encouraged them to play. On the other, they deplored the old woman's cannibalism and feared its consequences. In particular, they were disturbed by her habit of hanging up the genital organs of the dead men on a tree and proposing to the girls that they eat them—an invitation they steadfastly refused.
>
> Mumuna's grisly practices were finally put to an end by a man called Eaglehawk, a light sleeper who woke up in time to kill her before she killed him. The daughters ran away. As the old woman died, she called out . . . and her blood splashed onto every tree. (quoted in Hiatt, 1978, p. 257)

The negative conception of woman as devourer, a notion containing the seeds of mortal fear, was also manifest in the legend of the Murinbata people of Australia's Northern Territory (see Knight, 1988). This legend concerned the origins of the cult of the Old Woman, the most significant of all the Murinbata rituals.

> The people said to the Old Woman: "We shall leave the children with you while we find honey; you look after them." She agreed, and the people went off to hunt. After the children had bathed, they settled down to sleep near her.
>
> Bringing one close on the pretext of looking for lice, she swallowed it. The she swallowed the others, ten altogether, and left.
>
> A man and his wife returned to the camp for water and realised what must have happened. They gave the alarm, and the others came back. Ten men set off in pursuit and eventually overtook Mutjingga [the Old Woman] crawling along a river bed. A left-handed man speared her through the legs and a right-handed man broke her neck with a club. They then cut her belly open and found the children, still alive, in her womb.
>
> They had not gone where the excrement is. The men cleaned and adorned the children and took them back to the camp. Their mothers cried with joy on seeing them and hit themselves until the blood flowed. (quoted in Hiatt, 1978, p. 258)

Perhaps the most interesting myth, in terms of its connection with the development of initiation rites, was told by the Walbiri of Central Australia:

A long time ago there were two Mulga-tree brothers, each with a wife and several sons. Because the area they inhabited was suffering from drought, the two men decided to take their families and explore other regions for food. Before departing, they secretly circumcised their sons and inducted them into the clan totemic cult. Their wives heard about the ceremonies and became angry at their exclusion; and when the men refused to allow them to accompany them on their travels, saying they must stay behind and look after the boys, their anger increased. The husbands responded to their demands by soundly thrashing them with boomerangs. They then jumped into the air and began their journey.

After various adventures, they returned home. As they alighted from the sky, they called out happily to their wives, but there was no answer. Puzzled and apprehensive, they searched the vicinity of the camp site and to their alarm discovered evidence of a violent struggle. Leading away from the spot were two sets footprints, which they identified as their wives'. They then guessed what must have happened: the two women, furious at being excluded and left behind, had killed and eaten their sons.

The two men followed the tracks to a cave, around the mouth of which flies were swarming. Quickly fashioning torches they entered a large chamber where, among the boulders on the floor, they saw the putrescent remains of their sons. The flies, however, were streaming past the corpses and going further into the cave. The men raised their torches and cautiously advanced. At the end of the cave, they saw the two women, crouching like hideous demons, with flies swarming into their gaping, blood-stained mouths. The men realised that they had vomited up the lads and were ready to swallow them again. So terrifying was the scene of carnage that the men ran in terror from the stinking cavern. Outside, their courage returned. They rushed back in with armfuls of dry grass, threw it over the women and set fire to it. The women were completely destroyed.

Badly shaken by these events the two brothers returned to their original camp where they mourned the passing of their sons. They then pondered the question of how to replace the lads now that they were without wives and without prospects of acquiring more. That night the older brother dreamt of a magical formula that enabled the two men not only to resurrect their sons but to produce an unlimited supply of children without the aid of women. (quoted in Hiatt, 1978, p. 258)

The expression of such fear functioned, on one level, to afford the males the opportunity of disputing the existence of responsibility, of the right of women to be responsible for the children's welfare. These reactions, being derived from fear, allowed the men to displace the women by claiming, in ritual, that they could give birth to boys and safely tend them.

References

Allen, M. (1967). *Male cult and secret initiations in Melanesia*. Melbourne, Australia: Melbourne University Press.

Armstrong, T. (Ed.). (1996). *American bodies: Cultural histories of the physique*. New York: New York University Press.

Atwood, M. (1996). Alien territory. In L. Goldstein (Ed.), *The male body: Features, desires, exposure* (pp. 1-7). Ann Arbor, MI: University of Michigan Press.

Bakhtin, M. (1984). *Rabelais and his world.* (H. Iswolsky, Trans.). Bloomington, IN: Indiana University Press.

Bale, J., & Philo, C. (Eds.). (1998). *Body cultures: Essays on sport, space, and identity.* New York: Routledge.

Barker, F. (1984). *The tremulous private body: Essays on subjection.* London: Methuen.

Beall, A., & Sternberg, R. (Eds.). (1993). *The psychology of gender.* New York: Guilford.

Bederman, G. (1995). *Manliness and civilization: A cultural history of gender and race in the United States, 1880–1917.* Chicago: Chicago University Press.

Beemyn, B., & Eliason, M. (Eds.). (1996). *Queer studies: A lesbian, gay, bisexual, and transgender anthology.* New York: New York University Press.

Best, S. (1991). Foundations of femininity: Berlei corsets and the (un)raveling of the modern body. *Continuum: The Australian Journal of Media and Culture, 5,* 1-13.

Bhabha, H. (1995). Are you a man or a mouse? In M. Berger, B. Wallis, & S. Watson (Eds.), *Constructing masculinities* (pp. 57-65). New York: Routledge.

Bordo, S. (1993). *Unbearable weight: Feminism, Western culture, and the body.* Berkeley, CA: University of California Press.

Bordo, S. (1996). Reading the male body. In L. Goldstein (Ed.), *The male body: Features, desires, exposure* (pp. 265-306). Ann Arbor, MI: University of Michigan Press.

Bourke, J. (1996). *Dismembering the male: Men's bodies, Britain, and the Great War.* Chicago: Chicago University Press.

Bullough, B., Bullough, V., & Elias, J. (Eds.). (1997). *Gender blending.* Amherst, MA: Prometheus.

Burke, P. (1996). *Gender shock: Exploding the myths of male and female.* New York: Anchor.

Butler, J. (1990). *Gender trouble: Feminism and the subversion of identity.* New York: Routledge.

Butler, J. (1993). *Bodies that matter: On the discursive limits of "Sex."* New York: Routledge.

Butler, J. (1995). Melancholy gender/refused identification. In M. Berger, B. Wallis, & S. Watson (Eds.). *Constructing masculinity* (pp. 21-36). New York: Routledge.

Bynum, C. (1984). *Jesus as mother: Studies in spirituality of the high Middle Ages.* Stanford, CA: University of California Press.

Bynum, C. (1991). *Fragmentation and redemption: Essays on gender and the human body in medieval religion.* New York: Zone.

Cadden, J. (1993). *The meanings of sex difference in the Middle Ages.* Cambridge, MA: Harvard University Press.

Califia, P. (1997). *Sex changes: The politics of transgenderism.* San Francisco, CA: Cleis.

Carnes, M., & Griffen, C. (Eds.). (1990). *Meanings for manhood: Constructions of masculinity in Victorian America.* Chicago: Chicago University Press.

Chandler, T., & Nauright, J. (1996). Introduction: Rugby, manhood, and identity. In T. Chandler & J. Nauright (Eds.), *Making men: Rugby and masculine identity* (pp. 1-12). London: Frank Cass.

Chodorow, N. (1978). *The reproduction of mothering.* Berkeley, CA: University of California Press.

Clover, C. (1993). *Women, men, and chainsaws.* Princeton, NJ: Princeton University Press.

Cohen, J. J. (1997). Growth among the dogs: Becoming inhuman c. 1400. In J. J. Cohen & B. Wheeler (Eds.), *Becoming male in the Middle Ages.* New York: Garland.

Retrieved May 10, 1998 from the World Wide Web: http://www.gwu.edu/ ~humsci/bcom/gowther.html.

Cohen, J. J. (1994). *Interscripta archive,* Medieval Masculinities, week 3. Retrieved June 4, 1996 from the World Wide Web: http://www.georgetown.edu/labyrinth/ labyrinth-home.html.

Cohen, J. J., & Members of Interscripta. (1995). *Medieval masculinities: Heroism, society, and gender.* Retrieved June 4, 1996 from the World Wide Web: http:// www.georgetown.edu/labyrinth/labyrinth-home.html.

Comaroff, J., & Comaroff, J. (1992). *Ethnography and the historical imagination.* Boulder, CO: Westview.

Connell, R. (1983). *Which way is up?* Sydney, Australia: Allen and Unwin.

Connell, R. (1987). *Gender and power: Society, the person, and sexual politics.* Cambridge, MA: Polity.

Connell, R. (1995). *Masculinities.* Sydney, Australia: Allen and Unwin.

Creed, B. (1993). *The monstrous feminine: Film, feminism, and psychoanalysis.* New York: Routledge.

Csordas, T. (Ed.). (1994). *Embodiment and experience: The existential ground of culture and self.* Cambridge, UK: Cambridge University Press.

Davis, K. (1995). *Reshaping the female body: The dilemma of cosmetic surgery.* New York: Routledge.

Davis, L. (1997). *The swimsuit issue and sport: Hegemonic masculinity and Sports Illustrated.* Albany, NY: State University of New York Press.

Davis, R. (1998). *Duke: The life and image of John Wayne.* Norman, OK: University of Oklahoma Press.

Dawson, G. (1994). *Soldier heroes: Britishness, colonial adventure, and the imagining of masculinities.* London: Routledge.

Devor, H. (1997). *FTM: Female-to-male transsexuals in society.* Bloomington, IN: Indiana University Press.

Di Stefano, C. (1991). *Configurations of masculinity: A feminist perspective on modern political theory.* Ithaca, NY: Cornell University Press.

Diprose, R. (1994). *The bodies of women: Ethics, embodiment, and sexual difference.* London: Routledge.

Dockray-Miller, M. (1998). *Beowulf's* tears of fatherhood. *Exemplaria: A Journal of Theory in Medieval and Renaissance Studies, 10*(1), 1-28. Retrieved July 7, 1998 from the World Wide Web: http://web.english.ufl.edu/english/exemplaria.

Donaldson, M. (1993). What is hegemonic masculinity? *Theory and Society, 22,* 643-657.

Douglas, M. (1966). *Purity and danger.* New York: Penguin.

Dutton, K. (1995). *The perfectible body.* Sydney, Australia: Allen and Unwin.

Ehrenreich, B. (1997). *Blood rites: Origins and history of the passions of war.* New York: Henry Holt.

Eichenbaum, L., & Orbach, S. (1983). *Understanding women: A feminist psychoanalytic approach.* New York: Basic Books.

Ekins, R. (1997). *Male femaling: A grounded theory approach to cross dressing and sex changing.* London: Routledge.

Elias, N. (1994). *The civilizing process.* (E. Jephcott, Trans.). Oxford, UK: Basil Blackwell.

Ernst, T. (1991). Onabasulu male homosexuality: Cosmology, affect, and prescribed male homosexuality among the Onabasulu of the Great Papuan Plateau. *Oceania, 62,* 1-11.

Everest, C. (1994). *Interscripta Archive,* Medieval Masculinities, week 5. Retrieved June 4, 1996 from the World Wide Web:http://www.georgetown.edu/labyrinth/ labyrinth-home.html.

Fausto-Sterling, A. (1995). How to build a man. In M. Berger, B. Wallis, & S. Watson (Eds.), *Constructing masculinities* (pp. 127-134). New York: Routledge.

Ferree, M, Lorber, J., & Hess, B. (Eds.). (1999). *Revisioning gender.* Thousand Oaks, CA: Sage.

Foster, S. (1996). *Corporealities: Dancing, knowledge, culture, and power.* New York: Routledge.

Fradenburg, L., & Freccero, C. (Eds.). (1995). *Premodern sexualities.* New York: Routledge.

Francke, L. (1997). *Ground zero: The gender wars in the military.* New York: Simon & Schuster.

Franklin, C. (1988). *Men and society.* Chicago: Nelson-Hall.

Freud, S. (1953). Three essays on the theory of sexuality. In J. Strachey (Ed. and Trans.), *The standard edition of the complete psychological works of Sigmund Freud* (Vol. 7, pp. 25-39). London: Hogarth.

Fussell, S. (1996). Bodybuilder americanus. In L. Goldstein (Ed.), *The male body: Features, destinies, exposure* (pp. 43-60). Ann Arbor, MI: University of Michigan Press.

Gallop, J. (1988). *Thinking through the body.* New York: Columbia University Press.

Garton, S. (1995). Return home: War, masculinity, and reparation. In J. Damousi & M. Lake (Eds.), *Gender and war* (pp. 191-204). Melbourne, Australia: Cambridge University Press.

Gatens, M. (1983). A critique of the sex/gender distinction. In J. Allen & P. Patton (Eds.), *Beyond Marxism? Interventions after Marx* (pp. 143-160). Sydney, Australia: Intervention.

Gerster, R. (1995). A bit of the other: Touring Vietnam. In J. Damousi & M. Lake (Eds.), *Gender and war* (pp. 223-235). Melbourne, Australia: Cambridge University Press.

Gilligan, C. (1982). *In a different voice: Psychological theory and women's development.* Cambridge, MA: Harvard University Press.

Gorn, E., & Goldstein, W. (1993). *A brief history of American sports.* New York: Hill & Wang.

Grossman, D. (1996). *On killing: The psychological cost of learning to kill in war and society.* New York: Little, Brown.

Grosz, E. (1994). *Volatile bodies: Toward a corporeal feminism.* Sydney, Australia: Allen and Unwin.

Grosz, E., & Probyn, E. (Eds.). (1995). *Sexy bodies: The strange carnalities of feminism.* London: Routledge.

Halberstam, J. (1998). *Female masculinity.* Durham, NC: Duke University Press.

Halberstam, J., & Livingston, I. (Eds.). (1995). *Posthuman bodies.* Bloomington, IN: Indiana University Press.

Hall, M. (1996). *Feminism and sporting bodies: Essays on theory and practice.* Champaign, IL: Human Kinetics.

Hare-Mustin, R., & Marecek, J. (1988). The meaning of difference. *American Psychologist, 43,* 455-464.

Harrell, M., & Miller, L. (1997). *New opportunities for military women: Effects upon readiness, cohesion, and morale.* Santa Monica, CA: Rand.

Hatty, S. E. (1991, November). The dangerous sex: Men, women, and violence. Paper presented at the Annual Meeting of the American Society of Criminology, San Francisco, CA.

Hatty, S. E., & Hatty, J. (1999). *The disordered body: Epidemic disease and cultural transformation.* Albany, NY: State University of New York Press.

Hays, H. (1966). *The dangerous sex: The myth of the female evil.* London: Methuen.

Herbert, M. (1998). *Camouflage isn't only for combat: Gender, sexuality, and women in the military.* New York: New York University Press.

Heywood, L. (1998). *Bodymakers: A cultural anthropology of women's body building.* New Brunswick, NJ: Rutgers University Press.

Hiatt, L. (1978). *Australian aboriginal concepts.* Atlantic Highlands, NJ: Humanities Press.

Hogbin, H. (1970). *The island of menstruating men: Religion in Wogeo, New Guinea.* San Francisco, CA: Chandler.

Holsinger, B. (1994). *Interscripta Archive,* Medieval Masculinities, week 1. Retrieved June 4, 1996 from the World Wide Web: http://www.georgetown.edu/labyrinth/labryrinth-home.html.

Horrocks, R. (1994). *Masculinity in crisis: Myths, fantasies, and realities.* New York: St. Martin's.

Jackson, D. (1990). *Unmasking masculinity.* Winchester, MA: Unwin Hyman.

Johnson, L. (1996, March). Negative space and self-definition. Paper presented at the Intersections Conference, George Washington University, Washington, DC.

Karner, T. (1996). Father, sons, and Vietnam: Masculinity and betrayal in the life narratives of Vietnam veterans with post traumatic stress disorder. *American Studies, 37,* 63-94.

Katzman, J. (1993). From outcast to cliche: How film shaped, warped, and developed the image of the Vietnam veteran, 1967–1990. *Journal of American Culture, 16,* 7-24.

Kay, S., & Rubin, M. (Eds.). (1994). *Framing medieval bodies.* Manchester, UK: Manchester University Press.

Kessler, S. (1990). The medical construction of gender: Case management of intersexed infants. *Signs: Journal of Women in Culture and Society, 6,* 3-26.

Kimball, M. (1995). *Feminist visions of gender similarities and differences.* New York: Haworth.

Kimmel, M. (1994). Masculinity as homophobia: Fear, shame, and silence in the construction of gender identity. In H. Brod & M. Kaufman (Eds.), *Theorizing masculinities* (pp. 119-141). Thousand Oaks, CA: Sage.

Kimmel, M. (1996). *Manhood in America: A cultural history.* New York: Free Press.

Klein, A. (1993). *Little big men: Bodybuilding subculture and gender construction.* Albany, NY: State University of New York Press.

Knight, C. (1988). Menstrual synchrony and the Australian rainbow snake. In T. Buckley & A. Gottlieb (Eds.), *Blood magic: The anthropology of menstruation* (pp. 232-255). Berkeley, CA: University of California Press.

Kovel, J. (1997). *Red hunting in the promised land.* London: Cassell.

Laqueur, T. (1990). *Making sex: Body and gender from the Greeks to Freud.* Cambridge, MA: Harvard University Press.

Leder, D. (1990). *The absent body.* Chicago: The University of Chicago Press.

Lees, C. (1994a). *Interscriptia Archive,* Medieval Masculinities, week 3. Retrieved June 4, 1996 from the World Wide Web: http://www.georgetown.edu/labyrinth/labryrinth-home.html.

Lees, C. (Ed.). (1994b). *Medieval masculinities: Regarding men in the Middle Ages.* Minneapolis, MN: University of Minnesota Press.

Lingis, A. (1994). *Foreign bodies.* New York: Routledge.

Loeb, J. (1996). Childhood's end: Self recovery in the autobiography of the Vietnam war. *American Studies, 37,* 95-114.

Lomperis, L., & Stanbury, S. (Eds.). (1993). *Feminist approaches to the body in medieval literature.* Philadelphia: University of Pennsylvania Press.

Lorber, J. (1994). *Paradoxes of gender.* New Haven, CT: Yale University Press.

Loux, A. (1997). Is he our sister? Sex, gender, and transsexuals under European law. *Web Journal of Current Legal Issues, 3,* 1-10. Retrieved August 24, 1998 from the World Wide Web: http://webjcli.nci.ac.uk/1997/issue3/loux3.html.

MacKinnon, C. (1987). *Feminism unmodified: Discourses in life and law*. Cambridge, MA: Harvard University Press.

Madsen, D. (1994). *Visions of America since 1492*. London: Cassell.

Mangan, J. A. (1996). Games field and battlefield: A romantic alliance in verse and the creation of militaristic masculinities. In J. Nauright & T. Chandler (Eds.), *Making men: Rugby and masculine identity* (pp. 140-157). London: Frank Cass.

Mangan, J. A., & Walvin, J. (Eds.). (1987). *Manliness and morality: Middle-class masculinity in Britain and America, 1800–1940*. Manchester, UK: Manchester University Press.

Martin, A. (1993). *Perceptions of war: Vietnam in American culture*. Norman, OK: University of Oklahoma Press.

Matthews, J. (1984). *Good and mad women: The historical construction of femininity in twentieth-century Australia*. Sydney, Australia: Allen and Unwin.

McBride, J. (1995). *War, battering, and other sports*. Atlantic Heights, NJ: Humanities Press.

McKay, J., & Messner, M. (Eds.). (1997). *Managing gender: Affirmative action and organizational power in Australian, Canadian, and New Zealand sport*. Albany, NY: State University of New York Press.

Mead, M. (1935). *Sex and temperament*. New York: William Morrow.

Meigs, A. (1976). Male pregnancy and the reduction of sexual opposition in a New Guinea Highlands society. *Ethnology, 25,* 393-407.

Meigs, A. (1978). A Papuan perspective on pollution. *Man, 13,* 304-318.

Meigs, A. (1984). *Food, sex, and pollution: A New Guinea religion*. New Brunswick, NJ: Rutgers University Press.

Messerschmidt, J. (1993). *Masculinities and crime: Critique and reconceptualization of theory*. Lanham, MD: Rowman & Littlefield.

Messner, M. (1990). Boyhood, organized sports, and the construction of masculinities. *Journal of Contemporary Ethnography, 18,* 416-444.

Messner, M. (1992). *Power at play: Sports and the problem of masculinity*. Boston: Beacon.

Messner, M. (1994). *Sex, violence, and power in sports: Rethinking masculinity*. New York: Crossing.

Messner, M. (1997). When bodies are weapons. In M. Baca Zinn (Ed.), *Through the prism of gender: Readings on sex and gender* (pp. 257-272). New York: Allyn & Bacon.

Miller, W. (1998). *The anatomy of disgust*. Cambridge, MA: Harvard University Press.

Mimica, J. (1992). The incest passion: The logic of the Iqwaye social organization. Paper presented at the Social Science Colloquium, School of Social Sciences, Charles Sturt University, Bathurst, New South Wales, Australia.

Money, J., & Ehrhardt, A. (1972). *Man and woman: Boy and girl*. Baltimore, MD: Johns Hopkins University Press.

Moore, P. (Ed.). (1997). *Building bodies*. New Brunswick, NJ: Rutgers University Press.

Morgan, D. (1994). Theater of war: Combat, the military, and masculinities. In H. Brod & M. Kaufman (Eds.), *Theorizing masculinities* (pp. 165-182). Thousand Oaks, CA: Sage.

Nadeau, R. (1996). *S/He brain: Science, sexual politics, and the myths of feminism*. New York: Praeger.

Nilles, J. (1943). The Kuman of the Chimbu region. *Oceania, 14,* 25-65.

Oakley, A. (1972). *Sex, gender, and society*. Aldershot, U.K.: Gower.

Ortner, S. (1978). The virgin and the state. *Feminist Studies, 4,* 19-37.

Parker, A. (1996). Sporting masculinities: Gender relations and the body. In M. Mac an Ghaill (Ed.), *Understanding masculinities* (pp. 126-138). Buckingham, U.K.: Open University Press.

Paster, G. (1993). *The body embarrassed: Drama and the discipline of shame in early modern England.* Ithaca, NY: Cornell University Press.

Pleck, E., & Pleck, J. (1976). The male sex role: Definition, problems, and sources of change. *Journal of Social Issues, 32,* 155-164.

Pleck, J. (1981). *The myth of masculinity.* Cambridge, MA: MIT Press.

Poole, J. P. (1996). The procreative and ritual construction of female, male, and other. In S. Ramet (Ed.), *Gender reversals and gender cultures* (pp. 197-218). New York: Routledge.

Pugliese, J. (1995). The gendered figuring of the dysfunctional serviceman in the discourses of military psychiatry. In J. Damousi & M. Lake (Eds.), *Gender and war* (pp. 162-177). Melbourne, Australia: Cambridge University Press.

Rado, L. (Ed.). (1997). *Modernism, gender, and culture: A cultural studies approach.* New York: Garland.

Read, K. (1952). Nama cult of the Central Highlands, New Guinea. *Oceania, 23,* 1-25.

Roper, M., & Tosh, J. (Eds.). (1991). *Manful assertions: Masculinities in Britain since 1800.* London: Routledge.

Rotundo, A. (1993). *American manhood: Transformations in masculinity from the Revolution to the modern era.* New York: Basic Books.

Rubin, G. (1975). The traffic in women: Notes on the political economy of sex. In R. Reiter (Ed.), *Toward an anthropology of women* (pp. 159-180). New York: Monthly Review Press.

Russo, M. (1995). *The female grotesque: Risk, excess, and modernity.* New York: Routledge.

Said, E. (1991). *Orientalism.* New York: Penguin.

Schwartz, P., & Rutter, V. (1998). *The gender of sexuality.* Thousand Oaks, CA: Pine Forge Press.

Seidler, V. (1997). *Man enough: Embodying masculinities.* London: Sage.

Selig, M. (1993). Genre, gender, and the discourse of war: The a/historical in Vietnam films. *Screen, 34,* 1-19.

Shaffer, J. (1997). Molding women's bodies: The surgeon as sculptor. In D. Wilson & C. Laennec (Eds.), *Bodily discursions: Genders, representations, technologies* (pp. 69-84). Albany, NY: State University of New York Press.

Showalter, E. (1987). *The female malady: Women, madness, and English culture 1830–1980.* London: Virago.

Sillitoe, P. (1998). *An introduction to the anthropology of Melanesia: Culture and tradition.* Cambridge, UK: Cambridge University Press.

Simpson, M. (1994). *Male impersonators: Men performing masculinities.* New York: Routledge.

Smuts, B. (1992). Male aggression against women: An evolutionary perspective. *Human Nature, 3,*(1), 1-44.

Stiehm, J. (Ed.). (1996). *It's our military too! Women and the U.S. Military.* Philadelphia: Temple University Press.

Stoller, R. (1968). *Sex and gender.* London: Hogarth.

Strathern, A. (1979). Gender, ideology, and money in Mount Hagen. *Man, 14,* 42-54.

Strathern, A. (1996). *Body thoughts.* Ann Arbor, MI: University of Michigan Press.

Strathern, M. (1972). *Women in between.* London: Seminar.

Strathern, M. (1978). The achievement of sex: Paradoxes in Hagen gender thinking. In E. Schwimmer (Ed.), *Yearbook of symbolic anthropology* (Vol. 1, pp. 179-184). London: Hurst.

Taussig, M. (1995). Schopenhauer's beard. In M. Berger, B. Wallis, & S. Watson (Eds.), *Constructing masculinities* (pp. 107-114). New York: Routledge.

Theweleit, K. (1987). *Male fantasies* (Vols. 1-2). Minnesota, MN: University of Minnesota Press.

Tudor, D. (1997). *Hollywood's vision of team sports: Heroes, race, and gender.* New York: Garland.

Updike, J. (1996). The disposable rocket. In L. Goldstein (Ed.), *The male body: Features, desires, exposure* (pp. 8-11). Ann Arbor, MI: University of Michigan Press.

Ussher, J. (1997). *Fantasies of femininity: Reframing the boundaries of sex.* New Brunswick, NJ: Rutgers University Press.

Walsh, M. (1997). *Women, men, and gender: Ongoing debates.* New Haven, CT: Yale University Press.

Weiner, J. (1987). Diseases of the soul: sickness, agency, and the men's cult among the Foi of New Guinea. In M. Strathern (Ed.), *Dealing with inequality* (pp. 255-277). Cambridge, UK: Cambridge University Press.

Wherrett, P., & Wherrett, R. (1997). *Desirelines: An unusual family memoir.* Sydney, Australia: Hoddler Headline.

White, G. F., Katz, J., & Scarborough, K. E. (1992). The impact of professional football upon violent assaults on women. *Violence and Victims, 7,*(2), 151-171.

Wills, G. (1997). *John Wayne's America: The politics of celebrity.* New York: Simon & Schuster.

Wolff, J. (1990). *Feminine sentences: Essays on women and culture.* Cambridge, MA: Polity.

Young, K. (1997). *Presence in the flesh: The body in medicine.* Cambridge, MA: Harvard University Press.

Zapperi, R. (1991). *The pregnant man.* New York: Harwood.

Zimmerman, J. (1995). *Tailspin: Women at war in the wake of Tailhook.* New York: Doubleday.

5

Boys on Film
Masculinities and the Cinema

Masculinity is an effect of culture—a construction, a performance, a masquerade—rather than a universal and unchanging essence.
—*Steve Cohan and Rae Harke*

Emotions. There ought to be a law against them.
—*Judge Dredd*

Inspired by a boys' comic and situated in the future, the film *Judge Dredd* (1995) explores several themes: the rule of law, conformity and obedience, the kinship between flesh and machine, and the new reproductive technologies. The film also presents some clear and unequivocal images of masculinity. Threaded throughout the film are startling depictions of men—men as extraordinarily violent, men as domineering and brutal, and men as devoid of the taint of affect, to name a few.

The film describes an orthodox moral struggle between good and evil, manifest particularly in the bitter fight between two brothers. One, Dredd, represents law and justice. Dredd, played by Sylvester Stallone, first appears on screen encased in exaggerated body armor that provides hard coverage of genitals and shoulders. Designed by the late Gianni Versace, this haute couture outfit draws attention to the traditional signs of hegemonic masculinity. Along with the platform shoes, it also lends a playful and comic edge to the narrative. But Dredd's accessories leave us in no doubt that we are about to witness a serious drama in which gender plays a critical role. Dredd carries a weapon that he programs with verbal commands; the weapon repeats

Dredd's instructions in a deep, resonant male voice, suggesting a neat symbiosis between man and gun. Most importantly, however, Dredd is a judge.

The judges are an elite clan of highly trained specialists who prosecute, judge, and punish on the streets of a megacity (New York) in the third millennium. The judges have replaced the formal, state-controlled justice system, which has collapsed. The film tells of a renegade judge, Rico, who breaks out of the Aspen Penal Colony and proceeds cold-heartedly to murder his fellow judges. Rico is a test-tube product, the result of an experiment in genetic engineering, just like his brother, Dredd.

Through DNA evidence, Dredd is accused of his brother's crimes. Dredd escapes his punishment, and attempts to halt Rico's killing spree. Rico, meanwhile, is intent on cloning a new batch of judges to replace the diminishing number of original judges. Rico substitutes the existing DNA stock with his own sample, fires up the accelerated growth incubators, and prepares to spawn a myriad of adult clones within eight hours. "I'm about to be a daddy," he exclaims. Rico is foiled by the interventions of Dredd, who manages to blow up the partially hatched clones. Dredd emerges triumphant and in control at the close of the film. He is offered the position of Chief Justice. "I am the Law," declares Dredd.

Judge Dredd sketches the outlines of a dystopian future, a scenario in which the urban frontier is lawless, chaotic, violent, peppered by "block wars" and citizen riots. This urban zone is shut off from the "cursed earth"—the landscape beyond the megacities. Both zones are populated by artificial (i.e., non-natural) creatures: a giant robot brought to life by Rico, for example, and an outlaw who has metal woven into his flesh. The narrative combines the elements of the classic Western with those of the combat film. Rico, the male antihero who attempts to father himself many times over, is the antithesis of Dredd, the hypermasculine hero clothed in a ritualized and somewhat fetishistic costume. Rico is positioned in the narrative as the perfect criminal; an oppositional and disruptive figure pitted against his heroic and just brother.

The apocalyptic tensions in the narrative are worked out in the space of the future cityscape, and are shaped and ameliorated by the ascendancy and supremacy of hegemonic masculinity enshrined in the figure of Judge Dredd, a genetically engineered, "ideal" individual who restores order to this barbarous and anarchic public place. Here, we are witnesses to an extended cinematic portrayal of American masculinity.

In this chapter, I examine, in some detail, the representations of masculinity in American cinema. I look, in particular, at film genres in which masculinity is foregrounded: the Western, war films, and *film noir*. First, I consider the historical and structural conditions that shape contemporary representational practices and forms, particularly as these concern men and masculinity.

Public Masculinities

> We are no longer private. We are not private. For better and for worse, we, men, are public, and increasingly so.
>
> —*Jeff Hearn*

Men are now a highly visible and powerful presence in the public domain. We can speak of the mass collectivity of men and the universalizing of experience that has accompanied the social changes of the late 20th century. Men in public now exercise a wide range of powers: over women, whether located in the public or private domain; over some men in the public domain; and over all other men in the private domain. Furthermore, there is a silence surrounding the relationship between men's activity and experience in the public and private domains. Men are powerful and visible, yet fractured and disconnected; men's lives are split into compartments.

This expansion in men's power in the public domain has increased significantly since the latter part of the 19th century. Since that time, the private domain has receded and been dominated by the public domain. Private or family patriarchal formations have been displaced by public or social patriarchies (Hearn, 1992). It is in the public domain that new forms of masculinity have been culturally produced, enacted, and reflexively experienced.

The preeminence of a public domain, in which men exert control over economic production, labor, sexuality, and reproduction, is the result of a struggle to order the relations between the public and the private to ensure that the former is dominant. Moreover, this public domain is increasingly the sphere of display: Interactions with others are often more frequent and more visible; public selves are constructed for presentation in such interactions; and opportunities for interpersonal contact may be heightened by the expansive character of time and space in the public domain.

The discourses of consumption that supported the growth of industrialization in the late 19th century focused on the visual. The production and dissemination of the visual image propelled the development of modern retailing and marketing industries. The invention and propagation of visual artifacts, such as the photograph and, later, film, profoundly affected the character of popular culture. The photograph introduced fresh possibilities for the display and recording of masculine behavior and demeanors. Jeff Hearn (1992) describes this visual assertiveness on the part of men as the translation of the photograph into the "new public patriarch," a distillation of the rising power of public men (p. 188). However, film perhaps provided the greatest possibilities for the proliferation of varied images of masculinity. Referring to the present day, Hearn notes that "we, as masculinities, are partly, though no less profoundly, produced in/on film—the most *material* of media" (p. 222).

Public masculinities, represented in various configurations of imagery and text, have embraced new formations over time. This periodization of masculinity is reflected in the emergence of the "new man" in Britain in the late 1980s to early 1990s, and the subsequent celebration of "lad culture," with its emphasis on boozing and scoring.[1] Sean Nixon (1996) traces the rise of new man imagery in Britain across four key cultural sites: television advertising, press advertising, menswear retailing, and popular magazines for men. The latter have included *Esquire, Attitude, Arena Homme Plus,* and, of course, *Loaded.*

According to Nixon, this new man imagery was quintessentially metropolitan, calling up the distinct languages of the city, with its kaleidoscope of sights, sounds, and events. Specific technologies of self-presentation and specific techniques of looking, derived from particular sites of leisure and consumption, shaped this imagery. Male-to-male spectatorship and its attendant sexual ambiguity were coded into these representations of the new man. An explicit appeal to heterosexual men was also embedded in this imagery. The intense focus on the face and the body of the new man was achieved via the cropping and framing of images so that the onlooker's eye was drawn across the surface of the body and clothes on display. In this sense, the choice of models was of paramount significance. Nixon notes that the male models were frequently black or Italian in appearance, as if to signify both assertiveness and a heavy dash of sensuality.

The proliferation in the early 1990s of popular magazines aimed at a style-conscious male market added another dimension to the visualization of the new man. Sexualized references to women appeared in magazines such as *GQ* and *Arena,* and so the new man gave way to the new lad. Nixon describes the latter masculine formation as youthful heterosexuality combined with a reworking of the stock masculine interests of girls, sport, cars, and alcohol. Nevertheless, the lad culture lauded in various men's magazines simply perpetuated the old scripts about mateship, collective forms of masculine entertainment, and sexual exploitation. As we shall see, the discourses that underpinned masculinist lad culture continue to thrive in various arenas of popular culture.

So how does film capture and disseminate images of men and masculinity? What kinds of images are produced, and what is their significance?

Imagining Masculinities

No picture is pure image; all of them, still and moving, graphic and photographic, are "talking pictures," either literally, or in association with contextual speech, writing or discourse.

—*John Hartley*

Steve Neale observed in 1983 that screen representations of masculinity have rarely been studied (see Mulvey, 1975; Neale, 1993). However, in the last decade or so, there has been an explosion of interest in the depiction of masculinity in the mass media (see, for example, Cohan, 1997; Cohan & Hark, 1993; Kirkham & Thumin, 1995). This interest has been sparked by feminist theory, queer theory, and, more recently, cultural and media studies.

Robert Hanke (1992) suggests that we adopt Connell's conceptualization of masculinities as hegemonic, conservative, and subordinated, and apply this to an analysis of representations of men on the screen. Hanke argues that hegemonic masculinity, premised on the subordination of women within the gender order, is frequently articulated in mass media portrayals of men (see Hanke, 1990; Torres, 1989). Hanke nominates action-adventure films, the Western, and sports telecasts as vehicles that most clearly convey images of hegemonic masculinity. Television programs and films in these genres often present "a hypermasculine ideal of toughness and dominance" (Connell, 1987, p. 80; see also Tasker, 1993).

Images of subordinated masculinities (Connell, 1987, 1995) are also widely distributed in contemporary society. Here, we should turn to the example of African American men and the production and dissemination of depictions of black masculinity (see Harper, 1994). The history of representations of black men in American society is thick with portrayals of them as "criminal, lascivious, irresponsible, and not particularly smart" (Delgado & Stefancic, 1995, p. 210). This history is initially populated by figures of derision: Sambo and Jim Crow were childlike, slow-witted, often lazy, and sometimes entertaining; Uncle Tom and Uncle Remus were long suffering, pious, and wise (see Allen, 1994). Following Reconstruction, the liberty of the freed slave led to the production of a host of new images, in which male sexuality played a prominent role. African American males were often depicted as bestial and brutish, as reflected in films such as *The Birth of a Nation* (1915), in which a white woman was pursued to her death by an animalistic black male (see Kaplan, 1996). Popular images thus began to play on a fear of the sexual violation of white women and the resultant racial pollution from such "unnatural" couplings (see Bogle, 1994; Cripps, 1993; Richards, 1998; Sampson, 1998).[2]

Filmic images of black masculinity have often embraced the negative social constructions that circulate throughout society. However, the cinema also presented a sterilized portrait of black masculinity, a sterility reflected in the asexual leading roles offered such actors as Sidney Poitier. This resulted, according to Ed Guerrero (1995), in a binary construction of black manhood from which the intellectual, political, and cultural richness and diversity of black experience had been evacuated, leaving a "vast empty space in representation" (Guerrero, 1995, p. 397). The fact that the Hollywood machine has systematically excluded African Americans from key creative roles in the film industry has not helped to fill this representational void (Miller, 1996; see also Berry & Manning-Miller, 1996; Diawara, 1993; Guerrero, 1993; Martin, 1995; Smith, 1997).

Contemporary cultural images of black men are now more concerned with violence and crime. These are images that essentially signal profound levels of social anxiety and fear about the presence (and indeed circulation) of black men in civil society (Williams, 1995; Young, 1996). The black male body is now an icon of danger (Johnson, 1995), threatening to inflict extreme levels of personal harm on others or even to overturn the stability of the social order. Herman Gray (1995) refers to "the figure of the menacing black male criminal body" (p. 403), which is "the logical and legitimate object of surveillance and policing, containment and punishment" (p. 402).

Delgado and Stefancic (1995) assert that racist depictions of black men give society permission to perpetuate discrimination and bias. Moreover, such images cannot easily be dispelled by protest, exhortation, or counterexamples (see Read, 1996). bell hooks (1995) claims

that such representations of black males are also vital to the maintenance of the gender order; they ensure that hegemonic white masculinity remains dominant and that subordinated black masculinity
revolves, to some extent, around striving to emulate aspects of hegemonic white masculinity. Hence hooks talks about the generation of a
politics of envy and the circular loop of black male identity as lack.
Furthermore, says hooks, this politics of envy is shared with white,
heterosexual women (p. 105), who are also socialized to struggle for
approval and acceptance within a white, heterosexist social order.
hooks describes a 1994 issue of *Vogue* magazine that featured an
advertisement showing a young, black male boxer taking a punch
from a tall, white, fair-haired female model. The text of the advertisement announced, "Going for the knockout punch in powerfully sexy
gym wear." Such an advertisement, argues hooks, suggests that black
men should compete with white women for power and pleasure in the
gender order, and that access to this power and pleasure will be determined by white males (hooks, 1994, p. 105; see also Katz, 1995;
Kervin, 1990, 1991; Shields, 1990).

The issue of self-representation has assumed an urgency and a
significance in the African American community, particularly as hegemonic masculinity is continuously articulated and modified to accommodate the shifting nuances of public and private masculinities
(Hanke, 1992; Willis, 1997). These representations, produced from
within this community, mark out the "racial and cultural boundaries
of a counter-hegemonic blackness" (Gray, 1995, p. 403), a blackness
that opposes, resists, and attempts to displace the prevailing negative
constructions of black masculinity resident in the established gender
order (see Smith, 1998; Watkins, 1998).

How do the media, including the film industry, produce (and
reproduce) masculinity as a cultural category and as a social experience? Below, I look closely at how hegemonic masculinities are imagined in three different film genres: Westerns, war movies, and *film
noir*. I also explore the ways in which masculinity is being redefined
and reshaped, even as it is being performed and seen.

Frontier Nation: Men at the Edge

The Myth of the Frontier is our oldest and most characteristic myth,
expressed in a body of literature, folklore, ritual, historiography,
and polemics produced over a period of three centuries.

—*Richard Slotkin*

The western frontier is still the quintessential mythic site for demonstrating manhood. . . . [W]e come to the western to experience the initiation into manhood and the mythopoeic quest reinscribed into buckskin and revolvers. The search for authentic experiences, for deep meaning, has always led men back to the frontier, back to nature, even if it is inevitably the frontier of their imaginations.

—*Michael Kimmel*

After, all, the Old West is not really a time or a place but a state of mind.

—*Jim Janke's Old West Web page*

The idea of the West as a frontier populated by courageous and stoic settlers, ruthless outlaws, and hostile Indians is firmly entrenched in the American mythos. This idea serves as a metaphor for the national character, for the ideals of modernization and progress, for the expansion of the economy, and for the legitimization of imperialist interventions in the international arena.[3] It also serves as a justification for the subjugation and colonization of indigenous peoples and the exploitation of natural resources.

So great is the hold of this idea on the American imagination that the Western frontier continues to be fictionalized in literature and poetry; see, for example, *Roundup Magazine* produced by the Western Writers of America, *American Cowboy* magazine, and the novels of such authors as Louis L'Amour, Jack Schaefer, Luke Short, and Richard S. Wheeler. Museums preserve the history of the frontier and its colorful characters;[4] there is, for example, the Old West Museum, the Roy Rogers/Dale Evans Museum, the Gene Autry Museum of Western Heritage, the Buffalo Bill Historical Center, and even a Buffalo Bill Wax Museum. Significant among these memorials to the past is the National Cowboy Hall of Fame in Oklahoma, which is billed as a journey through the Old West. It is a place where visitors can experience a typical 19th-century frontier town—by walking the "streets" and looking at the building façades "filled with authentic . . . artifacts." The Hall of Fame also offers visitors the opportunity to participate in special events, such as the Cowboy Poetry Gathering and the Annual Chuckwagon Gathering. For those who wish to leave with a tangible piece of frontier history, the museum has a gift shop called, appropriately, Trappings of the West.

Such renderings of the past, sentimentalized and commodified for mainstream America, emphasize the significance of the cowboy as both masculine figure and as hero. Indeed, Michael Kimmel (1996) wryly observes, "The cowboy occupies an important place in American cultural history: He is America's contribution to the world's stock of mythic heroes" (p. 148; see also Hine & Bingham, 1972; Spence, 1966).

Central to the perpetuation of the myths and images of the Western frontier is the modern media. While the cultural project of manufacturing images of the West has a long history and has included written work, performance, and the visual arts, film and television have broadcast narratives about the pioneering days in a consistent process of production. The contours of the stories may change and the protagonists may vary, along with the extreme nature of their deeds, but the ideological underpinnings of these representations remain firmly in place. For example, the landscape is frequently represented as a site of renewal and of transformation, a place separate from the effete influences of the East (Mitchell, 1996; Tompkins, 1992).

Although the Western as a film genre has been both adaptable and flexible, its trajectory has followed some well-trod paths. For example, during the 1950s, Westerns were preoccupied with the biological requirements of manliness. In the 1960s, Westerns became more violent (Mitchell, 1996), as illustrated by the films of Sam Peckinpah, in which violence itself occupies center stage (see Chapter 3).

Westerns typically problematize a series of issues: progress, "envisioned as a passing of frontiers"; honor, "defined in a context of social expediency"; law and order, "enacted in a conflict of vengeance and social control"; and violence and "what it means to be a man, as aging victim of progress, embodiment of honor, champion of justice in an unjust world" (Mitchell, 1996, p. 3). Of all of the problems dealt with by the Western, masculinity is the most perplexing riddle nestled within the narrative. The Western novel and film have been described as "phallic discourses" taken to an extreme—as places where "men gaze at each other, pump bullets into each other's bodies, and lust after women" (Horrocks, 1995, p. 56).

Furthermore, the overt meanings of the Western are about law and order, patriarchal and colonizing law writ large on the male hero. They are also about violence—even "regeneration through violence" (Horrocks, 1995, p. 77)—and, of course, about death. Indeed, death is pivotal to the discourse of the Western. Horrocks (1995) notes that, here, "we find a worship of death, an eroticism around death, that is both disorderly and exciting" (p. 81). The covert meanings of the Western are concerned with men's capacity for love, men's suffering, and defiance of middle-class values. Horrocks claims that the male suffering depicted in some Westerns could be regarded as symbolic, representing the injury inflicted on men in patriarchal society. He further claims that this view is fraught with tension because it conflicts with the orthodox view that women are, rightfully, the suffering victims.

Westerns, according to Horrocks (1995), explore the contradictions in mainstream American masculinity and their alterations over time; they examine, for example, the expectation that men be "hard" or "tough," but remain within the confines of the law. We can thus see the changes in the depiction of masculinity in the post–World War II Westerns: Economic imperialism is often questioned, and the surfeit of masculine behaviors required in an earlier era is no longer seen as relevant.

At the same time, however, Westerns articulate a particular masculine ethos—one in which injury to the male body is an important and meaningful part of the narrative. Mitchell (1996) argues that male bodies are shown being whipped, beaten, flogged, and shot precisely so that they can be shown convalescing and recovering. It is the motif of rehabilitation that establishes the validity of masculine identity: Once recovered, men, in Western narratives, can maintain a strong, gendered presence. This idea is based on what Mitchell calls the "double logic of the male body visibly making itself, even as it needs to disappear *as a* body to ensure the achievement of masculinity" (p. 154). Masculinity is not simply a biological given, but must be asserted through the narrative as an achievement. As Mitchell notes,

> The frequency with which the [male] body is celebrated, then physically punished, only to convalesce, suggests something of the paradox involved in making true men out of biological men, taking their male bodies and distorting them beyond any apparent power of self-control, so that in the course of recuperating, and achieved masculinity that is at once physical and based on performance can be revealed. (p. 155)

The hero in the Western, more than any other genre, invites us to gaze upon his body. As we look, we see men in the process of fleshing out their identity, of finishing the creative process of self-construction. At the same time, we are encouraged to believe that all of this is unnecessary.

Paul Smith (1995) makes a similar point, claiming that, within the cultural productions of our phallocentric society, "masculinity is represented first of all as a particular nexus of pleasure," a pleasure produced through "a specific mode of objectifying and eroticizing the male body, and . . . fortified by a series of operations on that male body that, while they have the trappings of a resistance to the phallic law, are in fact designed to lead the male subject through a proving ground toward the empowered position that is represented in the Name of the Father" (p. 94).

Jane Tompkins (1992) asserts that Westerns are a masculine protest against feminine domesticity and the Christian sacrifice and reform celebrated in the late 19th-century woman's novel. Westerns, in Tompkins's view, can be seen as a counterpoint to the emotional sensibilities of this literature and also as an attempt to deny, or even eradicate, femininity in American popular culture. The novels of Western writers such as Zane Grey, Owen Wister, and others, and the film genre that evolved out of these work are thus, according to Tompkins, an expression of the attempt by American men to take back their manhood "from the Christian women who [had] been holding it in thrall" (p. 33). The Western, then, is principally about "men's fear of losing their mastery, and hence their identity" (Tompkins, 1992, p. 45); furthermore, the Western, as a cultural formula, "tirelessly reinvents" masculine identity as antithetical to the feminine values of mannered society.

We could conclude that the Western is concerned with the creation of an imaginary social space in which women are defined as a hindrance (or even as redundant), and in which talk, negotiation, and introspection are viewed as dangerous feminine practices. Moreover, violence is understood as integral to the Western; it tests the limits of masculine endurance, highlighting masculine prowess and bravery. Indeed, "the hero is *so right* (that is, so wronged) that he can kill with impunity," notes Tompkins (p. 229), and "vengeance, by the time it arrives, feels biologically necessary" (p. 228). In the Western, masculinity is protected from, and safeguarded against, the corrosive and polluting influence of femininity.

Warrior Spectacles:
Masculinity on Show

The only real thing was fighting. (You couldn't be a man without fighting, and being a man was the only way of being alive). When there is no more fighting, no more being a man, life ceases and everything (the man, the world) becomes a pulp.

—*Klaus Theweleit*

The war film encompasses a number of genres. Among them is the combat film, which explores themes such as nationalism, heroism, individual and collective morality, and the futility of war. The combat film, of necessity, depicts power relations between groups of men, struggle and resistance within groups of men, and the physical and psychological consequences of war. The combat film also negotiates a path between mythmaking and historical representation.

The combat film is a quintessential American genre. Its origins are in the infantry films of the World War I period. However, it was during World War II and the period thereafter that the combat film emerged as a genre in its own right. The combat film continues to be very popular in the post-Vietnam era.

The films made in the wake of World War I contained messages about the desecration of war: the waste of youth, the terrible injuries, the heavy death toll. Films such as *The Big Parade* (1925) and *What Price Glory?* (1926) were strongly pacifist. These post-war films also mapped out the identity of the professional soldier even as they emphasized the iconography of war: weapons, uniforms, and combat paraphernalia.

During World War II, the combat film was transformed into a cultural product with an ideological orientation. The films opened a narrative space for the dramatization of real events, and provided the audience with an opportunity to experience vicariously aspects of real combat. The reasons for attacking other nations, or defending our own, were important in these films, and the values and behaviors of the individual and the nation were, thus, bound together in a moral cohesion. In films such as *They Were Expendable* (1945) and *A Walk in the Sun* (1946), the idea of home provided the soldiers with a rationale to fight.

Women made occasional appearances in combat films during this time, usually as nurses (as in *They Were Expendable*), or during dream sequences or flashbacks. Women symbolized domesticity—home and family—and were usually included in the roles of wives and mothers. The film *A Walk in the Sun* was unusual because it focused on the individual emotions of the men and the sympathy felt for a commander who behaved in a stereotypically feminine way at a crucial moment. In the film, however, the mythologizing of death—the denial of mortality and the eulogizing of the bravery of the ordinary soldier—negated the fact that feminine qualities were admitted into the body of fighting men.

World War II combat films tended to represent masculinity in an unproblematic manner. The male subjects in the film were shown as actively engaged in warfare, as omniscient, as moving across physical terrain, and as disengaged from women as romantic partners (see Basinger, 1986). In post–World War II combat films, heroism was supplanted by the demands of conflict and war; duty and compassion also played a part, as did authoritarianism and the fear of responsibility. The moral purpose of these films was neither clear-cut nor direct; rather, they portrayed an equivocal and confused morality. Men in such films as *The Sands of Iwo Jima* (1949), *Fixed Bayonets* (1951), and *The Bridge on the River Kwai* (1957) struggled and did not always succeed in their individual and collective mission.[5]

With the advent of the post-Vietnam combat film, the presence of women assumed new significance. Furthermore, as we see below, the warrior mythology was reaffirmed in these films, and the confrontation with death was renewed as a rite of passage that validated masculinity.

Post-Vietnam films, produced in the knowledge of defeat, have typically employed the narrative strategies of mythologization and displacement. The script of the Vietnam war was effectively rewritten in films such as those in the *Rambo* series (1982, 1985, 1988), in which the eponymous hero immerses himself in the carnage of war but, nevertheless, emerges triumphant. In *The Deer Hunter* (1978) and *Apocalypse Now* (1979), the traumas of a humiliating loss were displaced by a transcendent interaction between the white culture of the West and the alien and exotic Other in the guise of the Vietnamese (Jeffords, 1990).[6]

Popular films produced about the Vietnam experience can also be understood as part of a larger cultural project, what Susan Jeffords (1989) has called "the remasculinization of America." Jeffords claims that "gender is the matrix through which Vietnam [can be] read, interpreted, and reframed in dominant American culture" (p. 53; see also Traube, 1992). This viewing of Vietnam through the lens of gender reflects the ways in which war itself provides an opportunity for the reconstitution and reassertion of formations of masculinity. Indeed, the "theater of war" may be regarded as the space in which masculinities are defined and performed anew, and in which the parameters of gender relations in civil society are articulated.

Indeed, the war zone is the discursive arena in which sexual difference is reaffirmed—in which elements associated with femaleness (bodies/desire) are, paradoxically, celebrated, denied, and disavowed. Thus Jeffords (1989) refers to the technologizing of the male body in narratives (and experience) of Vietnam, a maneuver that emphasizes the power and invincibility of the male body.

The body is clearly central to the discourses of war; it is around the body that gendered ideas about warfare are constructed. War, with its explicit and visceral violence, is often viewed as equivalent to the physical and psychic ordeal of childbirth. William Broyles, Jr., declared that "war was an initiation into the power of life and death. Women touch that power at the moment of birth; men on the edge of death" (quoted in Jeffords, 1989, p. 89). Ironically, representations of the Vietnam War in contemporary films often invoke a parturient masculinity; male characters in these films appropriate female reproductive functions. In these narratives, the male body is figured as life-giving as well as death-defying. The struggle over life and death inherent in warfare necessitates the radical separation of the "clean and proper" male body from the "mire" of the female body (see Theweleit, 1987); it also negates the reproductive capability of the female body, attaching these attributes to the warring male body—a body facing a crisis of transformation. Jeffords (1989) notes of these Vietnam narratives, "men do not *become* women in these narratives, they occupy them" (p. 105).

This crisis of bodily transformation assumes other forms. War stories in popular culture also address deeply held fears and anxieties about the literal loss of masculinity in warfare, signified by various degrees of castration or impotence resulting from injury. Peter Lehman (1993) states, "War, where men go to prove and affirm their masculinity, is perhaps not surprisingly also a literary and cinematic site of a great deal of anxiety precisely about losing that masculinity" (p. 71).[7] This observation is based on the distinction, drawn by Lehman (1993), between the penis and the phallus. He assumes that the latter "dominates, restricts, prohibits, and controls representations of the male body," and produces, in men, strong feelings of alienation from the body. Lehman cites the dramatic scene in the film *Born on the Fourth of July* (1989), in which the character Ron Kovick (played by Tom Cruise) learns of his paralysis, and immediately asks the doctor if he will be able to father a child. When the doctor replies in the negative, Ron is shattered.

Although such injuries are clearly a reality of war, the implications of these woundings are rarely depicted in Hollywood cinema. Here, the imperative of projecting the image of the technologized and invincible male body is in the ascendant. Indeed, Jeffords (1994) argues that Hollywood cinema responded to the political exigencies of the Reagan era with the production of images of hegemonic masculinity. While this has been a project of the American entertainment industry since at least the 1960s, Jeffords claims that the election of Ronald Reagan heralded the return of the "physical king" to the political stage. In the Reagan era, dominant constructions of masculinity dictated that assertiveness, toughness, decisiveness, and, when necessary, the capacity for violence should be at the core of what it means to be a man. This was depicted unequivocally in the action-adventure dramas of the 1980s, in which "heroism, individualism, and bodily integrity" were centered in the male body (Jeffords, 1994, p. 148).[8] Examples of this include the *Robocop* series (1987, 1990).

Films made subsequent to this wave of tales about machinelike heroes have tended, according to Jeffords (1993, 1994), to carry messages about men's capacity to experience emotional pain. These more recent portrayals, however, are contextualized within the narrative tensions between the utopian and dystopian discourses of society. Doyen (1996) observes that, in these cinematic dystopian depictions, the hero "through fearless action . . . still redeems and proves himself, but his victory is now dubiously impermanent and is taken away from him at the start of every sequel. . . . The modern hero is at war not just with the villains, but with a hostile society, which is repressive and dehumanizing." Despite these broader considerations, the image of the hard body persists. Jeffords (1994) states,

> The hard body has remained a theme that epitomizes the national imaginary. . . . [T]he hard body continues, in the post-Reagan, post–Cold War era, to find the national models of masculinity conveyed by some of Hollywood's most successful films. They have shown their resiliency as models because they appear to critique, at times even to reject, their earlier versions, only to renarrate them in ways more complex and more intimately woven into the fabric of American culture. (pp. 192-193)

The hard masculine body—taut with a musculature that resembles armor or mechanized in a simulation of the male form—reached its zenith in cinematic representations of combat. From World War II onward, depictions of men at war increasingly focused on the male body as the bearer of masculine meanings. The robotic masculinity still paraded in films such as *Judge Dredd* perpetuates and extends the crisis over gender relations in evidence at the close of World War II.

Ambiguous Masculinities:
Tough Guys and Crime Fighters

> In this dark world of crime, violence, and annihilation, nothing is certain. . . . Characters appear and disappear. . . . Violence and moral ambiguity, as well as murky character and action, create the

effect . . . [that] the spectator experience[s] what these desperate
characters feel: anguish and insecurity.

—*R. Barton Palmer*

Other cinematic genres can also be regarded, at least in part, as a
response to the disillusionment, alienation, and confusion produced
by large-scale military conflict. *Film noir,* which emerged in the early
1940s and was characterized, according to some critics, by "disruptions to the stylistic, narrative and generic norms of the 'classical' system of film-making" (Krutnik, 1991, p. x), is a case in point. Furthermore, *film noir* frequently offered "an engagement with problematic,
even illicit, potentialities within masculine identity" (Krutnik, 1991,
p. xiii). This is not surprising, as the topics dealt with in these films
often revolved around urban crime and corruption—quintessential
masculine activities (see Christopher, 1997; Forman, 1994; Martin,
1997; Muller, 1998; Server, Gorman, & Greenberg, 1998).

Film noir cannot easily be defined or categorized. Films in this
tradition capture a mood or an ambience, and draw on an eclectic
range of cinematic ideas and techniques. The thematic and stylistic
trends in *film noir* reflected the wider social criticism of moral and
sexual values in postwar American society. They also constituted an
acknowledgment of the significance of psychological aspects of char-
acterization, and expressed a fascination with sexuality, especially
predatory female sexuality. From a technical viewpoint, these films
often adopted the style of *chiaroscuro* visualization (see Krutnik,
1991).

Film noir can be divided into various stages. The early to mid-
1940s produced films in which the lead male character was alienated
and anxious, and in which events were overlaid by a dark, often foreboding, atmosphere. In many of these films, the male protagonist's
voice was privileged, and there was an attempt to contain and control
the excesses of sexual energy that threatened to unravel the social
order. The authority of the male protagonist, however, was often
undermined, and tensions were often introduced between loyalty to
other males and attraction to alluring and dangerous women.

The postwar years saw the production of many films that sprang
from the disruptions associated with returning veterans, the impending nuclear threat, the Cold War, anticommunist propaganda, and the
Korean conflict. Male protagonists in films of this period were often
violent and possessed of a hard-edged sexuality.

The 1950s witnessed the beginning of a decline in the utilization
of *noir* themes and techniques. Since this time, *noir* conventions have

been invoked to conjure a specific tone or create a milieu, as, for example, in *Chinatown* (1974), *Night Moves* (1975), and *Cop* (1987). However, the cultural context that made *film noir* possible—and even necessary—during the 1940s has altered radically in the last fifty years (see Crowther, 1988; Morrison, 1988; Thomas, 1988; Trelotte, 1989; Tuska, 1994).

It is the classic *film noir* thrillers from the 1940s that articulated vivid and highly delineated portraits of masculinity. In these "hard-boiled" crime and detective films, the male subject was located at the center of the narrative, and female subjects were positioned as erotic but marginal figures. Women in these films were highly sexualized. Krutnik (1991) claims that, "generally in the *noir* thriller, this kind of sexual objectification of the woman as body is a common strategy, occurring in a highly formalized and fetishistic manner and serving to deny the woman a subjective centering within the text" (p. 62). Frequently, the female protagonists were femmes fatales (see Allen, 1983; Bade, 1979; Dijkstra, 1996).

The introduction of the femme fatale into the *noir* thrillers permitted Hollywood to explore, in some detail, the topos of the manipulative, devious, and desiring woman (see Doane, 1991). This femme fatale character was both sought after and feared in the narrative (Maxfield, 1996), and was also censured (see Staiger, 1995). Christine Gledhill (1978) has noted that these female characters were subjected to intensive masculine scrutiny, followed by disapproval and punishment. Pam Cook (1978) has suggested that *film noir* thrillers were derived from the profound ambivalence about gender relations and the gender order in postwar America. The dislocation of cultural arrangements as a consequence of men's return from the war, women's entry into the workplace, and the subsequent rise in competence, skill, and ability in the previously subordinated female population, challenged the pre-war social order. As Krutnik (1991) argues,

> The postwar era required a reconstruction of cultural priorities, and one can see the postwar *noir* "tough" thrillers as being one of the principal means by which Hollywood, in its role as a cultural institution, sought to tackle such a project, by focusing attention upon the problems attending to the (re)definition of masculine identity and masculine role. (p. 64)

Hence the hard-boiled crime and detective thrillers emphasized the masculine through language (epigrammatic and controlled speech) and through action (tough, decisive, and often violent behaviors).

These films, according to Krutnik, sought to reorder "disruptions to and schisms in masculine identity" (p. 164). They were, ostensibly, consolatory tales.

Krutnik also argues that the ideological work of reconstructing beliefs and attitudes toward gender and power was extremely difficult and not always convincing. The continued popularity (and, sometimes, cult status) enjoyed by these films, however, is a testament to their cultural relevance today. The images of masculinity and femininity contained in these films resonate with the dominant constructions of gender in contemporary society. Witness, for example, the recent success of the droll, flashy, and violent film *L.A. Confidential* (1997), with its postmodern spin on the *noir* tradition.

Indeed, we should be aware that the three film genres examined here—the Western, the combat movie, and *film noir*—are interrelated in terms of their origins, especially Westerns and *film noir* (see Slotkin, 1992), and their explicit and implicit meanings regarding gender, power, violence, and the social order.

Masquerading: Icons of Masculinity

> Gender is a symbolic representation perceived in culture as a mimetic one; it always involves some element of masquerade.
>
> —*Steve Cohan*

As we have seen, it has been argued that masculinity is composed of acts, gestures, and enactments. Furthermore, the identity or essence that these public behaviors purport to represent might be regarded as a fabrication "manufactured and sustained through corporeal signs and other discursive means" (Butler, 1990, p. 136). This anti-essentialist view of the self implies that masculinity is performative—that gender (masculinity and femininity) is articulated and renewed in the interactions that occur between people. Gender is thus understood as public, visible, and changeable.

I have attempted to show, in this chapter, that the performative aspects of masculinity, concerned with exhibition and transaction, are mirrored on the screen. In film, or any public performance, whether rehearsed or spontaneous, masculinity becomes a corporeal display; it unfolds, as action, as violence, as omniscience, in a cascade of arrest-

ing images.[9] Holmund (1993) has written of the doubling of masculinity in some cinematic representations, suggesting that masculinity is
a "multiple masquerade" (p. 224).[10] Bingham (1994) claims that we
can see the "discontinuities of fabricated roles" and the "fragmentation that makes unitary masculinity a difficult—even impossible—
construction to maintain" if we look closely at the film careers and
public personas of celebrated male stars (p. 19).[11]

Bingham further argues that hegemonic (white, middle class) masculinity has been challenged and subverted in film. This has happened
more frequently since the fall of the studio system in Hollywood:
"Such subversions," according to Bingham, "take place in cycles—and
in different corners of an increasingly fragmented movie industry in
different eras" (p. 4).

According to Bingham (1994), we can interrogate the ruptured
surface that is masculinity as it is continually performed (both on and
off screen) by looking at the careers of such actors as James Stewart,
Jack Nicholson, and Clint Eastwood. Each of these actors, in their
performances, contradicts our deeply held cultural expectations that
gender identity is stable, fixed, and coherent. Stewart often manifested an "enraptured gaze" (p. 30), a "receptive look" (p. 31), often
combined with an open mouth, which gave him an ambiguous sexuality. Nicholson places great emphasis on anxiety-laden role-playing;
facial expressions become an exaggerated mask for emotions, an
ironic representation born of the epic acting tradition. Eastwood
evinces a kind of minimalism, a pastiche of frontier ideals and expres-
sionless heroics. Bingham maintains that this screen persona developed out of a recognition that "the foundations of masculine identity
had been lost and needed to be massively reconstructed and re-
performed" (p. 174). Charting the evolution of the roles played by
Eastwood, Bingham concludes that the film *Unforgiven* (1992) shifts
the threat to stability from the Other to the white male, undermining
his centrality in the narrative.

Specific films also play with these renegotiations around gender.
The recent British film *The Crying Game* (1993) has generated considerable controversy (see Simpson, 1994). Some believe the film invites
the audience to imagine gender disconnected from biology. Bordo
(1996) suggests that one scene in which a "female" character is shown
to have a penis is subversive to the degree that we, the audience, per-
sist with our original assumption that the character is a woman.
According to Bordo, the persistence of this belief undermines the
essentialist and masculinist readings of gender, which regard the pos-

session of a penis as the critical arbiter of maleness and, of course, of masculinity.[12] The film also features a male lead who is emotionally labile and open; a character described by Bordo as "probably the least phallic hero the screen has seen" (p. 302). Bordo insists that this character presents itself "not only as a revisioning of masculinity but as indictment of modern subjectivity" (p. 302).

One film that specifically explores the politics of masculinity and dominant schemas of representation is another British film, *The Full Monty* (1997). This film details the fortunes of six unemployed men "with nothing to lose" living in Sheffield, in the gray heart of industrial England. The six men include a middle-aged manager who cannot tell his wife that he has been made redundant (at least not until after their possessions are repossessed); an aging black man who can still perform a mean "funky chicken" dance; a young "lunchbox" (i.e., a well-endowed male) who can neither sing nor dance (and who may be gay); a temporarily suicidal young man who lives with his disabled, dying mother; and a thirty-something pair, one overweight and devoid of confidence, and the other a separated father behind in his child maintenance. This odd assortment of men elect to perform a one-night strip show, in which they go "the full monty"—that is, in which they strip completely. In this theatrical event, they expose their ordinary bodies (with one exception) to the local, mainly female, audience. They manage, in so doing, to turn adversity into advantage; their show is a triumph for a group of socially and economically redundant men. In preparing to stage their show, the men explore the construction of the sexualized and objectified body, and confront their own fears and inadequacies about their sexuality and the masculine status of their bodies. The film explores the pathos of the father denied access to his son and the emerging bond between generations of men. It is amusing, entertaining, and poignant.

What is the significance of these representations? I believe it is possible to argue that imagining and visualizing masculinities is a continuous and perpetual political process arising in response to social crises that imply changes to the gender order. Such processes are required to maintain the equilibrium within the structures and institutions of society, and to provide vehicles for the socialization of boys. Imagining and visualizing, through photographs, film, and video, produces maps of the masculine.

But what are these perceived crises within the gender order? Below, I explore the dimensions and scope of these crises, particularly as they affect masculinity.

The Felt Crisis of Masculinity

There seems to be a crisis of masculinities initiated through the feminist questioning of traditional forms of male power and superiority that have been structured into the very terms of an Enlightenment vision of modernity.

—*Victor Jeleniewski Seidler*

What is called the masculinity crisis involves the collapse of a common code for male role behavior and the intensification of gender role strain. . . . It also interacts in complex ways with what I have elsewhere termed the crisis of connection between men and women.

—*Ronald F. Levant*

It has been suggested that masculinity itself is in crisis. It has further been suggested that masculinity should be "reframed" (Betcher & Pollack, 1993), "revisioned" (Kupers, 1993), "redefined" (Kimmel, 1995), or "reconstructed" (Levant & Kopecky, 1995). It has even been suggested that we need to "end manhood" (Stoltenberg, 1993).

Ronald Levant (1996) claims that this felt crisis of masculinity takes several forms: the loss of the role of good provider; the inadequacy of the role of good family man, and its failure to replace the good provider role; the trend for heterosexual relationships to revert to stereotypical roles; and the patterns and dynamics of divorce. Levant claims that white, middle-class males are disproportionately affected by the dimensions and scope of this crisis. Not surprisingly, he notes the emergence of the phenomenon of the "angry white male" and the advent of organized public rallies involving men, such as the Promise Keepers.

Nowhere has the representation of the angry white male been so clearly articulated as in the movie *Falling Down* (1993). This ambiguously titled film portrayed the passage of a middle-class man, played by Michael Douglas, from success, self-control, and self-respect to failure, rage, and violence. Levant (1996) effectively describes the narrative of the film well when he states,

Divorced, restricted from seeing his child, and unemployed, [the film's protagonist] was unable to look at himself and examine the sources of his arrogant and abusive behavior. Instead, he focused on the loss of his (imagined) picture-perfect white English-speaking world to immigration, civic corruption, and urban decay, and began a one-day killing spree, taking out his venom on the ethnic minority people he encountered as he attempted an uninvited and very unwelcome "homecoming" to his wife and child.

Levant maintains that the economic restructuring of the workforce, which has led to employment instability and the disappearance of many manufacturing jobs, has brought many formerly privileged men closer to the experiences of working-class men. Consequently, white, middle-class men can no longer expect to reign supreme as economic providers for the family. A significant proportion of these men are now located in dual-career (or dual-job) families in which two incomes are imperative for maintaining an appropriate standard of living.

According to some commentators, these economic losses have fuelled the development of a climate of anger and hate. Joel Dyer (1998) argues that the devastation of the American farm economy, which has resulted in an unprecedented number of farm foreclosures, has threatened the very identity of those still left on the land. According to Dyer, this sowed the seeds of one of the worst terrorist incidents in the United States: the bombing of the Murrah Federal Building in Oklahoma City in April, 1995. Indeed, Dyer maintains that the antigovernment militia groups, many of which are dedicated to seceding from the United States and establishing alternative legal and administrative systems, have fed on the high levels of hostility toward the federal government in the farm sector.

This politics of hate and violence is the outcome, at least in part, of the growing gap between the rich and the poor in the United States. Arguably, it is also the expression of the frustrations experienced by impoverished males, now landless, devoid of identity and, in many cases, without reasonable income (see Eisenstein, 1997).

Other issues, aside from those of work and family, have propelled masculinity into the limelight. These issues include the impact of feminism and the women's movement. David Buchbinder (1992), writing in the Australian context, points to the unsettling and disturbing effects that the claims and, indeed, achievements of feminism with regard to equality and justice have had: Received masculine views and behaviors have become problematized, and individual men have sometimes felt compelled to justify or rationalize that which previously seemed natural or inevitable. This has made some men fearful, defensive, confused, and angry. Buchbinder refers to men's experience as "being embattled by feminism" (p. 137).

Other issues that have shaken the foundation of the prevailing constructions of masculinity include the advent of HIV/AIDS and the visibility accorded the gay men's movement. Both of these phenomena have, according to Buchbinder, radically affected male subjectivity, especially in the arena of sexuality and desire. The striving, hydraulic model of masculine sexuality so valorized in Western society has been exposed to examination and criticism. Ironically, it has become associated with disease, bodily decay, and death. Furthermore, the erotic relations between men—even avowed heterosexual men—have also become visible, calling into question the binary division between heterosexual and homosexual identifications.

Victor Jeleniewski Seidler (1997) writes of men's collective anxiety in the wake of social change:

> In the West heterosexual men have responded to the challenges of feminism and gay liberation in different ways, but they have left men feeling uncertain and confused about what it means "to be a man" as we approach the millennium. (p. 1)

What might this mean for a hierarchically organized gender order in which hegemonic styles of masculinity are focused on the possession of economic and social power, and in which heterosexuality is privileged? We have already seen how the threatened collapse of distinct but related categories provokes a crisis. Here, we are perhaps witnessing a crisis *within* the construct of masculinity, rather than a crisis between the masculine and the feminine. However, as we have seen, a crisis within constructions of masculinity has the potential to affect constructions of femininity.

The Politics of Masculinity

As we saw in Chapter 4, we can no longer speak of masculinity in singular terms in Western society. Instead, masculinities are now viewed as multiple or plural, with a number of different forms of masculinity coexisting in society at any one time. Connell (1995) argued that masculinities vary along a number of dimensions relating to power, privilege, and entitlement. Hegemonic or dominant masculinity embraces heterosexuality, homosociality (i.e., a preference for male groups), aggression, hierarchy, and competition.

The opportunity and capacity to dominate Others is integral to hegemonic masculinity. The use of force and violence is viewed as one of the instruments of power and as one of the modes of behavior by which hierarchy is perpetuated in society. Consequently, violence—

against gay men and women—is implicated within hegemonic masculinity. Subordinated masculinities, on the other hand, are central to the social experiences of gay men, men from non-English speaking backgrounds or other marginalized groups. Subordinated masculinities may still hinge on a strategy, albeit less effective, of excluding or denying social power to women.

The advent of a second-wave women's movement in the 1960s and 1970s, focusing on the frequency of sexual and other violence against women, threw the spotlight on hegemonic masculinity and its recourse to force. Connell (1997) notes that the association between violent actions and hegemonic masculinity is generally not problematized unless a crisis arises. In these circumstances, a formidable defense of hegemonic masculinity is mounted. We might call this a "backlash" politics (Connell, 1997). Connell (1995) refers to the institutional aspects of this defense when he notes,

> The consequences of this defense are not just the slowing down or turning back of gender change. . . . The consequences are also found in long-term trends in the institutional order that hegemonic masculinity dominates. These trends include the growing destructiveness of military technology (not the least the spread of nuclear weapons), the long-term degradation of the environment and the increase of economic inequality on a world scale. (p. 216)

Recognizing different, but coexistent, forms of masculinity helps to account for the wide range of responses to the contemporary crises affecting men and the masculine in Western society. It also helps to explain the emergence of a masculinity politics expressed in the idea of a men's movement. Some aspects of this movement are grounded in the politics of hegemonic masculinity; other aspects are based in the politics of subordinated masculinities. We might think here of the gay men's movement, or the profeminist movement dedicated to ending violence against women (see Clatterbaugh, 1997; Dench, 1996; Kimmel, 1995; Kimmel & Kaufman, 1994; Messner, 1997; Schwalbe, 1996; Seidler, 1997).

Risky Strategies

We began by noting that the desire to represent masculinity was accompanied by the expansion of the public domain in the 19th century and an increase in men's power within it. This desire was, of course, boosted by the invention of technologies of the visual.

Given that some now suggest that the public domain is synonymous with the media (see John Hartley, 1992), we can predict that images of masculinity will continue to saturate the entertainment and news media. Perceived crises in the gender order will continue to provoke an intensification of strategies of masculinization. *Judge Dredd* is undoubtedly an attempt to reassert dominant masculine values and to locate these in an aesthetic of hard, impenetrable (male) bodies remade in action-packed spectacles of difference. The risk in producing such extreme displays of masculine bravado is that they will then be viewed as parody; the performance will be revealed as excessive and ridiculous. Of course, women's skepticism about the masculine masquerade is nothing new. But will men be convinced by their own performance? Will acting be seen as mere dissimulation, and will the fabrications of gender be exposed as a sham? We can only wait and see.

Notes

1. The eponymous "lads" are the mainstay of Simon Nye's British comic success *Men Behaving Badly*, which has generated a huge international television audience and spawned an unsuccessful and heavily censored American imitation.

2. Of course, corporealizing the Other is not a strategy reserved for African Americans but has been consistently applied to women and socially marginal groups (see Adams & Donovan, 1995).

3. The frontier shapes American foreign policy and the deployment of U.S. power. Megan Shaw (1996) describes the way in which Vietnam was constructed in the American popular imagination and military consciousness as a new frontier. Shaw notes that the "mythic symbolism of the jungle . . worked on the American public to create an easily marketable mystique for the war. As lavishly detailed in numerous Hollywood productions, the Asian jungle is, for the American male, the last frontier of this world."

Of course, other frontiers have also been invented. Space, in particular, offers rich possibilities for frontier travel. This is so, irrespective of whether such travel (or exploration) occurs under the auspices of government funded scientific research or the mass-mediated entertainment industry. In either case, the imperial self prevails (see Fulton, 1994).

4. Michael Kimmel (1996) provides us with an insight into the seductiveness of this turn to nostalgia for the western frontier. He refers to the loss of certainty and predictability for American men: "As we face a new century, American men remain bewildered by the sea changes of our culture, besieged by the forces of reform, and bereft by the emotional impoverishment of our lives. For straight white middle-class men a virtual siege mentality has set in. *The frontier is gone* [italics added] and competition in the global marketplace is keener than ever" (p. 330).

5. Interestingly, this postwar period has been identified as a time of "phallic crisis." William Stern (1995) claims that

the art of physique photography . . . boomed in the 1950s, and while the
muscle men depicted often exhibited the hyper-masculinity so de rigueur in a

sissy-fearing society, they did so in a perverse way: implicitly critiquing the legitimation of certain forms of display (i.e., the sexualized and commodified female form).

6. For a discussion of Vietnam and the American imaginary, see the following sources: Adair (1981), Auster and Quart (1988), Devine (1995), Dittmar and Michaud (1990), Gilman and Smith (1990), Martin (1993), and Searle (1988).

7. This dilemma has its parallel in everyday life. Lake and Damousi (1995) acknowledge the significance of war, and its aftermath, for men:

> In wars men could attain heroism, but they might also be plunged into a crisis of masculinity as they in some way or other failed to measure up to the impossible standards. And, paradoxically, wars could destroy the very manhood they were meant to prove so that postwar repatriation policies were necessarily gendered restorative strategies, designed to make old soldiers feel like men again. (p. 5)

8. Jeffords (1994) notes that such figurations of the body are coded in terms of race as well as gender. She astutely observes that "masculinity is defined in and through the white male body and against the racially marked male body" (p. 148).

9. We might also think of dance here. Dance is an arena in which the dominant constructions of masculinity have been strongly contested. Dance can play with the limits of masculine behavior, the role of the viewer or spectator, and the idea of touch or bodily contact and its relationship to danger (see Burt, 1995).

10. The idea of gender as a masquerade was first posited by the psychoanalyst Joan Riviere in 1929. Riviere argued that femininity was essentially a mask or a façade erected to distract from or deny the absence of the phallus (see Riviere, 1986). More recently, the notion of femininity as a masquerade has been taken up by feminist film theorists and cultural studies scholars (see, for example, Fletcher, 1988; Heath, 1986).

However, to perceive masculinity as a masquerade is heretical to some. As Harry Brod (1995) explains,

> The masculine self has traditionally been held to be inherently opposed to the kind of deceit and dissembling characteristic of the masquerade. . . . Like the American cowboy, "real" men embody the primitive, unadorned, self-evident, natural truths of the world, not the effete pretences of urban dandies twirling about at a masquerade ball. (p. 13)

11. Steve Cohan (1995) notes that the

> understanding of a gender masquerade is especially pertinent to cinema because of its institutional reliance upon stardom. . . . In their performance of gender types, Hollywood stars . . . cross seemingly rigid binarized categories, such as the oppositions seeming/posing, natural/artificial, sincere/deceptive, which themselves carry a secondary gender inflection of masculine/feminine. (p. 58)

12. For an alternative reading of this film, see Simpson (1994).

References

Adair, G. (1981). *Vietnam and film: From the Green Berets to* Apocalypse Now. New York: Praeger.

Adams, C., & Donovan, J. (Eds.). (1995). *Animals and women: Feminist theoretical explorations.* Durham, NC: Duke University Press.

Allen, T. (1994). *The invention of the white race, Vol. 1: Racial oppression and social control.* London: Verso.

Allen, V. (1983). *The femme fatale: Erotic icon.* Troy, NJ: Whitson.

Auster, A., & Quart, L. (1988). *How the world was remembered: Hollywood and Vietnam.* New York: Praeger.

Bade, P. (1979). *Femme fatale: Images of evil and fascinating women.* New York: Mayflower.

Basinger, J. (1986). *The World War II combat film: Anatomy of a genre.* New York: Columbia University Press.

Berry, V., & Manning-Miller, C. (Eds.). (1996). *Mediated messages and African-American culture: Contemporary issues.* Thousand Oaks, CA: Sage.

Betcher, W., & Pollack, W. S. (1993). *In a time of fallen heroes: The recreation of masculinity.* New York: Atheneum.

Bingham, D. (1994). *Acting male: Masculinities in the films of James Stewart, Jack Nicholson, and Clint Eastwood.* New Brunswick, NJ: Rutgers University Press.

Bogle, D. (1994). *Toms, coons, mulattos, mammies, and bucks: An interpretive history of Blacks in American films.* New York: Continuum.

Bordo, S. (1996). Reading the male body. In L. Goldstein (Ed.), *The male body: Features, destinies, exposures* (pp. 265-306). Ann Arbor, MI: University of Michigan Press.

Brod, H. (1995). Masking a masquerade. In A. Perchuk & H. Posner (Eds.), *The masculine masquerade: Masculinity and representation* (pp. 13-20). Cambridge, MA: MIT Press.

Buchbinder, D. (1992). Editorial. *Southern Review, 25,*(2), 135-140.

Burt, R. (1995). *The male dancer: Bodies, spectacle, sexualities.* London: Routledge.

Butler, J. (1990). *Gender trouble: Feminism and the subversion of identity.* New York: Routledge.

Christopher, N. (1997). *Somewhere in the night: Film noir and the American city.* New York: Free Press.

Clatterbaugh, K. (1997). *Contemporary perspectives on masculinity: Men, women, and politics in modern society* (2nd ed.). Boulder, CO: Westview.

Cohan, S. (1995). The spy in the gray flannel suit: Gender performance and the representation of masculinity in *North by Northwest.* In A. Perchuk & H. Posner (Eds.), *The masculine masquerade: Masculinity and representation* (pp. 43-62). Cambridge, MA: MIT Press.

Cohan, S. (1997). *Masked men: Masculinity and the movies in the fifties.* Bloomington, IN: Indiana University Press.

Cohan, S., & Hark, I. R. (1993). Introduction. In S. Cohan & I. R. Hark (Eds.), *Screening the male: Exploring masculinities in Hollywood cinema* (pp. 1-8). New York: Routledge.

Connell, R. (1987). *Gender and power: Society, the person, and sexual politics.* Cambridge, MA: Polity.

Connell, R. (1995). *Masculinities.* Sydney, Australia: Allen and Unwin.

Connell, R. (1997). Men, masculinities, and feminism. *Social Alternatives, 16,* 7-10.

Cook, P. (1978). Duplicity in *Mildred Pierce.* In E. A. Kepler (Ed.), *Women in film noir* (pp. 52-74). London: Routledge.

Cripps, T. (1993). *Slow fade to black: The Negro in American film.* New York: Oxford University Press.

Crowther, B. (1988). *Film noir: Reflection in a dark mirror.* London: Columbus.

Delgado, R., & Stefancic, J. (1995). Minority men, misery, and the marketplace of ideas. In M. Berger, B. Wallis, & S. Watson (Eds.), *Constructing masculinities* (pp. 210-220). New York: Routledge.

Dench, G. (1996). *Transforming men: Changing patterns of dependency and dominance in gender relations.* New Brunswick, NJ: Transaction Publishers.

Devine, J. (1995). *Vietnam at twenty-four frames a second: A critical and thematic analysis of over four hundred films about the Vietnam War.* Jefferson, NC: McFarland.

Diawara, M. (Ed.). (1993). *Black American cinema.* New York: Routledge.

Dijkstra, B. (1996). *Evil sisters: The threat of female sexuality and the cult of manhood.* New York: Knopf.

Dittmar, L., & Michaud, G. (Eds.). (1990). *From Hanoi to Hollywood: The Vietnam War in American film.* New Brunswick, NJ: Rutgers University Press.

Doane, M. (1991). *Femme fatales: Feminism, film theory, and psychoanalysis.* New York: Routledge.

Doane, M. (1987). Film and the masquerade: Theorizing the female spectator. *Screen, 3,* 74-88.

Doyen, E. (1996). Utopia and apocalypse: The cultural role of Hollywood cinema. *Work in Progress, 3*(2). Retrieved November 15, 1997 from the World Wide Web: http://www.mcs.net/~zupko/popcult.htm.

Dyer, J. (1998). *Harvest of rage.* Boulder, CO: Westview.

Eisenstein, Z. (1997). *Hatreds: Racialized and sexualized conflicts in the twenty-first century.* New York: Routledge.

Fletcher, J. (1988). Versions of masquerade. *Screen, 29,* 43-69.

Forman, J. (1994). Men's worst fears: Exploring troubled masculinity in Mickey Spillane and the paperback novel. *Masculinities, 2,* 37-45.

Fulton, V. (1994). An other frontier: Voyaging west with Mark Twain and *Star Trek*'s imperial subject. *Postmodern Culture, 4*(3). Retrieved September 9, 1996 from the World Wide Web: http://jefferson.village.virginia.edu/pmc.

Gilman, O., & Smith, L. (Eds.). (1990). *America rediscovered: Critical essays on literature and film of the Vietnam War.* New York: Garland.

Gledhill, C. (1978). *Klute* Part I: A contemporary film noir in feminist criticism. In A. E. Kaplan (Ed.), *Women in film noir* (pp. 16-34). London: British Film Institute.

Gray, H. (1995). Black masculinity and visual culture. *Callaloo, 18,* 401-404.

Guerrero, E. (1993). *Framing blackness: The African American heritage in film.* Philadelphia: Temple University Press.

Guerrero, E. (1995). The black man on our screens and the empty space in representation. *Callaloo, 18,* 395-400.

Hanke, R. (1990). Hegemonic masculinity in *Thirtysomething. Critical Studies in Communications, 7,* 231-248.

Hanke, R. (1992). Redesigning men: Hegemonic masculinity and transition. In S. Craig (Ed.), *Men, masculinity and the media* (pp. 185-189). Newbury Park, CA: Sage.

Harper, S. (1994). Subordinating masculinities/racializing masculinities: Writing white supremacist discourse on men's bodies. *Masculinities, 2,* 1-20.

Hartley, J. (1992). *The politics of pictures.* London: Routledge.

Hearn, J. (1992). *Men in the public eye.* London: Routledge.

Heath, S. (1986). Joan Riviere and the masquerade. In V. Burgin, J. Donald, & C. Kaplan (Eds.), *Formations of fantasy* (pp. 45-61). New York: Methuen.

Hine, R., & Bingham, E. (1972). *The American frontier: Readings and documents.* Boston: Little, Brown.

Holmund, C. (1993). Masculinity as multiple masquerade: The "mature" Stallone and the Stallone clone. In S. Cohen & I. R. Hark (Eds.), *Screening the male: Exploring masculinities in Hollywood cinema* (pp. 213-229). New York: Routledge.

hooks, b. (1994). Doing it for daddy. In M. Berger, B. Wallis, & S. Watson (Eds.), *Constructing masculinities* (pp. 98-106). New York: Routledge.

Horrocks, R. (1995). *Male myths and icons: Masculinity in popular culture.* London: Macmillan.

Jeffords, S. (1989). *The remasculinization of America: Gender and the Vietnam War.* Bloomington, IN: Indiana University Press.

Jeffords, S. (1990). Fathers: Gender and the Vietnam War. In L. Dittmar & G. Michaud (Eds.), *From Hanoi to Hollywood: The Vietnam War in American film* (pp. 202-215). New Brunswick, NJ: Rutgers University Press.

Jeffords, S. (1993). Can masculinity be terminated? In S. Cohan & I. R. Hark (Eds.), *Screening the male: Exploring masculinities in Hollywood cinema* (pp. 245-262). New York: Routledge.

Jeffords, S. (1994). *Hard bodies: Hollywood masculinity and the Reagan era.* New Brunswick, NJ: Rutgers University Press.

Johnson, C. (1995). The phenomenology of the black body. In L. Goldstein (Ed.), *The male body: Features, destinies, exposures* (pp. 121-136). Ann Arbor, MI: The University of Michigan Press.

Kaplan, A. (1996). *Looking for the other: Feminism, film, and the imperial gaze.* New York: Routledge.

Katz, J. (1995). Advertising and the construction of violent white masculinity. In G. Dines & J. M. Humex (Eds.), *Gender, race, and class in media* (pp. 133-141). Thousand Oaks, CA: Sage.

Kervin, D. (1990). Advertising masculinity: The representation of males in *Esquire* advertisements. *Journal of Communication Inquiry, 14,* 1-51.

Kervin, D. (1991). Gender ideology in television commercials. In L. R. Vande Berg and L. A. Wenner (Eds.), *Television criticism: Approaches and applications* (pp. 235-253). New York: Longman.

Kimmel, M. (1995). *The politics of manhood: Profeminist men respond to the mythopoetic men's movement (and mythopoetic leaders answer).* Philadelphia: Temple University Press.

Kimmel, M. (1996) *Manhood in America: A cultural history.* New York: Free Press.

Kimmel, M., & Kaufman, M. (1994). Weekend warriors: The new men's movement. In H. Brod & M. Kimmel (Eds.), *Theorizing masculinities* (pp. 259-288). Thousand Oaks, CA: Sage.

Kirkham, P., & Thumin, J. (Eds.). (1995). *Me Jane: Masculinity, movies, and women.* New York: St. Martin's.

Krutnik, P. (1991). *In a lonely street: Film noir, genre, masculinity.* London: Routledge.

Kupers, T. A. (1993). *Revisioning men's lives: Gender, intimacy and power.* New York: Guilford.

Lake, M., & Damousi, J. (1995). Introduction: Warfare, gender, and history. In M. Lake & J. Damousi (Eds.), *Gender and war* (pp. 1-22). Melbourne, Australia: Cambridge University Press.

Lehman, P. (1993). *Running scared: Masculinity and representation of the male body.* Philadelphia: Temple University Press.

Levant, R. F. (1996). What is the status of manhood today? Paper distributed electronically to members of Division 51 of the American Psychological Association.

Levant, R. F., & Kopecky, G. (1995). *Masculinity reconstructed: Changing the rules of manhood.* New York: Dutton.

Martin, A. (1993). *Receptions of war: Vietnam and American culture.* Norman, OK: University of Oklahoma Press.

Martin, M. (Ed.). (1995). *Cinemas of the Black diaspora: Diversity, dependence, and oppositionality.* Detroit, MI: Wayne State University Press.

Martin, R. (1997). *Mean streets and raging bulls: The legacy of film noir in contemporary American cinema.* Lanham, MD: Scarecrow.

Maxfield, J. (1996). *The fatal woman: Sources of male anxiety in American film noir.* Madison, NJ: Fairleigh Dickinson University Press.

Messner, M. (1997). *Politics of masculinities: Men in movements.* Thousand Oaks, CA: Sage.

Miller, C. (1996). The representation of the Black male in film. Retrieved November 15, 1997 from the World Wide Web http://www.gti.net/cmmiller/blkfem.html.

Mitchell, L. (1996). *Westerns: Making the man in fiction and film.* Chicago: The University of Chicago Press.

Morrison, S. (1988). The (ideo)logical consequences of gender on genre. *CineAction!, 13*(14), 40-45.

Muller, E. (1998). *Dark city: The lost world of film noir.* New York: St. Martin's.

Mulvey, L. (1975). Visual pleasure and narrative cinema. *Screen, 16*(3), 6-18.

Neale, S. (1993). Masculinity as spectacle. In S. Cohan & I. R. Hark (Eds.), *Screening the male: Exploring masculinities in Hollywood cinema* (pp. 9-20). New York: Routledge.

Nixon, S. (1996). *Hard looks: Masculinities, spectatorship, and contemporary consumption.* London: University College London Press.

Palmer, B. (1994). *Hollywood's dark cinema: The American film noir.* New York: Twayne.

Read, A. (1996). *The face of blackness: Frantz Fanon and the visual representation.* London: Institute of Contemporary Art.

Richards, L. (1998). *African American films through 1959: A comprehensive illustrated filmography.* Jefferson, NC: McFarland.

Riviere, J. (1986). Womanliness as masquerade. In V. Burgin, J. Donald, & C. Kaplan (Eds.), *Formations of fantasy* (pp. 38-44). New York: Methuen.

Sampson, H. (1998). *That's enough folks: Black images in animated cartoons.* Lanham, MD: Scarecrow.

Schwalbe, M. (1996). *Unlocking the iron cage: The men's movement, gender politics, and American culture.* New York: Oxford University Press.

Searle, W. (Ed.). (1998). *Search and clear: Critical responses to selected literature and film of the Vietnam War.* Bowling Green, OH: Bowling Green State University.

Seidler, V. (1997). *Man enough: Embodying masculinities.* London: Sage.

Server, L., Gorman, E., & Greenberg, M. (Eds.). (1998). *The big book of noir.* New York: Carroll & Graf.

Shaw, M. (1996, March). Frontiers and pioneers. *Bad Subjects, 25.* Retrieved July 13, 1997 from the World Wide Web: http://english-www.hss.cmu.edu/bs/25/shaw.html.

Shields, V. (1990). Advertising visual images: Gendered ways of seeing and looking. *Journal of Communication Inquiry, 14*(2), 25-39.

Simpson, M. (1994). *Male impersonators: Men performing masculinity.* New York: Routledge.

Slotkin, R. (1992). *Gunfighter nation: The myth of the frontier in twentieth-century America.* New York: Atheneum.

Smith, P. (1995). Eastwood bound. In M. Berger, B. Wallis, & S. Watson (Eds.), *Constructing masculinity* (pp. 77-97). New York: Routledge.

Smith, V. (Ed.). (1997). *Representing blackness: Issues in film and video.* New Brunswick, NJ: Rutgers University Press.

Smith, V. (1998). *Not just race, not just gender: Black feminist readings.* New York: Routledge.

Spence, C. (1966). *The American West: A source book.* New York: Thomas Y. Crowell.

Staiger, J. (1995). *Bad women: The regulation of female sexuality in early American cinema.* Minneapolis, MN: University of Minnesota Press.

Stern, W. (1995). Aesthetizing masculinity: The example of physique photography. *Threshold: Viewing Culture, 9*. Retrieved June 17, 1997 from the World Wide Web: http://www.arts.ucsb.edu/~tvc/v09/section2/v09s2.stern.html.

Stoltenberg, J. (1993). *The end of manhood*. New York: Plume.

Tasker, Y. (1993). *Spectacular bodies: Gender genre, and the action cinema*. London: Routledge.

Theweleit, K. (1987). *Male fantasies* (Vol. 1). Minneapolis, MN: University of Minnesota Press.

Thomas, D. (1988). Film noir: How Hollywood deals with the deviant male. *CineAction!, 13*(14), 18-28.

Tompkins, J. (1992). *West of everything: The inner life of westerns*. New York: Oxford University Press.

Torres, S. (1989). Melodrama, masculinity, and the family: *Thirtysomething* as therapy. *Camera Obscura, 19*, 86-106.

Traube, E. (1992). *Dreaming identities: Class, gender, and generation in 1980s Hollywood movies*. Boulder, CO: Westview.

Trelotte, J. (1989). *Voices in the dark: The narrative patterns of film noir*. Chicago: University of Illinois Press.

Tuska, J. (1994). *Dark cinema: American film noir in cultural perspective*. Westport, CT: Greenwood.

Watkins, C. (1998). *Representing: Hip hop culture and the production of black cinema. Chicago: The University of Chicago Press*.

Williams, P. (1995). Meditations on masculinity. In M. Berger, B. Wallis, & S. Watson (Eds.), *Constructing masculinities* (pp. 238-249). New York: Routledge.

Willis, S. (1997). *High contrast: Race and gender in contemporary Hollywood film*. Durham, NC: Duke University Press.

Young, L. (1996). *Fear of the dark: "Race," gender, and sexuality in the cinema*. London: Routledge.

6

Traumatic Crossings

On the one side, . . . there is the erosion of the boundaries between body and world, body and image, body and machine. On the other, there is its direct pathologization: trauma as the collapse of the distinction between inner and outer, observer and scene, representation and perception, as the failure of the subject's proper distance with respect to representation . . . , a collapse of proper boundary maintenance—the opening and wounding of bodies and persons.

—*Mark Seltzer*

To many, it seems as if the boundaries that frame the conceptual categories underpinning Western society are now dissolving. We might think here of the manifold anxieties about place and identity that have generated debates about the disappearance of the boundaries around nation, community, the public and private spheres, and, of course, identity—including sexual identity (see Radhakrishnan, 1996; Seelye & Wasilewski, 1996).

Sometimes, this process of boundary collapse is pathologized—viewed as a sign of aberrance or deviance, and labeled a "trauma." However, discourses of nondifferentiation or boundary crossing can be articulated in terms of either negative or positive shifts in knowledge and experience. Consequently, the erosion of the boundaries of the established order offers both a threat, in terms of its potential to pathologize, and a promise, in terms of its potential to refuse the idea of a center that is premised on the exclusion and devaluation of the Other (Hatty & Mills, 1998).

In this chapter, I return to the principal concern of this book: the relationship between violence and masculinity. I begin by examining the centrality of violence to American culture; specifically, I discuss one of the most extreme, but emblematic, forms of violence evident today: serial killing. Analyzed in academic writing, aestheticized in film, and popularized in television shows, serial killing has become the litmus test of public morality, private desires, and social tolerance. As a type of predation often linked to sexuality, serial killing condenses a range of issues and anxieties revolving around self, bodies, instruments/weapons, and the administration of justice. Serial killing, as the limit case of the human (and, perhaps, the masculine), is the lens through which I examine the interplay between violence and gender. I conclude with some thoughts on responsibility, care, and justice.

Violated Bodies

Let us begin by noting that we live in an era in which violation is one of our primary cultural metaphors. We live in a culture in which violence is spectacular, immediate, and entertaining (Bok, 1998; Fisher, 1997; Goldstein, 1998). This translates into an appetite for visual and experiential intimacy with exaggerated forms of violence, such as serial killing. Holmes and Holmes (1998) note that "serial killers have become a part of America's cultural heritage" (p. 35), and that "to many Americans, serial murderers are seen as icons" (p. 29). Indeed, as Holmes and Holmes argue,

> Serial murder has mesmerized the attention of American society. It has become a focus of attention, and some may even call it fascination. The media have devoted pages and books, TV documentaries and large-screen movies to the topic of serial killers. Each killer occupies a space in the memory of us all to one degree or another. (p. 46)

In a similar vein, Steven Egger (1998) declares,

> American culture as a whole has cultivated a taste for violence that seems to be insatiable. . . . The violence of our popular culture reflected in movies, TV programs, magazines, and fact or fiction books in the latter part of the twentieth century has made the shocking realism of this violence a routine risk that we all face. (p. 89)

And, in a most extraordinary series of statements, Egger declares,

> We desire to learn more about the killer. The killer becomes our total focus. We want to hear or read about the torture and mutila-

tion deaths of female victims as if such acts were an *art form* [italics added]. The serial killer becomes *an artist* [italics added], in some cases performing a reverse type of sculpturing by taking the lives of his victims with a sharp knife. (pp. 89-90)

Bodies are violated in other ways as well. We might think here of the discourses of viral infection that abound in the contemporary context (Hatty & Hatty, 1999). Such discourses embrace fiction and popular entertainment, as well as the worlds of science and politics. One arena in which we can see this language at work is biotechnological warfare. Here, we can witness the cultural preoccupation with the possibility that a malevolent and disturbed individual or group might inflict massive injury or death on a large number of people through the release of a contagious and lethal virus. This fear relates to the risks of unpredictable and undetectable acts of catastrophic harm— harm that takes the form of extreme injury to the body.

In an address given before the National Academy of Sciences in January, 1999, President Clinton (1999, p. 2) noted, "Last May . . . I said terrorist and outlaw states are extending the world's fields of battle, from physical space to cyberspace, from our earth's vast bodies of water to the complex workings of our own human bodies" (p. 2). So seriously did Clinton view this threat that he expressed relief that panels of experts are now speaking out on the threat of bioterrorism and deflecting suspicion from the idea that he, Clinton, "was just reading too many novels late at night" (p. 1).

It has been suggested that the bioterrorism threat might not be confined to the individual terrorist or the rogue state, but might be an extension of the modus operandi of the serial killer. Steven Egger (1998) poses this question: "What kind of serial killers will hunt our world in the next century? . . . Possibly they will be mass-serial killers, using letter bombs, poison in our water supply, or poison gas in the subways of our urban centers" (p. 263). The American public is currently consuming a wide variety of imagined accounts of this scenario. One example is Richard Preston's recent book, *The Cobra Event* (1997): a fictional narrative of a secret, counterterror operation mounted by a disgruntled scientist who uses biological weapons, developed through genetic engineering, to spread a highly contagious virus throughout the civilian population of New York. The technology he uses is a known as "black biology," and the weapon he employs is the so-called cobra virus. The descriptions of the bodily disintegration in Preston's book are intense; they include vivid scenes depicting the viral amplification processes within the body and horrific acts of self-cannibalization provoked by the virus. The reader is deliberately confronted by the visceral experience of bodily breakdown and the ensuing reaction of disgust.[1] (See Miller, 1998; see also Cole, 1998; Peters & Olshaker, 1997; Radetsky, 1995; Rhodes, 1997; Ryan, 1997.)

It is possible to argue that, on the brink of the 21st century, we are located in both a *viral* culture, in which we are preoccupied with fears about bodily disintegration, and a *violent* culture, in which we are inundated with increasingly explicit images of wretched, broken bodies. Our dominant impulses and anxieties revolve around the forced breaching of the body's boundaries. These tropes of human experience have in common the violation of the body by an external agent: an involuntary and nonconsensual intrusion or invasion resulting in injury and, perhaps ultimately, individual extinction.

These attacks from beyond the borders of the body may result in corporeal disintegration: the spilling out of the body's viscera and organs, and a radical failure of the body's border (that is, the skin) to hold. If this occurs, the person loses her or his integrity as an individual, and is transformed into an undifferentiated, bloody pulp. And proximity to this monstrous body—indeed, the very process of *becoming* monstrous—produces a reaction of horror. This reaction of horror is fundamental to the experience of abjection: the threatened encroachment of that which is defined as abject (excreta, bodily fluids, or the corpse itself), and the potential collapse of the border between the pure and the impure (Kristeva, 1982).

However, some now welcome the abject; some now wish to know it intimately, to experience its impurity at close range. This, of course, is linked to discourses of sex, sexuality, and desire.[2] We can see these impulses at work in popular culture: for example, in news media and in film. In the book *Offensive Films,* Mikita Brottman (1997) discusses the genre known as "cinema vomitif," which involves acts of cannibalism, unsuspected slaughter, and ritualized killing, acts that violate various taboos surrounding the body. This film genre enjoys a certain cachet among a growing array of audiences. We might compare it with the photographic genre of the New Grotesque, pioneered by Joel-Peter Witkin. Witkin's celebrated photos of anatomical anomalies, body parts, and decorated, augmented, and transformed bodies are visual experiences born of the medical museum and the gothic imagination (see Witkin, 1989, 1994, 1998; see also Akin & Ludwig, 1989).

As a result of these cultural trends and practices, infection/contagion and violence are linked in a ritualized attack on the "clean and proper" body. This body, the idealized and masculinized body of modernity, is now under threat; external forces impinge on the integrity of this body, threatening to turn it into something Other, something monstrous. And we know that the monstrous body is "always in a state of decomposition, . . . constantly threaten[ing] to unravel, to fail to hold together" (Halberstam, 1995, p. 47).

Below, I explore the ways in which the linked emotions of fear, panic, and trauma shape our experience of the social, especially our engagement with the public sphere. As I do this, it might be useful to reflect on the relationship between the crises of gender and embodiment. How do the boundaries that mark out embodied differences shift under the pressures of such crises? How is this played out in public fear or panic?

The Rise of Wound Culture

According to Mark Seltzer (1998), the public sphere is now a space in which perverse and violent desires are given expression. Moreover, the public sphere is a space in which participation in or witnessing of acts of violence constitutes the lines of communication, the bonds that link people and communities.

This witnessing of violent events may take many forms, from the well-rehearsed activities of pornography, to disasters of various magnitudes, and, of course, to crime. This last form now involves the technologies of the image: for example, the use of video cameras to capture private transactions occurring in public or to provide surveillance of commercial spaces. We might think here of the freezing on film of the unforgettable image of young James Bulger being led out of a shopping mall to his violent death by two 10-year-old boys in Liverpool, England, in 1993. The visibility of James's walk to his imminent demise—and its availability for endless repetition on our television screens—constituted a significant portion of the horror attached to this crime. Imagining his small, torn body left lying on the railway tracks following the crime constituted another significant aspect. Indeed, many people in the local community and beyond were linked together by the affective experience of witnessing this killing-in-the-making, what Alison Young (1996) calls "the trauma of the visible" (p. 111).

The representations of violated bodies in media, fiction, and film, as well as in official state discourse and academic accounts constitute what Mark Seltzer (1998) calls "atrocity exhibitions" (p. 21). These exhibitions make up "the contemporary pathological public sphere, our wound culture" (p. 1). This "wound culture"—in which the traumatic, the injurious, and the violent are not only visible, but also an integral aspect of individual and social functioning—is premised on the pathologization of the public sphere, the rendering of the public sphere as a place of abjection. Traumatic violence, in which bodies are ripped open, emptied out, or taken apart, flows through the public sphere connecting all who are involved in these processes of corporeal annihilation. Agency, desire, and spectatorship are interlinked in a bizarre logic of shared pleasure and singular pain.

Acts of spectacular violence, whether murders, accidents, or suicides, are the sites in which public fantasy and private desire interact. This collective fascination with violence takes the form of prurient interest in such crimes as serial killing, and a fascination with the collision between bodies and technologies; both represent "a shock of contact that encodes, in turn, a breakdown in the distinction between the individual and the mass and between private and public registers" (Seltzer, 1998, p. 253). Of course, this prurient interest is only possible in a culture in which the distinction between inside and outside threatens to collapse or indeed has disappeared altogether.

What are the origins of this fascination with grotesque violence?

Gothic Traces

> There is no consensus in the psychiatric community that Dr. Lecter should be termed a man. He has long been regarded by his professional peers in psychiatry, many of whom fear his acid pen in the professional journals, as something entirely Other. For convenience they term him "monster."
>
> —*Thomas Harris,* Hannibal

The 19th century witnessed the birth of the American gothic imagination. It was a time when constructions of killers and killing were realigned; the prevailing religious and spiritual interpretations of crime and violence, with their emphasis on original sin and innate human depravity, were replaced to a large extent by new readings focusing on the secular and the sensational (Halttunen, 1998). The gulf between the gothic imagination, premised on mystery and revelation, and the legal imagination, founded on rationality and prosecution, was encapsulated in the figure of the killer. The killer, viewed from the perspective of the gothic cultural frame, was transformed from a sinner to a monster. The killer became defined as radically different from the norm, outside social relations, and threatening to the social order. Fundamentally, the killer became incomprehensible and morally strange: a representative of the realm of horror (Halttunen, 1998). Society could no longer make sense of acts of violence in terms of narratives of personal failure, moral lassitude, or corruption of values. The unfathomable killer became a figure of terror who haunted society and challenged the limits of the permissible.

What is the significance of this gothic response to transgression? Elizabeth Grosz (1996) points out,

> Fascination with the monstrous is testimony to our tenuous hold on the image of perfection. . . . The viewer's horror lies in the recognition that this monstrous being is at the heart of his or her own identity, for it is all that must be ejected or abjected from self-image to make the bounded, category-obeying self possible. (p. 65)

As we have already noted in Chapter 2, the 19th century also witnessed the birth of the idea of the dangerous individual. The character of the actor rather than the character of the acts themselves took precedence, as is most evident in the production of the figure of the sex criminal. Here, issues of sexual identity and individual functioning came to the fore, which provided ripe terrain for the emergence of the serial killer. Mark Seltzer (1998) notes that

> the serial killer emerges at the dark intersection of these strands. By the turn of the 20th century, serial killing has become something to do (a lifestyle, or career, or calling) and the serial killer has become something to be (a species of person). The serial killer becomes a type of person, a body, a case history, a childhood, an alien life form. (p. 4)

Today, serial killing can be regarded as a cultural formation typical of the late 20th century. As such, it is emblematic of the motifs of machine culture: the mass-produced images, the multiple representations and simulations, and the retreat of the ideals of humanism. The insertion of graphic violence at the heart of society and its replication in numerous visual forms provides the optimum context for the generation of the "logic of killing for pleasure" (Seltzer, 1998, p. 7).

Moreover, as I have argued throughout this book, it is now assumed that serial killers (and other "predators") are nestled at the core of civic society. They are concealed *inside* the ordinary machinery of everyday life, obscured within institutions and able to crisscross various sites without detection. Our inability to visually identify these predators by looking for signs of physical anomaly only increases our fear. Ironically, our technologies of identification, such as psychological profiling, are neither instantaneous nor reliable. Judith Halberstam (1995) observes,

> The postmodern monster is no longer the hideous other storming the gates of the human citadel, he has already disrupted the careful geography of human self and demon other and he makes the peripheral and marginal part of the center. Monsters in postmodernism are already inside—the house, the body, the head, the skin, the nation— and they work their way out. Accordingly, it is the human, the façade of the normal, that tends to become the place of terror in postmodern Gothic. (p. 162)

Egger (1998) recently wrote, "As we move about among strangers, we have little control over these strangers. As we become the ever-increasing prey for these strangers, we are reminded that *predators are all around us* [italics added]. We feel truly isolated and very alone" (p. 39). This imagery of penetration and enclosure is reminiscent of that used by President Clinton in 1996 to warn the sexual predators of America that the state would not tolerate their activities, and would declare war on the predators lurking within society.

Presence and Absence

Jack the Ripper, who murdered a series of women in London at the end of the 19th century, could be regarded as the prototypical serial killer. Many of the women he killed were sex workers, their mutilated bodies testament to the dangers of their encounters. Jack the Ripper, however, is a mythic figure, unknown and unknowable, an inspiration for books, films, and much public speculation. As Joan Smith (1989) states, "Jack the Ripper is not a person but a *label* connecting a set of related acts; he has no proper name, no address, no biographical details" (p. 117).

As we saw in Chapter 2, contemporary constructions of the serial killer embrace the idea of psychological types or statistical phenomena. We now have technologies of knowing: ways of quantitatively mapping the characteristics of the serial killer. As we saw, the U.S. Federal Bureau of Investigation has a unit devoted to accumulating psychological and criminological data on serial killers. Robert Ressler, cofounder of the FBI's Behavioral Science Unit (BSU), published an influential book on the psychological profiling of serial killers (Ressler & Schachtman, 1992). Ressler's colleague, John Douglas, has also published in this field (Douglas & Olshaker, 1995, 1998).[3]

Despite this intense interest in cataloguing the traits, tendencies, and behaviors of serial killers, there is, paradoxically, a claim that some of these offenders are characterized by lack, by a kind of psychological vacuum. For example, the British serial killer Dennis Nilsen was diagnosed as suffering from False Self Syndrome, which implied that he had failed to develop an autonomous, mature sense of self. Nilsen had been in the army, the police force, and the civil service: To those who diagnosed him, these occupational choices seemed to prefigure his *modus operandi,* which involved piling the bodies of his victims onto a huge fire. He described this as "a mixing of flesh in a common flame and a single unity of ashes, . . . a uniform and anonymous corporation cemetery" (quoted in Seltzer, 1998, p. 19). This act was as "a mass spectacle of pathology and abjection" (Seltzer, 1998, p. 19). Furthermore, it has been said that Nilsen was "a black hole of violation and pollution about which the contemporary national body gathers, spectates, and discharges itself; in his words, he was 'a national receptacle into which all the nation will urinate'" (Seltzer, 1998, p. 19). We can recognize these excessive performances, apparently inspired by lack, as characteristic of the monstrous (see Chapter 3).

Ironically, these killers are situated in a culture saturated with media representations of the serial killer and those who stalk him. An example of this might be the television show *Profiler,* in which a forensic psychologist with the ability to visualize aspects of the crime or crime scene works as part of an elite team pursuing serial killers, perpetrators of hate crimes, arsonists, and other offenders. Serial killing figures prominently in the series: According to the story line, the lead character, the gifted forensic psychologist, once became too entangled with a serial killer nicknamed Jack of All Trades, and her husband was abducted and murdered as a consequence. In recent episodes of *Profiler,* Jack, the serial killer, has been caught, and so the main character is no longer stalked. Interestingly, the television network responsible for the show (NBC) hosts a website, *Jack's Killer Website,* that invites visitors to enter an on-screen game with Jack. The site contains statements such as the following:

This is Jack speaking. . . .

Relish my pleasure. The hunter and the hunted. The Quick and the Dead.

I am stirred to the hunt by my hunger, like a Lion in search of its prey. . . .

It's a dog eat dog world . . . and I am the Alpha Male. . . .

What more Power can you have than controlling Life and Death? I will do as I see fit.

Visitors to the site are invited to enter the game, pit their wits against the mind of the serial killer, and solve the riddle by assembling a series of black and white photographs scattered throughout the site.

Real serial killers are not isolated from these cultural representations, but come to know themselves through exposure to the range of available instructional and mass-mediated materials. This produces a kind of circular process of incorporation and imitation, a mimetics of desire and violence. The film *Copycat* (1995) depicts this mimetic relationship in detail. In this film, an imprisoned serial killer threatens a criminal psychologist who has written the definitive text on the psychology of serial killing. He induces a young man to reenact murders committed by various infamous offenders, such as Ted Bundy. The *modus operandi* of the copycat killer changes as the chosen identity of each notorious offender changes. The psychologist and the copycat killer are aware of the actors and the circumstances of each replicated murder, as this information is contained in the psychologist's definitive text and in her numerous public lectures. The psychologist is drawn into the police investigative process in her status as expert, and becomes embroiled in a plot to take her life. Here, the mimetics of desire and violence are literalized in the film: Not only are the convicted serial killer and his follower exposed to professional knowledge about serial killing, but the actions central to the film revolve around reenactments of prior acts of violence.

Trashing Bodies and Boundaries

As we saw in Chapter 1, the issue of boundaries and their dissolution is central to the construction and lived experience of the self. As we saw subsequently, the self is both gendered and embodied; furthermore, the body is sexed, and cannot be regarded as mere neutral matter. Grosz (1994) discusses the idea of sexual difference as it is played out on the terrain of the body, posing some compelling questions about the distinctive ways in which men's and women's bodies are conceptualized in contemporary Western society. She asks,

> Can it be that in the West, in our time, the female body has been constructed not only as lack or absence but with more complexity, as a leaking, uncontrollable, seeping liquid; as formless flow; as viscosity, entrapping, secreting; as lacking not so much or simply the phallus but self-containment—not a cracked or porous vessel, like a leaking ship, but a formlessness that engulfs all form, a disorder that threatens all order? (p. 203)

Referring to men's bodies, she asks a similar set of provocative questions:

> Could the reduction of men's body fluids to the by-products of pleasure and the raw materials of reproduction, along with men's refusal to acknowledge the effects of flows that move through various parts of the body and from the inside out, have to do with men's attempt to distance themselves from the very corporeality—uncontrollable, excessive, expansive, disruptive, irrational—they have attributed to women? (p. 200)

What, then, might be the uses (psychological, social, and cultural) of this differentiation between sexed bodies? What is the significance of the erection of this constantly patrolled boundary? How is extreme, repetitive violence implicated in this system of difference? I explore below some of the consequences of the threatened collapse of this boundary and the potential of formlessness to engulf all form and to unleash disorder.

Seltzer (1998) claims that the preoccupation with boundaries colors the discourses of serial killing; experts and killers alike make sense of their behavior in terms of these discourses. For the serial killer, this anxiety about boundaries "shapes the panic about the 'fusion' with other bodies and bodily masses—as the threat of self-dissolution; and shapes the desire for this fusion—the desire for self-dissolution that, at the extreme, takes the form of the killer's black out at the moment of violence" (Seltzer, 1998, p. 139). Furthermore, Seltzer alleges that the impulse to open bodies and skin and to preserve bodies can be viewed as "panics about and desires for the dissolution of boundaries that make it possible for the killer to derive identity from, and take pleasure in, destruction and self-destruction" (p. 140).

The anticipation of mergence or fusion with another is molded by the cultural construction of sexed bodies. Consistent with the discourses of serial killing, heightened anxiety about self-dissolution may be played out on the victims' bodies; sexual difference is literally (re)imposed on the bodies of the women who are killed. The sexed bodies of these women may be rendered different from the killer through acts of violence. Furthermore, attempts on the part of serial killers to rework the self may be attempts to annihilate femaleness. For example, the serial killer Henry Lee Lucas announced, "I am death on women."

However, in the discourses of serial killing, a kind of strange inversion is presumed to be at work in the relationship between the killer and his victim. There is an identification with the victim; the tearing open of the body of another and the externalization of the body's interior can be seen as a response to the desire to see inside one's own body. There is also the refusal to identify with the victim, the exclamation of victory over death, especially another's death. As Seltzer (1998) notes, "the drive to survive [the] opening of interiors" is profound indeed (p. 273). As the serial killer Ed Kemper expressed it, "What I wanted to see was the death, and I wanted to see the triumph, . . . the triumph of survival and the exultation over death" (quoted in Seltzer, 1998, p. 272).

In an orgy of killing, Kemper extinguished the lives of several young female college students, and dismembered their bodies, literally acting out his desire to turn women's bodies inside out. Kemper acknowledged this urgent impulse to view the interior of women's bodies: Of one victim, he said, "She had a rather large forehead and I was imagining what her brain looked like inside" (quoted in Seltzer, 1998, p. 273). The act of detaching the head from the body—of depriving the young women of their "personality," as he called it— was both compulsive and deeply satisfying to Kemper. We cannot fail to notice the historical and cultural precedents for Kemper's desires and actions: We might think here of the association of violence with the acquisition of knowledge, particularly hidden or secret knowledge; we might think, also, of the link between sight and knowledge, and the acquisition of medical knowledge through the practices of dissection (see Chapter 1).

Not surprisingly, Kemper was apparently driven by a desire to possess and incorporate aspects of his victims' identities. He said, "I wanted them to be a part of me—and now they are" (quoted in Seltzer, 1998, p. 274). Here, another breakdown in boundaries becomes evident: The self/Other distinction is displaced by an ultimate self-sameness. Kemper's penultimate act of violence, the killing and dismembering of his mother, points to a mergence between the murderous acts of female obliteration and the imperative of male self-genesis, of continually recreating a new identity through incorporation. This coalesces with the fantasy of genderless reproduction that underlies many of the acts of male serial killers. Jeffrey Dahmer, who killed and dissected a series of young men, literalized his identification with one victim by consuming a part of his body. Egger (1998) claims that Dahmer experienced "an addiction to bodies" (p. 254). Dahmer himself declared, "My consuming lust was to *experience* [italics added] their bodies" (quoted in Egger, 1998, p. 263).

Dahmer also conducted grotesque chemical and anatomical experiments on the bodies of his victims. Of these experiments, Seltzer (1998) says,

> These are, above all, experiments in the lifelike: experiments in reduplicating bodies and persons. Seeing how things work involves, most basically, a fascination with what makes subjects go—something like an attempt to isolate and to make visible "life itself."
> (p. 191)

This fascination with "life itself" took hold in public culture in the 19th century. Biology, as the science of life, was propelled by the search for the life force through a mechanistic visualization of physiology and anatomy. Foucault, among others, pointed out the deep irony of the biological sciences gaining their credibility by taking apart and studying the dead body—the techniques of the corpse, Foucault called it.

We could conclude that the desires and fears of the (male) serial killer regarding bodies and gendered differences have been transposed into a constellation of cultural desires and fears. These emotions are no longer confined to the small band of "postmodern monsters." This small company of killers now act out the desires of a significant proportion of mass society; these postmodern monsters embody the violent, murderous desires that transect parts of American society.

Ironically, this identification with the serial killer—the self-sameness evident in the literature on serial killing and in media and film—is literally horrifying. It produces anxiety in the population. Arguably, this anxiety takes a very different shape for men and for women: While men may enjoy a vicarious thrill at the "hunting" of the serial killer, women may experience a range of emotions, including the terror of being hunted.

How, then, does femininity intersect with the dictates of wound culture? Below, I look at how the feminine is constructed in contemporary culture, and examine the relationship between the feminine and violence.

Femmes Fatales:
Figuring the Feminine

We have already seen in Chapter 1 that the boundaries of the subject and the body are no longer either secure or predictable. Consequently, cultural images and representations of womanhood in the fin-de-siècle context are multiple and diverse (Griggers, 1997). We have the persistence of old images of woman as inherently dangerous: We might think here of the witch, that contradictory and complex figure symbolic of all that is dark and foreboding (Purkiss, 1997). Of course, central to the historical constructions of the witch is female sexuality.[4] Another reading of the feminine that prevails at the brink of the 21st century is that of the threatening or violent woman, a reading that has been given expression in film, literature, and television in recent decades. We could cite here the figure of the femme fatale that haunted *film noir* in the 1930s and 1940s (see Chapter 3). The literal interpretation of this figure is the woman who kills, especially the woman who kills a stranger (i.e., whose killings occur in the public rather than the private domain).

One of the most notorious female serial killers in recent American memory is undoubtedly Aileen Wournos. The FBI labeled Wournos America's first female serial killer. Convicted in 1992 of killing Richard Mallory, a white middle-class man, Wournos is suspected of killing at least six other men from similar backgrounds between December 1989 and November 1990. Their bodies had been discovered scattered amongst the trees along Florida's highways. Wournos was a prostitute who worked these highways. Judge Uriel Bount, Jr., sentenced Aileen Carol "Lee" Wournos to death in Florida's electric chair.

During her trial, Wournos was portrayed by the defense as a prostitute who had suffered serious violence and humiliation at the hands of the men who were her clients. The prosecution portrayed Wournos as a "predatory prostitute" whose "appetite for lust and control had taken a lethal turn." (quoted in Mills, 1995, p. 1). Wournos was described as a woman who was "no longer satisfied with just taking [sic] men's bodies and their money, but who was now seeking the ultimate gratification of taking men's lives" (quoted in Mills, 1995, p. 1). The prosecution emphasized the notion of control and the power inherent in the possession and exercise of that control. This control was viewed as the prerogative of the prostitute. Moreover, the power involved in "taking" men's bodies provided the basis for usurping men's very existence. The power of the prostitute was understood as potentially life-threatening; it was viewed as an extension, in part, of the presumed vulnerability experienced by men in noncommercial sexual encounters with women. This vulnerability supposedly delivers high levels of control to the female, who may take advantage of it in various ways: As we have seen, the "predatory prostitute" may even kill. The prosecution concluded its case against Wournos by declaring that female sex workers are driven by a need for "tremendous control," a need to "take all that a man has physically . . . [and] spiritually" (quoted in Mills, 1995, p. 2). State Prosecutor John Tanner announced, "There's only one thing left—and that's to kill. . . . [T]hat's what [Wournos] wanted and that's what she *took* [sic]" (quoted in Mills, 1995, p. 2).

The defense, on the other hand, directed attention to Wournos's experiences of repeated abuse as a child, her poverty, and the violence and torture meted out regularly by the men she engaged as clients. Public Defender Tricia Jenkins portrayed Wournos as a victim of men's savagery: "You will hear evidence of bondage, rape, sodomy and degradation," Jenkins told the jury (quoted in Mills, 1995, p. 1). Provoked beyond endurance, according to Jenkins, Wournos eventually defended herself with fatal consequences. In her own legal defense, Wournos said,

> In my confessions, I stated thirty-seven times . . . thirty-seven times [I stated] that they raped, or beat and then began to rape—and had intentions of killing. And what I did was what anybody else would do, defended myself. . . . And I had no intention of killing anyone. . . . *I'm not that type of person.*" (quoted in Mills, 1995, p. 2)

As a prostitute who had contact with 200 to 250 men a month, who avowed a liking for sex, and who derived a good income from her work, Wournos is representative of a raft of taboos. She disrupts the usual division between masculine and feminine roles in sexual encounters, in relationships, and in commercial transactions. She can also be seen as a figure of disease and contagion; the multiple exchanges of body fluids during the many encounters to which Wournos was a willing or unwilling party transform Wournos into a metaphor for the implied danger associated with the female body and with female sexuality. Yet Wournos is aberrant in a number of ways: She is a lesbian, she knows a great deal about men's desire and men's bodies, and she traverses public space with an eye to a profit.

Wournos exceeds the boundaries of "proper" femininity; she epitomizes abjection in her embrace of the abnormal and the strange.

In this sense, Wournos's character—and her body—are a material reality and also a collective fiction. Too far from the normalizing category of the feminine and too close to the prohibited category of the masculine, Wournos, as female serial killer, represents one aspect of "becoming-Woman" in contemporary U.S. culture (Griggers, 1997). Female predation—more terrible than its male counterpart—is the specter that threatens the social order. And according to the dominant discourses of gender, it must be expunged.

The masculine postmodern monster affords many the opportunity for identification, and hence is a source of desire as well as fear. The *feminine* postmodern monster is the living expression of the capacity of her gender to wreak havoc in civic society (see Chapter 1). She inspires dread; she is more frightful than her male counterpart. The famed Italian physicians Lombroso and Ferrero (1958) claimed that the female criminal was "more terrible than any man" (p. 150).

Cultural Discourses of Violence

I have argued throughout this book that it is possible to identify a persistent and pervasive cultural narrative about violence in Western society. We explored some of the historical catalysts to the development of this narrative in Chapter 1, and we examined the specific accounts of violence, the specific explanations of gender constructs, and the linkages between the two in subsequent chapters. In these chapters, we noted that the construction of modern selfhood is supportive of and consistent with the imperative to violence in the West; indeed, that violence, in its many forms, is installed within the machinery of the modern self. We acknowledged the social and psychological contingency of the *masculine* sense of self, composed as it is of an illusory "inner masculine knot of selfhood" (West, 1997, p. 284), and noted that this "fiction of unambivalent self-possession," peculiar to masculine subjectivity, is "always shadowed by disavowed reminders that it is borrowed, simulated, relative—more a costume than an essence" (Kramer, 1997, pp. 6, 7).

One question remains: What are the components of this dominant cultural narrative about gender and violence in the West? Barbara Whitmer (1997) describes this narrative as the "violence mythos:" "a collection of beliefs that articulates attitudes in Western culture about violence" (p. 1). According to Whitmer, this belief system and its attendant attitudes are premised on two assumptions: first, that violence is central to human nature, and its expression is inevitable; and, second, that it is necessary to apply legal and cultural sanctions to prevent or curb violent individual behaviors.

The matrix of beliefs and attitudes that make up the violence mythos are consistent with the gendered, cultural ideas we discussed in Chapter 1. These ideas revolve around dualist hierarchies: the mind/body split; the dissociation of culture from nature; and, of course, the radical separation of male from female. The violence mythos, as outlined by Whitmer (1997), also privileges the concept of control—control of self (especially emotions and desires); and control of Others (especially those deemed likely to provoke unsettling or disturbing emotions or desires). We discussed the significance of control to Western knowledge systems, and lived experience, in Chapter 1. We also noted that dominant constructions of masculinity—that is, hegemonic masculinity—are grounded in notions of (self) control (Seidler, 1997). We explored the motif of loss of control, and its implications for modern masculinity, in Chapter 4.

According to Whitmer (1997), it is imperative that we replace the violence mythos with another set of cultural discourses that turn on the construct of *interdependence*. These alternative discourses would disavow dualist thinking and all that it implies, and would embrace instead the interconnectedness of life and experience. Whitmer claims that we need a "richer, broader lexicon to accommodate the language of somatic interchange" (p. 237): a language founded on trust and mutuality; a language that recognizes the inherent limitations of the binary logic of either/or, the logic of inclusion and exclusion; a language that shifts to a positive evaluation of femaleness, emotions, and bodies. Furthermore, we need to withdraw support for a hero mythology and to develop a set of practices for acknowledging and addressing vulnerability and suffering. These practices should be contextualized within a framework in which attachment rather than hierarchy is the hallmark of relations. The emergence of this mythos of interdependence would finally show that "the hero has no armor, only skin, and the perpetrator no shadow, only face, and the victim no violence, only a need to live" (Whitmer, 1997, p. 239).

Moira Gatens (1996a, 1996b) also proposes the development of fresh approaches to the twin concepts of justice and responsibility. She talks of the need for an ethic of embodied responsibility. Drawing on the work of the philosopher Spinoza to extend her argument, Gatens notes that, although definitions of morality vary by historical and social context, it is nevertheless at the level of community or civil society that we should attempt to make sense of the concepts of justice and responsibility. Gatens suggests that, in order to rework the relationship between individual acts of harm and the larger society, it is important to rethink the composition and functioning of the civil body. This would involve paying more attention to the aspects of Spinoza's juridical and political theory that focus on the benefits of sociability among citizens. On a practical level, it would involve ensuring that all those traditionally excluded from civil society are accorded both social position and status. This practice would have an impact on legal (and other social) systems, which have encoded—and embodied—the link between secondary status and heightened vulnerability. As we have seen, this traditional focus on individual harms, narrowly defined (see West, 1997), distracts attention from the harms embedded in the structures and everyday practices of governments, corporations, and associations. As we have also seen, our current moral and legal order encourages us to see the criminal offender as different, thereby stressing the Otherness of the offender and effecting a radical separation between the offender and the civil body.

As Gatens (1996b) observes, however,

> It is this fabricated difference that contributes to the marked fascination/repulsion that so many, encouraged by the media, appear to have for serial killers or those convicted of particularly violent or shocking crimes. The frequent finding of such media exposés is that, according to neighbors and acquaintances, the so-called monster was a quiet, polite "ordinary sort of guy." This ordinariness adds to rather than undermines his monstrosity. The spectacular cruelty of such crimes only serves to mask the underlying banality of a largely unchallenged *structural* cruelty in many of our social relations. (p. 42)

If, instead of cleaving the world into monsters and ordinary men, we concerned ourselves with the structural dimensions of harm, and violent behavior generally, we would be diverted from our preoccupation with the criminal offender as a particular type of person—something Other, something monstrous. For, as Gatens (1996b) cautions us, "So long as the law continues to treat the criminal as an aberrant individual or as a monster and as the sole locus of responsibility, our civil body will continue to structure human relations in ways which systematically encourage violence" (p. 40).

This alternate approach to justice and responsibility would turn on the development of a morality of care (West, 1997), an ethic of embodied justice. Such a stance would recognize that our dominant constructions of masculinity both shape and are shaped by our understandings of morality (May, 1998), that our conceptions of legal rationales for behavior and our conceptions of judicial decision-making are affected by the ideals of hegemonic masculinity. It would also recognize that notions of justice and care are not mutually exclusive, but should be mutually constitutive (West, 1997).

Most significantly, such an approach would recognize both that our connective relationships, especially those that imply responsibility and protection, are often profoundly abusive and violent, and that it is this nexus of connection—the articulation of need and emotion in this context—that may be fraught with violence. This nexus has the potential to produce what Levant (1996) calls the "crisis of connection" between men and women. These relationships, however, are suffused with moral meaning as surely as they contain the potential for harm. We need to exercise an ethic of care in order to encourage positive moral value to flourish within these relationships. It is only when we invoke the virtues of nurturance, compassion, and commitment that justice will prevail.

Notes

1. Despite being fictional, Preston's book is not science fiction. The advent of black biology—the creation and use of genetically engineered biotech weapons of mass destruction—has generated a new politics of fear surrounding invisible but deadly weapons and also the social proximity of bodies (see Hatty & Hatty, 1999). There is now a demonstrable relationship between terrorism and contagious viruses, and there is a new tide of anxiety about the potential effects of insidious and lethal weapons released within an unsuspecting urban population.

The expression of cultural anxiety about bioterrorism so lucidly portrayed in Preston's book has a parallel in real-life politics. It is now widely accepted that a major biowarfare terrorist attack cannot be prevented, and that thorough preparation and training are our *only* defense. Jeffrey Simon (1997) notes, "By improving our readiness to respond to biological terrorism, many lives can be saved and terrorists denied their goal of creating panic and crisis throughout the country" (p. 428). The U.S. Department of Defense is currently spending $50 million to provide crisis training for police, fire, medical, and ambulance workers in the event of a chemical or biological weapons attack. Specific cities are preparing for the possibility of a nuclear, chemical, or biological weapons attack: New York City, for example, began this training in earnest in 1998. President Bill Clinton recently announced a comprehensive strategy to strengthen U.S. defenses against terrorist attacks during the 21st century—including attacks on infrastructure, computer networks, and through the use of biological weapons. With regard to this last form of attack, Clinton announced that the entire armed services will be inoculated against anthrax, and that medicines and vaccines to fight biological attacks will be stockpiled. Clinton (1998) declared that it is necessary to "approach these 21st century threats with the same rigor and determination we applied to the toughest security challenges of this century."

2. Nowhere are these impulses more obvious than in the recent scandal involving the president and the former White House intern. Here, we were witnesses to the prurient fascination with the sexual transgressions of President Clinton. Described as both

"contagious" and "hysterical," the recent response to the vigorous inquiry into President Clinton's private life by Special Prosecutor Kenneth Starr was an instance in which media interest in sex and sexuality approached the extremes of obsession (Kroker & Kroker, 1998). Despite the slippery semantics surrounding Clinton's definition of sex, this "outrageous farce" (Said, 1998), with its exaggerated attention to the tawdry antics of the president, took on the dimensions of a "national trauma" (Said, 1998). The catapulting of private acts into the public domain ultimately compromised the office of the president and exposed the United States to international ridicule. The violation of the boundaries between private and public and the sensationalist interest in intimate behaviors propelled the nation into a state of anxiety that could be alleviated only by a penitential ritual. The necessity for the production of a sacrificial victim is commonplace in U.S. culture—a culture in which the moral lessons of confession, contrition, forgiveness, and redemption are of paramount significance.

3. For more on the psychological profiling of serial killers, see Fox and Levin (1996), Giannangelo (1997), Jackson and Bekerian (1997), and Keppel and Birnes (1997).

4. Witches, according to the *Malleus Malificarum*, were possessed of extraordinary sexual powers. Witches, as carriers of the manifold anxieties, fantasies, and desires of both men and women, continue to exert a profound influence on contemporary cultural institutions and discourses. Moreover, constructions of female sexuality as powerful but potentially malevolent are still with us. We may think of the wave of cultural anxiety unleashed by the actions of Lorena Bobbitt (and the rendering of her as "mad"). For more on this subject, see Dijkstra (1996).

References

Akin, G., & Ludwig, A. (1989). *Grotesque: Natural, historical and formaldehyde photography*. Amsterdam: Fragment Uitgeverij.

Bok, S. (1998). *Mayhem: Violence as public entertainment*. Reading, MA: Addison-Wesley.

Brottman, M. (1997). *Offensive films: Toward an anthropology of cinema vomitif*. Westport, CT: Greenwood.

Clinton, W. (1998, May 22). Meeting the Terrorist Threats of the 21st Century. [White House press release]. Washington, DC: The White House, Office of the Press Secretary.

Clinton, W. (1999, January 22). Remarks by the President on keeping America secure for the 21st century. [White House press release]. Washington, DC: The White House, Office of the Press Secretary.

Cole, L. A. (1998). *Eleventh plague: The politics of biological and chemical warfare*. New York: Freeman.

Dijkstra, B. (1996). *Evil sisters: The threat of female sexuality and the cult of manhood*. New York: Knopf.

Douglas, J., & Olshaker, M. (1995). *Mindhunter: Inside the FBI's elite serial crime unit*. New York: Scribner.

Douglas, J., & Olshaker, M. (1998). *Obsession*. New York: Pocket Books.

Egger, S. A. (1998). *The killer among us: An examination of serial murder and its investigation*. Englewood Cliffs, NJ: Prentice Hall.

Fisher, J. (1997). *Killer among us: Public reactions to serial murder*. New York: Praeger.

Fox, A. J., & Levin, J. (1996). *Overkill: Mass murder and serial killing exposed*. Boston: Dell.

Gatens, M. (1996a). *Imaginary bodies: Ethics, power and corporeality*. London: Routledge.

Gatens, M. (1996b). Spinoza, law and responsibility. In P. Cheah, D. Fraser, & J. Grbich (Eds.), *Thinking through the body of the law* (pp. 26-42). New York: New York University Press.

Giannangelo, S. J. (1997). *The psychopathology of serial murder.* New York: Praeger.

Goldstein, J. (Ed.). (1998). *Why we watch: The attraction of violent entertainment.* New York: Oxford University Press.

Griggers, C. (1997). *Becoming-woman.* Minneapolis, MN: University of Minnesota Press.

Grosz, E. (1994). *Volatile bodies.* Sydney, Australia: Allen and Unwin.

Grosz, E. (1996). Intolerable ambiguity: Freaks as/at the limits. In R. Thomson (Ed.), *Freakery: Cultural spectacle of the extraordinary body* (pp. 55-66). New York: New York University Press.

Halberstam, J. (1995). *Skin shows: Gothic horror and the technology of monsters.* Durham, NC: Duke University Press.

Halttunen, K. (1998). *Murder most foul: The killer and the American gothic imagination.* Cambridge, MA: Harvard University Press.

Harris, T. (1999). *Hannibal.* New York: Delacorte.

Hatty, S. E., & Hatty, J. (1999). *The disordered body: Epidemic disease and cultural transformation.* Albany, NY: State University of New York Press.

Hatty, S. E., & Mills, R. (1998). *Ways of knowing: Modern and postmodern perspectives* (Rev. ed.). Lismore, Australia: Southern Cross University.

Holmes, R., & Holmes, S. (1998). *Serial murder* (2nd ed.). Thousand Oaks, CA: Sage.

Jack's killer website. (1999). Retrieved December 14, 1998 from the World Wide Web: http://www.nbc.com/profiler/index.html.

Jackson, J. L., & Bekerian, D. A. (Eds.). (1997). *Offender profiling: Theory, research and practice.* New York: John Wiley.

Keppel, R. D., & Birnes, W. J. (1997). *Signature killers.* New York: Pocket Books.

Kramer, L. (1997). *After the lovedeath: Sexual violence and the making of culture.* Berkeley, CA: University of California Press.

Kristeva, J. (1982). *Powers of horror: An essay on abjection.* (L. Roudiez, Trans.). New York: Columbia University Press.

Kroker, A., & Kroker, M. (1998, January 26). Void reports: 1. The oral office. *CTHEOR.* Retrieved on December 18, 1998 from the World Wide Web: http://www.ctheory.com/.

Levant, R. F. (1996). What is the status of manhood today? Paper distributed electronically to members of Division 51 of the American Psychological Association.

Lombroso, C., & Ferrero, W. (1958). *Female offender.* New York: Philosophical Press.

May, L. (1998). *Masculinity and morality.* Ithaca, NY: Cornell University Press.

Miller, W. I. (1998). *The anatomy of disgust.* Cambridge, MA: Harvard University Press.

Mills, R. (1995, March). "May God have mercy on your corp . . . ," Woman without a soul. Paper presented at the Representing Sexualities Conference, University of Sydney, Sydney, Australia.

Peters, C. J., & Olshaker, M. (1997). *Virus hunter: Thirty years of battling hot viruses around the world.* New York: Anchor.

Preston, R. (1997). *The cobra event.* New York: Random House.

Purkiss, D. (1997). *The witch in history: Early modern and twentieth-century representations.* New York: Routledge.

Radetsky, P. (1995).*The invisible invaders: Viruses and the scientists who pursue them.* Boston: Little, Brown.

Radhakrishnan, R. (1996). *Diasporic mediations: Between home and location.* Minneapolis, MN: University of Minnesota Press.

Ressler, R., & Schachtman, T. (1992). *Whoever fights monsters.* New York: St. Martin's.

Rhodes, R. (1997). *Deadly feasts: Tracking the secrets of a terrifying new plague.* New York: Simon & Schuster.

Ryan, F. (1997). *Virus X: Tracking the new killer plagues out of the present and into the future.* Boston: Little, Brown.

Said, E. (1998, September 17-23). The President and the baseball player. *Al-Ahram Weekly.* Retrieved on December 18, 1998 from the World Wide Web: http://www.ahram.org.eg/weekly/.

Seelye, H. N., & Wasilewski, J. H. (1996). *Between cultures: Developing self-identity in a world of diversity.* New York: NTC.

Seidler, V. (1997). *Man enough: Embodying masculinities.* London: Sage.

Seltzer, M. (1998). *Serial killers: Death and life in America's wound culture.* New York: Routledge.

Simon, J. D. (1997). Biological terrorism. *Journal of the American Medical Association, 278,* 428-430.

Smith, J. (1989). *Misogynies.* London: Faber & Faber.

West, R. (1997). *Caring for justice.* New York: New York University Press.

Whitmer, B. (1997). *The violence mythos.* Albany, NY: State University of New York Press.

Witkin, J-P. (1989). *Gods of heaven and earth.* Pasadena, CA: Twelvetrees.

Witkin, J-P. (Ed.). (1994). *Harm's way: Lust and madness, murder and mayhem.* Santa Fe, NM: Twin Palm.

Witkin, J-P. (1998). *The bone house.* Santa Fe, NM: Twin Palm.

Young, A. (1996). *Imagining crime.* London: Sage.

Index

About the Author

Suzanne E. Hatty is Associate Professor of Culture, Epistemology and Medicine in the Department of Social Medicine at Ohio University. She has a Ph.D. in Psychology from the University of Sydney, Australia. Her research interests include the cultures of medicine, the body and society, bioethics and biotechnologies, posthumanism and future studies, and crime and popular culture. Her most recent book, co-authored with James Hatty, is *The Disordered Body: Epidemic Disease and Cultural Transformation.*